What Your Colleagues Are Saying . . .

Kelly, Laminack, and Vasquez have provided a treasure trove of detailed lessons and resources designed to help justice-minded teachers not only understand the need for literacy learning rooted in efforts to address issues of injustice, but also better understand what it might look like in their own classrooms. My hope now is that teachers are brave enough to do the work that needs to be done!

—Chris Hass, **Author of *Social Justice Talk***

Wow. Kelly, Laminack, and Vasquez have created a blueprint for critical comprehension that needs truly to be in the hands of all educators—preservice and veteran. It's the book I want to share with my undergraduate students and the book I want my children's teachers to have. It is rife with concrete examples and beautiful questions to springboard the critical thinkers we all aim to cultivate.

—Nawal Qarooni, **Educator, Author, and Literacy Coach**

Katie Kelly, Lester Laminack, and Vivian Vasquez wrote the book I wish I had when I was first studying critical literacy in grad school many years ago. Not only does this book define critical comprehension for teachers, but it masterfully supports teachers in putting the work of critical comprehension into practice in the classroom. The lessons are practical, meaningful, and highly engaging for students. This is a book I will turn to again and again in my work as a classroom teacher and writer.

—Christina Nosek, **Author of *Answers to Your Biggest Questions About Teaching Elementary Reading***

Critical Comprehension: Lessons for Guiding Students to Deeper Meaning offers teachers a powerful look at ways to support young readers to read with criticality. The book is full of tools, teaching resources, lessons, book lists and questions to help us, as educators, examine our classrooms and practices. I feel fortunate to have this team thinking together and sharing their expertise. The combination of their personal stories and classroom anecdotes makes for very powerful learning as we all work to create inclusive classrooms.

—Franki Sibberson, **Author of *Beyond Leveled Books***

Critical Comprehension: Lessons for Guiding Students to Deeper Meaning encourages educators to read critically, take action, and be part of a necessary global change. Kelly, Laminack, and Vasquez describe opportunities that will allow learners to construct a deeper meaning of texts through a critical literacy lens while moving forward to take social action. This book uses a leading-edge instructional framework to center children of all ages as agents of their own learning. I believe this book will leave you with an overwhelming desire to work alongside young learners and will give you the inspiration and knowledge required to "be the change."

—Carolyn Clarke, **Assistant Professor,**
St. Francis Xavier University

Critical Comprehension

Lessons for Guiding Students to Deeper Meaning

Katie Kelly

Lester Laminack

Vivian Vasquez

FOR INFORMATION:

Corwin

A SAGE Company

2455 Teller Road

Thousand Oaks, California 91320

(800) 233-9936

www.corwin.com

SAGE Publications Ltd.

1 Oliver's Yard

55 City Road

London EC1Y 1SP

United Kingdom

SAGE Publications India Pvt. Ltd.

B 1/I 1 Mohan Cooperative Industrial Area

Mathura Road, New Delhi 110 044

India

SAGE Publications Asia-Pacific Pte. Ltd.

18 Cross Street #10-10/11/12

China Square Central

Singapore 048423

President: Mike Soules

Vice President and Editorial
  Director: Monica Eckman

Executive Editor: Tori Mello Bachman

Content Development Editor: Sharon Wu

Editorial Assistant: Nancy Chung

Project Editor: Amy Schroller

Copy Editor: Heather Kerrigan

Typesetter: C&M Digitals (P) Ltd.

Proofreader: Christine Dahlin

Indexer: Integra

Cover Designer: Janet Kiesel

Marketing Manager: Margaret O'Connor

Copyright © 2023 by Corwin Press, Inc.

All rights reserved. Except as permitted by U.S. copyright law, no part of this work may be reproduced or distributed in any form or by any means, or stored in a database or retrieval system, without permission in writing from the publisher.

When forms and sample documents appearing in this work are intended for reproduction, they will be marked as such. Reproduction of their use is authorized for educational use by educators, local school sites, and/or noncommercial or nonprofit entities that have purchased the book.

All third-party trademarks referenced or depicted herein are included solely for the purpose of illustration and are the property of their respective owners. Reference to these trademarks in no way indicates any relationship with, or endorsement by, the trademark owner.

Printed in Canada

ISBN 978-1-0718-7933-7

This book is printed on acid-free paper.

23 24 25 26 27 10 9 8 7 6 5 4 3 2 1

DISCLAIMER: This book may direct you to access third-party content via web links, QR codes, or other scannable technologies, which are provided for your reference by the author(s). Corwin makes no guarantee that such third-party content will be available for your use and encourages you to review the terms and conditions of such third-party content. Corwin takes no responsibility and assumes no liability for your use of any third-party content, nor does Corwin approve, sponsor, endorse, verify, or certify such third-party content.

Contents

For downloadable resources related to
Critical Comprehension,
visit the companion website at
resources.corwin.com/criticalcomprehension.

Acknowledgments

To our partners at Corwin Press: Tori Bachman, you are an editor extraordinaire and a really cool person. Your enthusiasm for this book project, your encouragement, and your consistent support from start to finish are greatly appreciated. You helped sustain the joyfulness of our writing experience. Thank you! Nancy Chung, your gentle nudges and attention to detail helped keep us on schedule and organized as the book moved into production.

To the teachers (Chris Hass, Daniel Hoilett, Alyssa [Cameron] Likens, Reilly Mahan, and Hannah Reyes) who opened their doors to share their spaces of learning with us (and our readers), thank you! This book could not have happened without you.

KK—I first learned about critical literacy during my doctoral studies (which was far too late in life and why this book is needed!). The work of many scholars, including Vivian Vasquez, shaped my understanding of critical literacy and supported my dissertation and future research. To come full circle and write this book with Vivian is incredibly humbling and exciting. And her love for the movie *Elf* always makes for fun GIF exchanges! "VV . . . I love you! I love you! I love you!" To Lester, I'm thrilled to be writing a second book with you! Not only are you my writing partner, but you are like a big brother. I am forever grateful for our friendship, the laughs, the advice, and the space to process the work and the world. To my family, friends, and colleagues, thank you for supporting me, inspiring me, and nudging me to think critically and curiously to continually learn, unlearn, and relearn.

LL—When you write a book with other folks you form a bond. You think together, you negotiate meaning and word choice, and you push your own understanding. Together you create something that is more precise, more crisp, more insightful, and more helpful than any of you would have produced alone. In writing this book I have had the great pleasure of collaborating with two dear friends. We have laughed out loud, we have layered ideas and language, we have refined thought and expression, and we have formed greater bonds of friendship. Katie, we *are* like siblings. We talk every week, we bounce ideas off one another, and we seek advice from one another. We are indeed family. It is a joy to write with you.

Vivian, we have known each other for more than thirty years. I have followed your work and have long admired your integrity and scholarship. It has been an honor to finally work with you and a great pleasure to think and write and laugh with you. Working with you and Katie has been an absolute joy. The three of us working together have been a perfect team.

And writing a book always means that there are times when you just lose yourself in the work. That, at times, means that you are squirreled away in your office, totally unaware of the passing of time. I am grateful to my husband, Steve, who is always patient and kind and supportive of my work.

VV—Katie and Lester, working on this book with you has been an intellectually stimulating and extremely enjoyable experience. It was the writing adventure I didn't know I needed. Katie, I'm so happy that I was able to experience close-up your enthusiasm and unassuming brilliance. Elfing with you is proof that you can live in academia with humility and love! Lester, you were there on the first day, more than thirty years ago, when I became involved in the world of literacy beyond the preschool and elementary school classroom. Your creativity and way with words, your profound knowledge and understanding of literacy teaching and learning with teachers and students, and your wit and sense of humor have enriched our joint writing experience in ways that have made it a fun-filled adventure. It has truly been a pleasure to work with the two of you!

Andy and TJ, you are my heart. Thank you for always being there for me and reminding me "Things are only impossible until they're not."

Publisher's Acknowledgments

Corwin gratefully acknowledges the contributions of the following reviewers:

Elaine Shobert
Literacy Coach
Monroe, North Carolina

Melissa Black
Elementary ELA Teacher
Washington, DC

Darius Phelps
Middle Grades Teacher
New York, New York

Fran McVeigh
Literacy Consultant and Academic Coordinator
Unionville, Iowa

Krista Geffre
Graduate Instructor
Hillsboro, Oregon

About the Authors

Katie Kelly is a professor of education and coordinator of the Literacy Graduate Program at Furman University in Greenville, South Carolina. As a former teacher and literacy coach, Katie's teaching and research interests include engaging children in meaningful literacy experiences and practices to foster lifelong literacy, equity, and justice. She is widely published in several peer-reviewed journals, including *The Reading Teacher* and *Voices from the Middle*. She has coauthored three other books: *Reading to Make a Difference: Using Literature to Help Students Think Deeply Speak Freely and Take Action* (Heinemann), *From Pencils to Podcasts: Digital Tools to Transform K-12 Literacy Practices* (Solution Tree), and *Smuggling Writing: Strategies That Get Students to Write Every Day, in Every Content Area (3–12)* (Corwin). She can be contacted on Twitter @ktkelly14 and by email katie.kelly@furman.edu.

Lester Laminack, professor emeritus, Western Carolina University in Cullowhee, North Carolina, is now a full-time writer and consultant working with schools throughout the United States and abroad. He is the author of more than twenty-five books for teachers and children. His academic publications include *Climb Inside a Poem* (Heinemann), *Cracking Open the Author's Craft* (Scholastic), *Bullying Hurts: Teaching Kindness Through Read Aloud and Guided Conversations* (Heinemann), *The Writing Teacher's Troubleshooting Guide* (Heinemann), *Writers ARE Readers: Flipping Reading Strategies into Writing Instruction* (Heinemann), and *The Ultimate Read Aloud Collection Fiction and Nonfiction* (Scholastic).

Lester is also the author of several children's books, including *The Sunsets of Miss Olivia Wiggins, Trevor's Wiggly-Wobbly Tooth, Saturdays and Tea Cakes, Jake's 100th Day of School, Snow Day!, Three Hens and a Peacock* (2012 Children's Choice K–2 Book of the Year Award), and *The King of Bees,* all published by Peachtree Publishers. His new book, *Three Hens, a Peacock, and the Enormous Egg,* is expected in February 2023, and *A Cat Like That* is expected in 2024.

His newest works are *Reading to Make a Difference* (Heinemann) and *The Ultimate Read Aloud Resource,* 2nd Edition (Scholastic). Lester is available for professional development and school author visits. You can contact him via his website, www.LesterLaminack.com, and follow him on Facebook or on Twitter @Lester_Laminack.

Vivian Vasquez is a professor in the School of Education at American University in Washington, DC. She is a former preschool and elementary school teacher. Her interest in creating spaces for critical literacies, in early years classrooms, began while she was a kindergarten teacher in the early 1990s. She has published numerous articles and book chapters, and she has authored or coauthored fifteen other books, including the award-winning *Negotiating Critical Literacies with Young Children*. Vivian's honors and awards include the Outstanding Elementary Educator in the English Language Arts Award, the NCTE Advancement of People of Color Award, the AERA Division B Outstanding Book of the Year Award, and the James N. Britton Award. The NCTE Early Childhood Assembly honored her with a scholarship in her name, the Vivian Vasquez Teacher Scholarship. She can be reached at vvasque@american.edu.

This book is for all educators who work tirelessly to support the future generation to develop as critical citizens who strive for a better, more equitable, and just world.

It is for teachers who are entering the profession, for those with experience teaching with a critical lens and it is for those who have come to this work later in life, who are seeking an accessible avenue into making it real for themselves and their students.

We hope this book challenges you, supports you, and strengthens your teaching and learning practices. And for those of you who face the pushback against access to books and information, we hope this book gives you strength to advocate for the right to read and seek and speak truth.

Introduction

Our classrooms are microcosms of the larger more pluralistic society, so it is necessary for us as educators to consider how *who* we are affects *how* we create inclusive spaces where all children thrive. In other words, it's important to recognize how our identities as literacy educators are shaped by our histories. Consider Vivian's experience as a young literacy learner. Vivian was born in the Philippines, to Filipino parents, and her family immigrated to Canada when she was in elementary school.

> *It was 1965. I was five years old. I remember hurrying home after school one day, rushing to the kitchen and opening the freezer door. I was sure I could scrape off enough frost from the sides of the freezer to make a snowball like Dick and Jane had done in my school primer. I had barely scraped off enough frost to make a tiny ball of ice when it all began to melt in my hand in the heat of that summer day in the Philippines.*

For almost half a century, until 1946, the United States governed the Philippines as a colonial power (Casambre, 1982) during which time the United States pursued policies believed to promote the social and material well-being of the people of the Philippines. These policies included the imposition of the American system of education and the use of English as the only language of instruction. The use of the Dick and Jane primer at Vivian's school is one way that elements from the American colonization of the Philippines in the past continued to be entangled in the lives of Filipinx children for many years with remnants that continue to be felt today. Against this historical backdrop, what may, at first, come across as a banal literacy story takes on new life. For a child growing up in the Philippines, the use of the Dick and Jane primer and its stories of life in America in no way took into account Vivian's knowledge and understanding of the world around her. Instead, the use of such books resulted in what Campano and colleagues (2016) describe as the formation of Vivian as a *racialized other*, in the very country in which she was born. In curricular terms, through the stories of Dick and Jane, she attempted the impossible task of living the experiences of individuals who were not like her, such as playing in the snow. Whose stories were getting told and by whom to Vivian and her classmates? What are the effects when children are not able to see themselves in the books they engage with in their classrooms?

Vivian and her family immigrated to Canada in 1970. Multicultural education, which can be traced historically to the Civil Rights Movement, was only beginning to take root. Similar to her school experiences in the Philippines, there was a disconnect between the texts used in her classroom and her lived experiences. Imagine what a difference it could have made for Vivian and her classmates to engage with books that were culturally sustaining, in which she could see herself, in which others could see her.

Five years before Vivian and her family emigrated from the Philippines to Canada, Lester was attending fourth grade in Alabama.

> *I was in fourth grade in 1965. Fourth grade was the year children in Alabama studied state history and geography. And each year all the fourth graders loaded on school buses with packed lunches, teachers, and a few mothers for the long drive to Montgomery. The 112-mile trip was a highlight of fourth grade. We toured the monuments and the state buildings and met legislators from our part of the state. We felt grown-up and important that day.*

On May 17, 1954, two years before Lester was born, the US Supreme Court issued its landmark decision that struck down the doctrine of "separate but equal" and ordered an end to school segregation. Ten years later, July 2, 1964, the summer before he entered third grade, the Civil Rights Act was signed to end segregation in public places and ban employment discrimination on the basis of race, color, religion, sex, or national origin. Yet, Lester attended all-white public schools in three different states until sixth grade when Black students were allowed to attend the school he attended. It was that same year, in sixth grade, that he had his first Black teacher.

Like Vivian, Lester learned to read with the Dick and Jane primers. However, Lester saw reflections of the world he knew: white faces, heteronormative families, and children playing with friends and going to school with others who look like them. All schoolbooks, television pro-grams, commercials, movies, magazines, advertisements, and so on reflected that world. Bishop (1990) reminds us that

> Children from dominant social groups have always found their mirrors in books, but they too have suffered from the lack of availability of books about others. They need the books as windows onto reality, not just on imaginary worlds. They need books that will help them understand the multicultural nature of the world they live in, and their place as a member of just one group, as well as their connections to all other humans. In the United States, where racism is still one of the major unresolved social problems, books may be one of the few places where children who are socially isolated and insulated from the larger world may meet people unlike themselves. If they see only reflections of themselves, they will grow up with an exaggerated sense of their own importance and value in the world—a dangerous ethnocentrism. (p. 1)

Lester's reflection on fourth grade confirms this:

> As a nine-year-old child, it never occurred to me that I should question why everyone on that bus was white. Or why everyone in the school was white. Or why the focus of our study and textbooks was whitewashed with the portrayals of enslaved African Americans as happy folks working in the rows of cotton, singing gospel songs, and living in the small cottages surrounding the big plantation houses. We did not delve into the capture, transport, or sale of human beings. We did not consider the pain and indignity of forced labor or the unbearable horror of seeing your children or spouse sold and taken away. In fact, we weren't even aware of it. In fourth grade we were taught that once there were four tribes of Native Americans in Alabama—Cherokee, Choctaw, Chickasaw, and Creek. We didn't delve into the forced removal of the people who had been on the land for generations before the arrival of Europeans. We didn't have conversations or stories revealing where they went, what they lost, and where they are today. As a nine-year-old I never questioned why we didn't learn more about the contributions of the Native people or Black people in the history of our state. As a nine-year-old I accepted what I was given by textbooks and adult authority figures as the truth.

Lester's experience demonstrates the impact of living in a curriculum of mirrors. When everything you read reflects only the world as you know it, you live with a distorted worldview. That narrow view limits curiosity and breeds contempt for, or fear of, difference, and if left unchallenged often results in naive acceptance that perpetuates itself.

Almost two decades later, in the 1980s, Katie attended an elementary school that was fully integrated. Children at Katie's school included white children from her neighborhood and Black children who were bussed into the northside school from Syracuse's southside and the nearby apartments. As a young person she was taught that the Jim Crow era of segregation and racism was part of the past and something that occurred in the South. She developed a color-evasive view of the world, passively accepting the idea that people of color had the same rights and opportunities as whites. It did not occur to her what it might have been like for her classmates to get up early and catch the bus to ride to the other side of town to attend school where the faces of your classmates, teachers, and even characters in the basal readers did not look like your own.

Although schools were integrated, neighborhoods were not. Katie wondered, "Why did we live in different areas? Why were there such socio-economic differences in these neighborhoods? Why did the Onondaga people live on a reservation just five miles south of downtown Syracuse?" When Katie asked these questions, the typical response from adults was "that's just the way things are." That response left her with unanswered questions and curiosity.

Growing up just a few miles away from Onondaga Lake and living in Onondaga County, why wasn't there a greater emphasis on the name-sake of the area? The Onondaga people are one of the Six Nations of the Haudenosaunee Confederacy. The capital of the Iroquois Confederacy was founded on the shores of Onondaga Lake. Katie recalls her school experiences learning about the history of Native Americans:

> In school, we read about "Indians" in our social studies textbooks depicted from a historical lens. We built longhouses out of popsicle sticks and made construction paper feather headdresses for Thanksgiving. We learned the whitewashed version of Thanksgiving depicting the Pilgrims and Native Americans as peaceful and friendly neighbors. We visited Sainte Marie Among the Iroquois (known as the French Fort), a living history museum along the shores of the sacred, yet heavily polluted Onondaga Lake. Here we were told the history of the Haudenosaunee people from the

perspective of the French Jesuits who lived in the fort for just two years. We didn't learn about the history of colonization, the forced removal of the Onondaga from 95 percent of their own land, and the abuse and assimilation at the Indian boarding schools.

We learned about George Washington, the first President of the United States and Revolutionary War general who fought with the separatists against the British. We didn't learn that he launched an attack against the Haudenosaunee people ordering total destruction, burning and looting their villages, destroying their food sources, and capturing men, women, and children as prisoners.

Today, the French fort has been renamed the Skä•noñh—Great Law of Peace Center and focuses on telling the story of the Native people of central New York through the lens of the Onondaga people, and efforts are being made to clean up the heavily polluted Onondaga Lake. Changes such as these are a step forward. However, there is still much work to be done. For instance, the Syracuse City School District is among the most segregated in the country (Kucsera & Orfield, 2014). According to Edbuild (2020), the percentage of nonwhite students in 2016–2017 in Syracuse was 78 percent compared to 13 percent in neighboring Westhill School District. As the city of Syracuse increases in its diversity, the number of whites fleeing to the suburbs has also increased, resulting in a return to greater segregation than when Katie attended school in the 1980s and early 1990s. Shifting population from within the city of Syracuse to the suburbs in the same county has resulted in resegregated schools (Fernández, 2017).

Redlining

Redlining is a discriminatory practice of denying services (e.g., mortgages) to people from certain neighborhoods based on race or ethnicity. Syracuse, like other cities across the country, has a long history of redlining as is demonstrated in a 1919 map (Mulcahy, 2021) (Figure I.1). This map shows the evolution of redlining with labels for various ethnic groups which eventually morphed into color-coded neighborhoods with coded labels such as "best," "desirable," and "hazardous."

FIGURE I.1   1919 Map of Syracuse (CNY Central)

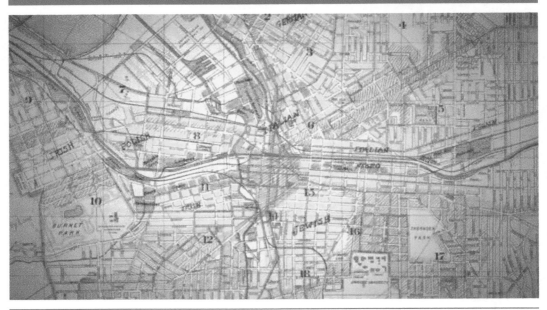

Source: National Archives and Records Administration. Public Domain.

Examining Our Personal Histories

When we examine our personal histories, we can stop perpetuating the false—and harmful—patterns of white-centered schooling that are so common in the United States.

We must begin by decolonizing ourselves, our curriculum, and our instruction by doing things like questioning who is included in the books and textbooks we bring into our classrooms and who is excluded. We must disrupt the perpetuation of dominant narratives that privilege some people at the expense of others. We must examine texts critically and consider whether individuals and groups are portrayed in authentic ways or if harmful stereotypes send implicit messages. We must be critically conscious and question the world around us from a historical and current lens.

- Why are these changes happening?
- Who benefits from these changes?
- Who is harmed by these changes?
- What changes should be happening but are not?
- Who benefits from maintaining the status quo?
- Who is harmed by keeping things the way they are?

- What do we need to do differently?

- What action can we take to right any wrongs and create greater equity?

We are currently a part of history, and we have the power to shape it.

If we do not ask critical questions such as these, we risk contributing to inequities that favor dominant cultural groups and contribute to the perpetuation of color-evasive attitudes, behaviors, and discourses that negatively impact systems such as education.

Who we are and how we perceive ourselves are shaped by intersecting and converging factors, including our histories. How we move through the world is also shaped by many factors, including when we were born, where we have lived and with whom, events we experienced in our social worlds, and texts that we encountered.

Pause to Reflect

What moments in your history and what experiences with texts have contributed to shaping who you are today? How have these influenced the beliefs that you hold? Here are some questions to help you reflect on your earliest memories of reading.

- Did the characters look like you?

- How often did you see nations or cultures that were relatable to you?

- How often were representations of your nation or culture accurate?

- How often were representations of your nation or culture inaccurate?

- How often did you see representations of your gender identity?

- How often did you see representations of your religious beliefs?

- Did the family structures parallel yours?

- Did the characters' or their families' experiences mirror yours?

- Do you recall wondering or questioning the portrayal of family?

- Do you recall the celebrations, the food, or the social activities of those characters? Did they reflect those of your family? Were they accurate representations or were they offensive representations?

- Were there certain celebrations that you felt were private and should not have been included?

Reflecting on Our Reading Histories

We remember reading in school as a task assigned by the teacher rather than meaningful, purposeful, or critical practice. Reading was often followed by a set of questions to answer, a book report, or some sort of written task. Opportunities for authentic reading where we chose books based on our interests and read for our own purposes were limited. Further, any efforts to nudge our thinking beyond surface-level understanding to find the "right" answers were nonexistent. In all subjects, including social studies, science, and health, we were typically assigned to read a chapter from the textbook and then directed to answer the questions at the end of the chapter. A single text for each subject area was the source of information.

Pause to Reflect

Reflecting on Your Own School Experiences

Think back to the curriculum from your own schooling.

- What was taught?

- Who was teaching?

- How was it taught?

- Whose perspective was centered?

- Was there representation of the contributions of people of color? If so, how were they represented?

- What nations or cultures were missing from the texts you read?

- Was there equal representation of the contributions of men, women, and gender nonbinary individuals?

- Was the representation of the contributions of people who were considered "famous" mostly white? Mostly men?

- Was there an inordinate focus on governance written by white male leaders?

- Were there policies and practices that placed limitations on people of color?

Astute readers may have noticed that the presentation of questions, usually found at the end of each chapter, moved through the chapter sequentially and were often interrogative versions of the topic sentence, some key detail, or fact. If you had similar experiences, then you may remember that those questions were often keyed to statements in the chapter. Reading like this could become a mindless process of lifting language from the text to match the wording in the question. It could feel somewhat like a steam shovel scooping up details from the text, dropping them into the dump truck driven by the questions, and dumping those onto a clean page for the teacher. We remember dutifully reading (and sometimes skimming) the chapter, writing each question then searching for and copying the answer before moving on to the next question. Reading was reduced to fact-finding, shuffling information, and filling in the blanks as an act of compliance where the teacher was the authority and holder of knowledge.

Without a meaningful purpose for reading, there were times when we "fake read" our way through the assigned reading at school. We began by skimming the questions and then looked up the answers without ever really reading the material. Did you do that too? This suggests that for many of us, reading in school was simply a task to complete with limited opportunities or guidance to delve into purposeful reading for deeper understanding, constructing meaning, exploration, and critical thinking.

When thinking back on our K–12 schooling experiences (even though we attended schools in different locations and in different decades), none of us can remember being taught to question the information we read or people in positions of authority (such as the teacher or the author). It was never suggested that an alternative version of this information could exist or that some stories and perspectives were left out, let alone why this happens. In fact, the notion that a textbook issued by the state or texts selected by a teacher could contain information that was in any way biased or incomplete was just unfathomable to us. As children we consumed the "facts" we were fed and assumed the teacher and the author of the text were authorities on the topic. We never realized how malnourished our reading lives were. This is how our families were taught and the generations before them as well. This instructional history created generations of readers who consume text without question.

Pause to Reflect

Considering Your Literacy History

Pause a moment to consider your own literacy history.

- What do you recall about the way you were taught reading in school?
- What kinds of spaces did your teacher create for you to question or confront the text?
- What kinds of spaces did your teacher create for you to challenge the text or to push back against the information in a text and seek counternarratives?
- Was there a time when your teacher told you the text was only one version of the truth and assigned you the task to find the stories of the missing voices or perspectives?
- Recall a book or text that caused you to question the intentions of the author, or the accuracy of historical events, or consider alternate perspectives.
- Recall a book or text that resulted in an "aha" moment for you that had an impact on you in some way. Where did you encounter the text? What effect did this text have on you and your actions?
- What factors influenced the reader and person you are today?
- What is your personal literacy legacy?
- What is the literacy legacy of your family?
- How does it position you to accept or challenge text?
- How does it position you with power and privilege?
- In what ways do you question texts and the world around you?

We All Start Somewhere

In order to teach children to read critically, we must first be critically literate ourselves. We came to this understanding as adults when we were first introduced to and embraced a critical literacy stance as a vehicle to seek and understand a broader, more equitable, and just version of truth. From a critical literacy perspective, we learned that examining our own assumptions, values, and beliefs is part of "understanding the position(s) from which we speak, the position(s) from which we teach and the Discourses (ways of being, doing, acting, talking, and thinking) that shape those positionings" (Vasquez et al., 2013, p. 23). Prior to this awakening and development of a critical lens, none of us routinely questioned the word and the world around us (Freire & Macedo, 1987). With critical literacy as part of our theoretical toolkit, we learned to use our past experiences to question our assumptions about what we read, who wrote it, what their intentions were, or how the text benefits some while harming others.

As with other experiences that broaden our perspective and deepen our understanding, new insight alters the way we view text and the world ever after. Even young children can learn to notice that a story is being presented in a way that favors one character, voice, or perspective. Young children are naturally curious about themselves, others, and the world around them. They often pose questions to seek more information or greater understanding. Consider how often young children ask "why" and "how" questions about their worlds. For example, one of the books that Vivian's kindergarten students enjoyed reading was *Baby Beluga* by Raffi. The children loved that it was such a happy story about Beluga whales until one of the children saw a news clip about how these whales were on the decline in the St. Lawrence River as a result of pollution, reduced food resources, disturbance by humans, and habitat degradation. With Vivian's support after many discussions and research, the children decided they needed to do something to help the plight of the Beluga. One of the things they did was to create an alternate version of the text (see Figure I.2) which they shared with the other kindergarten classrooms as a way to offer a perspective that was different from the original book (Vasquez, 2014).

FIGURE I.2   Example of Revised *Baby Beluga* Text

Original Text	Alternate Version Text
Baby Beluga in the deep blue sea swim so wild and you swim so free heaven above and the sea below and a little white whale on the go.	Baby Beluga in the deep blue sea please help us so we can be. The garbage in the water doesn't let us be free. Please save us from this pollution.

As educators, we have a responsibility to help children move beyond a passive acceptance of text and the world around them. Rather than dismissing the children's questions and issues, let's embrace their inquiries, assist them with seeking answers, and nurture their ongoing natural critical curiosity as Vivian did with her students. If children are taught to accept all that is presented to them at face value without ever questioning the content or the intention, the inclusion/exclusion of voices, and their assumptions; if they are not provided opportunities to deconstruct text(s) to examine social, cultural, and political issues, they are more likely to be indoctrinated into the dominant ideology (McDaniel, 2004). In other words, when readers fail to question texts or authorities, they are more likely to be manipulated by them. "For too long kids have felt powerless in their classrooms because they spend their days being told what to learn, how to learn it, and what to think about this all afterwards" (Hass, 2020, p. 21). When reading critically students broaden their thinking, expand their perspectives, and deepen their understanding. When empowered with these insights, children are more likely to take a stand against injustices and take action to make a difference for a better world (Bomer & Bomer, 2001; Laminack & Kelly, 2019).

> When readers fail to question texts or authorities, they are more likely to be manipulated by them.

Further, traditional approaches that center teachers' interests rather than students' interests rob children of important learning experiences to develop critical thinking and a sense of agency to take action in the future (Hass, 2020, p. xv). Literacy is empowering and transformative. Learning to question information, power structures, and/or people in positions of power is essential to a just society. Learning to uncover alternative perspectives opens the potential for more authentic and purposeful conversations within a community and fosters greater action for justice and equity. Learning to seek out the voices and stories of the underrepresented is a step toward excavating truths, even when it challenges what we have always believed.

Critical Comprehension in Action

Our goal in writing this book is to offer opportunities for children to think beyond what is presented in a single text, as a single truth to seek counternarratives that can help them construct a more nuanced, complicated, informed, and accurate truth. When we teach children to be critical readers—to question the commonplace, to evaluate text for stereotyping and tokenism, to disrupt biases, and to seek counternarratives—they begin to weave threads to create more complete tapestries of truth. We can begin to do this work by asking questions such as those listed in Figure I.3.

FIGURE I.3   Critical Questions

CRITICAL QUESTIONS
For Thinking Beyond a Single Text

- How does the text position the reader?
- Who is included or featured in the text/image? How are they represented? Why? Who benefits? Who is harmed?
- What information is featured? Is it presented as "the" truth, or does it make clear there are other perspectives to consider? Who benefits from this portrayal of information? Who is harmed or made invisible?
- Who/what is excluded from the text? Why? How does this exclusion position who/what is included? Why? Who benefits? Who is harmed?
- What are the counter narratives?
- What could be a more accurate/complete representation of the story? Where might I find those alternate perspectives?
- What questions might an alternate perspective answer?

Engaging in conversations based on questions like these results in a shift away from the passive acceptance of, and search for, "the" correct meaning and is the basis of what we refer to as critical comprehension. This book is our attempt to demonstrate how to create spaces for critical conversations to develop critical comprehension using a series of lessons.

Each lesson features one book but also includes a list of alternatives for additional work to extend thought and insight. As is the case with all of the lessons in this book, we offer these ideas as a starting point and encourage you to adapt them based on the interests and inquiries of students.

What Is Critical Comprehension?

1

Critical comprehension entails an active interrogation of words, images, and other presentations of ideas to challenge existing forms of power that privilege some and disadvantage others. When we read critically, we

- question the text, the author's intention, and our own assumptions and biases;

- consider whose perspectives are included or excluded and who benefits from or is harmed by the narrative;

- seek alternate narratives and counternarratives to develop a deeper, broader, and more informed understanding that leads to heightened awareness of inequity and positions us to take action in pursuit of social justice;

- acknowledge that all texts are constructed by a person, or group, with their own biases and intentions;

- recognize that the effects of texts on readers are shaped by a reader's identities, background knowledge, and the perspectives they bring to the text; and

- engage in reading with the text and reading against the text. We must first read with the text to better understand what it is we are reading against (see Figure 1.1).

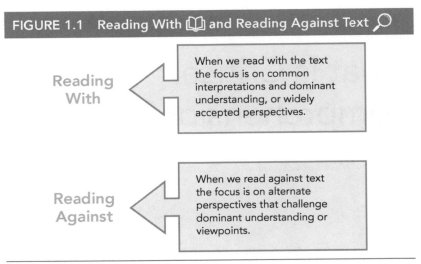

FIGURE 1.1   Reading With 📖 and Reading Against Text 🔍

Reading With — When we read with the text the focus is on common interpretations and dominant understanding, or widely accepted perspectives.

Reading Against — When we read against text the focus is on alternate perspectives that challenge dominant understanding or viewpoints.

Source: Harste, J. C., Vasquez, V., Alberts, P. (2021). *Using Art Critically: Volume 2.* Bloomington, IN: CCCPress.

To become critically literate is to develop the ability to examine

- whose stories are told and whose are omitted;
- whose voices are represented and whose are ignored;
- what topics or issues (e.g., racism, sexism, ableism) are avoided or misrepresented;
- how structures position some in power while marginalizing others; and
- ways to disrupt systems of inequities.

Critical readers and consumers

- question and problematize text;
- examine what the text says, how it is said, who created it, and why it was created; and
- examine what texts omit, and who benefits from such omissions.

Questioning text helps readers reveal power relations and inequities also mirrored in society (Jones, 2006; Vasquez, 2010). Critical readers bring this work beyond the pages of the text and apply it to the way they live their lives: always seeking the full truth and questioning factors that may impede the whole truth from being revealed. Critical readers avoid being manipulated by the dominant perspective as they confront stereotypes and bias (Boutte, 2008) and work toward greater equity and justice.

Critical comprehension, then, is an approach to deeper reading that moves beyond the passive acceptance of text and literal levels of meaning to question the word and the world (Freire, 2000; Freire & Macedo, 1987; McLaughlin & DeVoogd, 2004a, 2004b). And as we read critically, we recognize that meaning resides neither in the text nor in the reader. Instead, meaning is created by the interactions with the text as filtered through a reader's identities, background knowledge, and the perspectives they bring to their reading of a text (Rosenblatt, 1995). There are multiple ways of responding to or generating meaning from a text.

Rather than looking for the correct meaning of a text, critical readers

- read *with* and *against* the text (Janks, 2010);

- recognize that people who produce texts make choices that are not always in everyone's best interest;

- understand that texts have different social effects; and

- read from multiple perspectives to make more informed decisions about what information to take away, what information to question, and what information to leave behind (Janks, 2014).

> Meaning is created by the interactions with the text as filtered through a reader's identities, background knowledge, and the perspectives they bring to their reading of a text (Rosenblatt, 1995).

Luke and Freebody's (1997) Four Resources Model of reading as social practice suggests the need for readers to be code breakers, meaning makers, text users, and *text critics*. Their model was based on an examination of existing and proposed literacy curricula and pedagogical strategies across numerous classroom settings (see Figure 1.2). One of their findings was that supporting children as text critics is an area that was addressed minimally if at all in classrooms.

It is as text critics that we dig beneath the surface level of literal understanding to excavate issues of power and privilege and begin to question our assumptions and expand our perspectives. Acknowledging that both reading and writing are never neutral and are shaped by our ideologies and beliefs, critical comprehension works to help us interrogate and unpack our own assumptions and the messages conveyed in texts (Luke & Freebody, 1999; Vasquez, 2010). As readers deconstruct text, they examine the relationships of power, privilege, and position in text.

Critical readers also reconstruct text to represent multiple perspectives and truths. This approach not only positions the reader to dig deeper beneath the surface level of the text, but also considers the information from other perspectives as they imagine and seek out counternarratives in search of a more complete truth.

FIGURE 1.2   Luke and Freebody's Four Resources Model

Code-Breaking Practices

Skills required to break the code of written texts such as, spelling, alphabet sounds in words, structural conventions and patterns

Meaning Making Practices

Opportunities to participate with text—including understanding and composing meaningful written, visual, and spoken texts—in relation to a reader's available knowledge and experiences

Text User Practices

Using texts functionally by knowing about and acting on different cultural and social functions that various texts perform and understanding that these functions shape the way texts are structured, such as their tone or degree of formality

Text Critic Practices

Practices that include critical analysis of text and the transformation of texts based on the understanding that texts are not natural or neutral and that they represent particular points of views that can silence some people, privilege others, and influence individuals and groups

In the Four Resources Model, each set of practices described above is needed for literacy learning but none in isolation is sufficient. Each of the four is inclusive with each being integral to the achievement of the others.

The Word "Critical"

The word "critical" applies to various ways of thinking:

Critical Thinking—A focus on deeper, analytical thinking (e.g., asking complex questions).

Critical Race Theory—The term was initially applied to legal studies in the 1970s (Bell, 1976). It is a cross-disciplinary way to examine and make sense of ongoing and systemic disparate outcomes (e.g., in real estate or educational opportunity) based on race (Baker-Bell et al., 2017; Bell, 2018; Crenshaw, 1989; Ladson-Billings, 2021; Love, 2021).

Critical Literacy—A way of thinking and being that is focused on both text consumption and text production as well as the relationship between the two (Janks, 1993, 2012; O'Brien, 2001; Vasquez, 1994; Vasquez et al., 2019).

Critical Comprehension—A framework for engaging with texts using a critical literacy lens. This is a term that we have coined to extend critical literacy and its application in elementary classrooms.

The following chart delineates what we mean and what we don't mean regarding critical literacy.

CRITICAL LITERACY IS . . .	CRITICAL LITERACY IS NOT . . .
• Centered on student issues and concerns • Responsive • A lens/framework for teaching, learning, and living • Embedded in our everyday teaching • Contextualized • Participatory justice-seeking learning • Fluid and evolving • Grounded in our own practice • Consciousness of power, privilege, and intention • A way to engage and empower active citizens • Liberating and transformative • A way of reading the word and the world (Freire & Macedo, 1987)	• Teacher-centered • An add-on • Isolated lessons taught out of context • One-size-fits-all curriculum • Linear and step-by-step • Finding the "right" answers to someone else's questions • Taking a single source as the whole truth • Accepting what is said or written without question • Indoctrination of beliefs or ideas

Central to critical comprehension instruction is a focus on students' interests, passions, and ideas as they engage with texts featuring critical dialogue and examination of both knowledge and the gatekeepers of that knowledge. This stance is in direct opposition to what Freire (2000) refers to as the "banking method" where teachers act as a dispenser of knowledge.

Critical comprehension is not a scripted program, and it does not follow a step-by-step sequence. Therefore, the focus of lessons will vary because it should be responsive to students' needs, interests, curiosities, and concerns. It also varies based on the context in which texts are being used to offer perspective for teaching and learning (Comber & Simpson, 2001; Comber et al., 2001; Vasquez, 2014).

Criticality calls for teachers to connect their teaching to the human condition and to frame their teaching practices in response to the "social and uneven times in which we live" (Muhammad, 2020). As teachers, we aim to prepare children to be successful in school-based literacy practices and to use literacy as a tool to become engaged and empowered citizens. When children learn to read with a critical stance, they begin to identify and examine problems, become more socially conscious, and work for social action to make a difference in their lives, the community, and the larger world around them (Vasquez, 2010, 2017).

Central to critical comprehension instruction is a focus on students' interests, passions, and ideas as they engage with texts featuring critical dialogue and examination of both knowledge and the gatekeepers of that knowledge.

A Framework for Critical Comprehension

In each chapter that follows you will find a collection of lessons with intentionally selected text to help readers of all ages engage with texts for critical comprehension.

We recommend asking the following questions when selecting texts. If you find these questions challenging, we recommend doing this work with a friend or colleague as a way to begin the process of critically analyzing texts.

- How does the book reflect students' identities and cultures?
- How does the book move beyond a "single story" and a "single truth"?
- Have the books received culturally specific awards (e.g., Coretta Scott King, Stonewall, Pura Belpré, etc.)?
- Is the text authentic and accurate?
- Does the text include harmful stereotypes?
- Does the book offer multiple perspectives?
- What other texts could provide alternate perspectives?
- Could the text cause harm? If so, for whom?
- What other texts can be layered to deepen understanding?

Reliable Sources for Book Recommendations

Social Justice Books: A Teaching for Change Project
www.socialjusticebooks.org

American Indians in Children's Literature by Debbie Reese
https://americanindiansinchildrensliterature.blogspot.com/

Learning for Justice
https://bit.ly/3vFdcA2

Equity Through Education Collaborative
https://bit.ly/3d7XzL5

Our Story: Exploring Diversity
http://ourstory.diversebooks.org/pro/1.05/

International Latino Book Awards
https://www.latinobookawards.org/

Rethinking Schools
https://rethinkingschools.org

Coretta Scott King Book Awards
bit.ly/3UISnTC

Stonewall Book Awards List
bit.ly/3OXnLXB

The lessons throughout this book are possibilities of what you may design for your own classroom practice. They are not intended to be scripted lessons or sequential in nature as we believe this work should ultimately emerge from the interests, concerns, curiosities, and questions posed by students. Each lesson features an intentionally selected text to be read aloud by the teacher and revisited for follow-up reads for deeper examination or excavation of a topic, idea, or issue.

Each lesson makes use of a framework that we have developed for supporting critical comprehension. The framework includes multiple reads of a text. The elements of the framework are described below and summarized in Figure 1.3.

 First Read: Movie Read

This first visit, the "movie read" (Laminack, 2019), focuses on taking in the story without interruption. In a movie theater, no one hits pause or stops to share their thoughts. Instead, the movie keeps going, and we keep watching and listening and making meaning individually. When the movie is over, we likely chat about our connections, confusions, interpretations, and questions. Our discussions often spark thoughts we hadn't considered and may raise new questions, confusion, or understanding. And that may result in viewing the movie again. If you return to the movie, you bring a new frame of reference, an understanding of the whole that enables you to tune in more closely and examine bits with new insight.

This first reading of the text is intended to be much like that first viewing of the movie and may be a full uninterrupted reading or a picture walk if the art is sufficient to provide a gestalt for the book, an overview of the whole. This experience offers insight into how the text is organized and the perspective from which it is told, and it provides a contextual frame in terms of time and place. It leaves students with budding knowledge of the issue(s), problem(s), or conflict(s). This positions you to revisit the text guided by their questions, knowing where they want to pause and examine more closely, and which ideas they want to challenge and excavate.

Read-Aloud Tip

When reading aloud, take the time to rehearse the book so that you have a feel for the pacing of the text and know the spots where you will shift your voice to reflect the tone and evoke the mood.

Before beginning the read aloud or picture walk, make sure the students are comfortably gathered near the book so they can clearly see the illustrations. Remember that some children may prefer to sit and listen while others need to sketch or jot ideas as they listen. Allow those who like to think with pencils or crayons to bring their tools with them.

 Second Read: Reading With the Text

The second read focuses on the common interpretations and dominant understanding, or widely accepted perspectives (Figure 1.1). When reading with the text, consider engaging with the text in one or more of the following ways:

- Summarize the text.
- Say something about the text:
  - Share a comment.
  - Make a connection.
  - Pose a question.

- Comment on a decision, change, action or reaction, or a wondering.
- Share a quote or phrase that resonates or makes you think about something differently.
- Do a quick write in response to a segment of the text.
- Make a quick sketch to visualize.
- Create a bumper sticker or theme statement for the text.

Reading with the text reveals students' current understanding and the skills or tools they use for engaging with text, along with what is on their minds. This can offer a starting point for framing the return read to read critically.

 Return Read: Reading Critically

Return read is a term we use to describe revisiting a text after the second read with a specific focus to question the text, examine whose voices or experiences are centered or decentered, or challenge the status quo. Through reading critically, we hope to create a space for students to "name and critique injustices to help them ultimately develop the agency to build a better world" (Muhammad, 2020, p. 12). In other words, during the return read, teachers and students are reading against the text, asking and answering questions about the word and the world.

When reading critically, consider engaging with the text in one or more of the following ways:

- Focus on alternate perspectives that challenge dominant understanding or beliefs.
- Read against the text by questioning the text, the author's intent, and our own stances as a reader.
- Explore how the text centers certain groups and ideas while marginalizing others.
- Consider how our identities influence the perspectives we bring to the text and how that shapes our understanding.
- Deconstruct the text to examine whose perspectives are included and whose are omitted and how that shapes our thinking.
- Consider how the historical perspective, the social and political climate of the setting, and the publication date may influence our thinking.

Return Read: Reading Critically Tip

As you read against the text, consider how your ideas and observations shift or change and whether you are encouraged to act on your new understanding. Are you eager to learn more? Are there gaps that need to be examined and shared? If so, where are they, and with whom should they be shared? How can you use the knowledge gained from exploring alternate perspectives to create a more complete narrative? Can you right any injustices? If so, how? What steps will you take to advocate for change and greater equality and justice?

Figures 1.3 through 1.5 provide questions to consider when reading for critical comprehension to support your work as you and your students read against the text.

You may need to scaffold, adapt, or rephrase some of these questions for your students.

FIGURE 1.3   Text Factors

Questions to Consider When Reading for Critical Comprehension

- ❑ How is the text organized in a way that highlights certain ideas and values over other ideas and values?
- ❑ How does the text work to highlight certain individuals or groups or make them seem more important?
- ❑ How does the text work to make certain individuals or groups less visible or make them seem unimportant?
- ❑ Who is the author? Does the author have credibility? Can they be trusted? Why or why not?
- ❑ How would the text be different if written by someone else? Who?
- ❑ How might the text help me challenge my perceptions and assumptions or my thoughts and ideas about a certain topic or issue?
- ❑ Does the text help me to think of a topic or issue in a different way?
- ❑ How is the text attempting to influence my thinking about this topic?
- ❑ How does the text perpetuate or disrupt stereotypes?
- ❑ Is the text accessible or understandable for all readers? If not, who would be able to easily make sense of the text? Who would find it hard to make sense of the text?
- ❑ How are words or images used to make the text easy or hard to understand?
- ❑ Who is missing and not represented or visible in the text? What purpose does it serve to exclude certain individuals or groups in a text?

FIGURE 1.4   Unpacking the Text

Questions to Consider When Reading for Critical Comprehension

☐   Whose perspective is included?

☐   Are there perspectives that were not included?

☐   Whose voice is heard?

☐   Whose voice is not heard?

☐   How do the different perspectives advantage some individuals and groups?

☐   How do the different perspectives disadvantage some individuals and groups?

☐   Whose story/voice is missing or misrepresented?

☐   What issues are being explored in the text?

☐   How/why do the issues being explored in the text present a problem or difficulty?

☐   How does the setting influence the story and the view or perspective I am offered?

☐   How do past causes that led to the event or idea in the story influence the view I am given?

☐   How does the social and political climate of the time period, or what is going on in the world and in my community, influence the view I am given?

☐   How can I use information from reading and talking about the text to inspire me to take action?

☐   What more can I read or research to give me other perspectives to consider?

online resources

FIGURE 1.5   Reader Factors

Questions to Consider When Reading for Critical Comprehension

☐   How does the text position me as a reader?

■   How does it make me feel as an individual?

■   Do I find it easy to make sense of the text or do I find it hard to make sense of the text?

■   Do my past experiences help me to make sense of the text?

■   What kinds of experiences would help me to make sense of the text?

☐   From what perspective am I reading the text?

☐   What experiences come to mind when I read the text?

☐   When assumptions do I make, or what understanding do I come away with based on reading the text?

☐   How does my position influence these assumptions?

online resources

⭐ Reading for Action

At the end of each chapter, we include a Reading for Action section to help bring together the big ideas from across the collection of lessons and make space for taking action. At this point you have read *with the text*, and you have read critically *against the text*. You and your students have done the work of reading critically to question the text and examine ways in which the text positions some in power while marginalizing others; you have engaged in robust conversations, further reading, and research to excavate more complete truths. Now is the time to ask, "So what? Now that we have done this work, how are we different and how do we use what we learned to outgrow our current selves?"

Invite students to reflect on the actions that seem most appropriate for them regarding the issue or topic under exploration. For example, students may make a commitment to conscious language use or a change of attitude or behavior. They may decide to create a public service announcement, reconstruct the text to provide an alternate version to share a more complete truth, design posters for the school or community, or launch a campaign to rally support for a particular cause (Laminack & Kelly, 2019). Remain open to what students feel inspired to do and help facilitate their decisions and actions.

Reading for Action

Reading for action may occur after reading one text or a collection of texts from a given chapter. If a particular text inspires children to act, follow their lead. Invite them to consider what an alternative text or counternarrative might offer. Ultimately, we aim to help children consider how to become agents of, rather than victims of, text.

Creating a Space for Critical Comprehension

The First Days of School

Although our intent in this section is to offer insight into ways of creating a classroom community as part of laying the groundwork for critical comprehension, we believe that fostering a classroom community is something that should happen as a prelude to learning together. One way to do this is by sending each child a handwritten letter or an email with information about yourself, including photos, and what you most look forward to in the coming year together. To learn more about the students, provide them with a self-addressed stamped envelope for their response or ask them to record a video. Invite them to share about themselves, their interests, and what they most look forward to.

Communicating With Families

Invite the parents/caregivers to share information about their child and their family's culture and lifestyle. By honoring students' and their families' funds of knowledge (Moll et al., 1992), we position their ways of being and knowing as valid and valuable. Powerful information about children and their families can help develop a culturally responsive curriculum, select culturally relevant resources, and build positive social identities for each child (Hass, 2020). To learn more about the children and their families, invite parents/caregivers to complete a survey (print or digital) at the beginning of the year and when new students join the class. Sample questions may include "What languages are spoken in your house?," "What are your memories of learning as a child?," and "What are your fears or concerns about your child this year in school, if any?" (Kleinrock, 2021).

Culturally Responsive Teaching

Culturally relevant and responsive teaching is an asset-based approach to empower students as capable learners by bridging their cultural learning styles and tools in the classroom (Hammond, 2015; Ladson-Billings, 2014).

Morning Meeting

Once school begins, we recommend starting each day with a morning meeting. In this meeting, everyone gathers in a comfortable spot where they can see each other. Begin the first meeting by naming it as a morning meeting and explaining that this is a routine that will occur daily. Explain that the purpose of the meeting is to come together in community to share what is on our minds and in our hearts and the many connections we will make to the learning happening throughout the day both in and out of the classroom. For the first meeting, we recommend getting to know each other.

The morning meeting is the bedrock for establishing a classroom community where children can feel comfortable being themselves. This includes being brave to be uncomfortable, to take risks, and to participate in critical conversations to grow as learners and human beings. Students need safe spaces where they can be vulnerable to speak their minds, share their truths, ask their questions, and push boundaries to disrupt, consider, and offer various perspectives. Trust must be established and maintained for children to be brave to participate in courageous conversations and foster critical comprehension.

Co-Constructing Agreements

After you have spent some time getting to know each other in morning meetings, have a conversation with students to co-construct a class agreement.

- **Tell students:** *We will have a lot of conversations this year and there will be times when some of us will have different opinions and ideas. No matter what each of us believes, we must listen and respond to each other respectfully. So, we need guidelines to help us know what to do when we disagree or when we have hard conversations. To help us do so, we will create a class agreement together.*

These agreements help establish a sense of belonging and shared ownership in the class community where students can participate without fear of judgment. When conversations explore sensitive topics, remind students of class agreement statements, such as "speak honestly about our experiences and feelings," "use I statements," or "listen with compassion," previously established and agreed on by all stakeholders.

The co-constructed classroom agreements can facilitate respectful conversations to provide opportunities for critical thinking and expand students' perspectives beyond their own experiences. A space created in this way gives students a voice, empowers them with confidence, and provides them the agency to make their own decisions. It also actively prepares students to become engaged citizens by embracing and practicing democratic values, active listening, communicating with others, working together to reach a compromise, and learning how to disagree or share an unpopular perspective while respecting others' views—all important skills for critical comprehension and life. "We the Kids" (Figure 1.6) is an example of a class agreement.

FIGURE 1.6   We the Kids

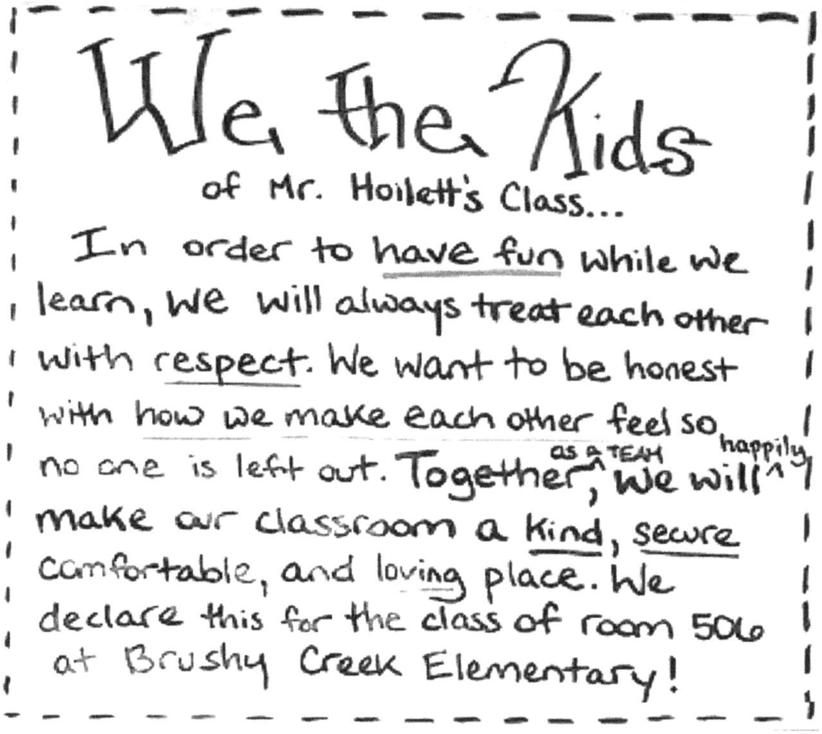

> We, the Kids
>
> of Mr. Hoilett's Class...
>
> In order to have fun while we learn, we will always treat each other with respect. We want to be honest with how we make each other feel so no one is left out. Together, as a TEAM we will happily make our classroom a kind, secure comfortable, and loving place. We declare this for the class of room 506 at Brushy Creek Elementary!

Individual and Class Affirmations

With a class agreement established, another way to build the foundation for critical comprehension work includes the use of individual and class affirmations. Affirmations are words or phrases to remind ourselves of key principles and values that matter to us individually and as a collective community.

Students in Alyssa (Cameron) Likens's fifth-grade class begin each day by reciting a co-constructed class pledge comprised of agreed-on affirmations (Figure 1.7).

The process for co-constructing this class pledge began with a read aloud of Grace Byers's *I Am Enough* (Figure 1.8).

After reading, students created individual affirmations to highlight what makes them who they are and finished each statement with "I Am Enough." Then the students placed the affirmations where they could see them as a daily reminder (Figure 1.9). After students created individual

FIGURE 1.7   Class Pledge

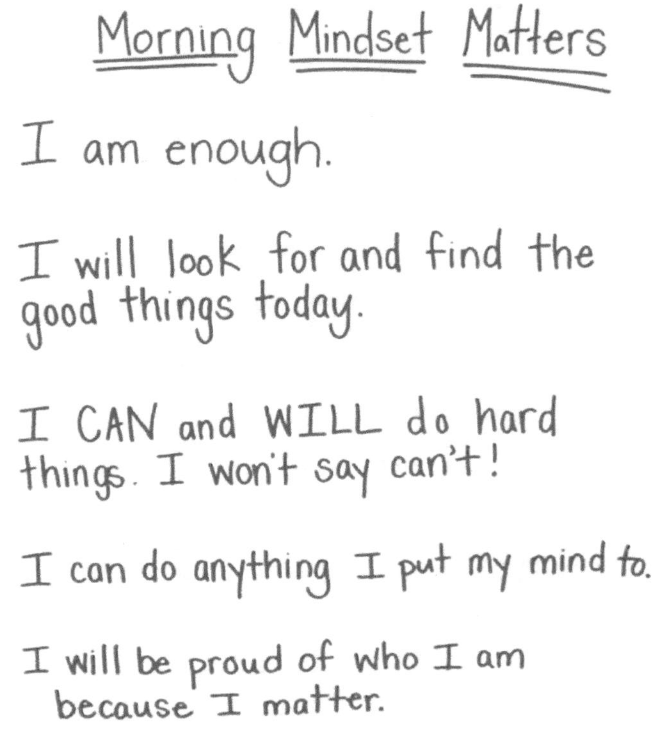

<u>Morning</u> <u>Mindset</u> <u>Matters</u>

I am enough.

I will look for and find the good things today.

I CAN and WILL do hard things. I won't say can't!

I can do anything I put my mind to.

I will be proud of who I am because I matter.

affirmations, they brainstormed classroom affirmations as a group. Then they narrowed the big list down to five agreed-on statements for the class pledge. Each morning, a student leads the class in repeating them together.

Trusting Ourselves and Each Other

Our stories matter and we must make space for students to share their own stories. Knowing who we are and who we share space with is essential to building the trust necessary to engage in courageous and critical conversations. Feltman (2009) defines trust as choosing to risk making something you value vulnerable to another person's actions. According to Brown (podcast on trust, November 2021), trust is built on the everyday small moments and interactions with others. She tells the story of how her daughter was heartbroken and in tears one day after coming home from school. She confided in her third-grade peers only to have them turn around and tell the whole class who then laughed at her. Brown uses the analogy of the classroom marble jar to ask her

FIGURE 1.8 *I Am Enough*

GRACE BYERS

I Am Enough

PICTURES BY
KETURAH A. BOBO

Source: Byers, G. *I Am Enough*. Balzer & Bray (2018).

daughter which friends contribute marbles and in what ways. Her daughter responds by saying that one friend saves her a seat in the cafeteria, and another acknowledges and greets her grandparents when they attend their soccer game. These seemingly small moments are exactly the kinds of things we can do to build trust. When we offer our stories and listen to others' stories without judgment, we are building trust.

Daniel Hoilett tells his students, "We are bridge builders, but we can't build bridges and make connections if we don't have two ends to start from." Students in Ms. (Cameron) Likens's class brainstorm and share ways they want their peers and teacher to treat them (Figure 1.10).

Books as Mirrors, Windows, Doors, and Curtains

With a class agreement, class pledge, and steps to build trust, we've begun the necessary foundational work to engage in critical conversations. Additionally, we must ensure that all children have

Scan the QR code to watch Courtney Farrell's 2018 TED Talk, when she says, "The shortest distance between two people is a story."

FIGURE 1.9   Individual Affirmation: "I Can Do Anything I Put My Mind To"

FIGURE 1.10   Ms. (Cameron) Likens's Students Build Trust by Sharing How They Want to Be Treated

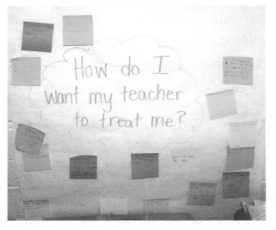

opportunities to see themselves reflected in the curriculum in positive and affirming ways. This includes in the pages of the books they read and have read to them, in images posted on walls and on screens, and in the topics being explored in the classroom. Books, for instance, must be *mirrors* (Bishop, 1990) where students can see reflections of themselves. When readers see themselves reflected in the texts they read, they are affirmed and valued (Bishop, 1990; Boyd et al., 2015). This leads to greater engagement in reading as they make connections and interpretations of text (Au, 1980; Christ & Sharma, 2018; Keene & Zimmerman, 2007; Tatum & Muhammad, 2012).

It is also important that children have opportunities for text to serve as *windows* (Bishop, 1990). Literature as a window allows a reader to stand safely in their own identity while exploring a world beyond their current view or demographic and holds the potential to expand their perspectives and understanding of others in the broader society.

Books can also serve as *sliding glass doors* (Bishop, 1990). These books invite the reader to step inside the world unfolding in the book as if they are walking alongside the character.

Dr. Debbie Reese (2019a) has expanded Bishop's metaphor. She writes,

> I have been adding a "curtain" to Bishop's (1990) "mirrors, windows, and sliding glass doors" metaphor when I talk or write about Native stories. This is a way to acknowledge and honor the stories behind the curtain—those that are purposefully kept within Native communities. Native communities resisted historical oppression and continue to preserve our culture by cultivating our ways in private spaces—behind the curtain. While Native people share some of our ways publicly in the present day, there is a great deal that we continue to protect from outsiders. Furthermore, it conveys the importance of [knowing] what belongs within the community and what knowledge can be shared outside of our communities. (pp. 390–391)

The addition of Reese's curtain creates a space for us to better understand what it means to support Native children with the use of children's books about Native American nations that best represent their experiences. The same can be said of books that represent other cultural groups.

For more information on the influential work of Rudine Sims Bishop and Debbie Reese, you can visit these websites:

Bishop's article, "Mirrors, Windows, and Sliding Glass Doors"
https://scenicregional.org/wp-content/uploads/2017/08/Mirrors-Windows-and-Sliding-Glass-Doors.pdf

Reese's blog, American Indians in Children's Literature
https://americanindiansinchildrensliterature.blogspot.com

Creating Safe Spaces for Critical Conversations

According to Learning for Justice's *Let's Talk* (Teaching Tolerance, 2019), critical conversations include "any discussions about the ways that injustice affects our lives and our society. It's a conversation that explores the relationship between identity and power, that traces the structures that privilege some at the expense of others, that helps students think through the actions they can take to create a more just, more equitable, world" (p. 2).

To foster safe spaces for all students to participate in critical conversations, Mr. Hoilett frames his teaching with the Children's Defense Fund Freedom School Partners model for emotional, mental, physical, and spiritual safety (EMPS).

EMPS	FOR TEACHERS	FOR STUDENTS
Emotional safety	How might this book make my students feel?	Can I trust my class with all my feelings?
Mental safety	What mirror or window can I offer to set the stage?	Do I feel comfortable being vulnerable here?
Physical safety	How will I react if conflict arises?	Will I still be okay after I open up to my class?
Spiritual safety	How will I ensure that all hearts and minds are clear?	Am I going to want to share in this way again?

Before doing this work with his students, Mr. Hoilett does his own work. He considers each question from the teacher's standpoint while planning for read alouds and critical conversations, especially when tackling tough topics. He devotes time during the morning meeting and throughout the instructional day to ensure that students' hearts and minds are ready to be open and vulnerable to learn together in respectful and collaborative ways.

One day while discussing the impact westward expansion had on Native Americans, one student in Mr. Hoilett's class exclaimed, "Mr. H, please tell me this all is fake!? No offense to you [pointing to the white students in the room] but this is why I really get frustrated!"

Mr. Hoilett remained calm and paused to ponder how to move the conversation forward. He considered the EMPS questions "How will I react if conflict arises?" and "How will I ensure that all hearts and minds are clear?" He began by referring to the class agreement "We the Kids" (Figure 1.6) and reminded the class that they agreed to create a classroom rooted in respect and love. He then reiterated that although the past is inseparably linked to the present, the white students in his class were not responsible for what occurred in the past, including the impact of westward expansion on Native Americans, and they should not feel a sense of guilt. He explained that although systems of inequality have existed for a long time, we can all work together to end them.

He then reminded the class of an earlier conversation they had about how they wanted to be treated when there is a conflict. "Let's remember that we can't deny our friend's feelings. Can we work toward understanding his perspective and what led to his reaction?" The students' heads nod. Mr. Hoilett then asks the student if he would like to say more about why he was frustrated. The student revealed that he was thinking about the treatment of the Native Americans and how it reminded him of the way the Black community is treated in the United States. He explained how his family regularly discusses current events in the news like the Black Lives Matter protests in response to the killings of unarmed Black men and women. As a Black boy himself, he was highly aware of race relations and racism in his life and in the world around him.

The space created by Mr. Hoilett, for students like this boy to share his reality, is invaluable.

This conversation reveals the relationship between identity and power and how some groups have been and continue to be marginalized. To help students delve deeper into these important conversations, we've developed a series of lessons that you'll find in the chapters that follow.

In this chapter, we defined what we mean by critical comprehension and outlined a framework we developed for use with texts from picture books to print ads and commercials. The elements of the framework were

FIGURE 1.11   Mr. Hoilett Reads to His Class

highlighted, and suggestions were offered for using the lessons to create space for critical comprehension in the curriculum.

Chapters 2 through 7 include easy-to-implement lesson series for multiple reads of texts, each focused on different topics:

- Chapter 2, with its focus on identity, is the bedrock for the remaining chapters. We encourage you to do the work alongside your students. To teach critical comprehension, we must first be critically conscious ourselves.

- With the foundation established on identity, Chapter 3 launches an exploration of perspective. This lesson series begins with the exploration of perspective using a wordless picture book to show how more information can be revealed as we widen our lens and then moves to more complex concepts around perspective, including the role of power in decision making and considering other perspectives.

- Chapter 4 begins with an introduction to the concept of stereotypes and then moves to an exploration of different ways stereotypes shape our thinking and understanding.

- In Chapter 5 we have selected a collection of books to explore bias. Each book creates a space for helping children to learn what it means to read books (the word) and the world from an antibias perspective.

- The lessons in Chapter 6 focus on historically marginalized groups to help students broaden perspectives, challenge stereotypes, and expand their understanding of the past and the present.

- In Chapter 7 we focus on consumerism and make use of picture books and everyday texts like ads and commercials to help students develop an awareness of the intent of product manufacturers and become critical consumers who question and make conscious and informed decisions about their needs and wants.

The lessons were chosen based on feedback from teachers regarding topics they want to address in their classrooms, that they find challenging, or topics for which they would like support. How to work with issues of identity was one such topic so we started there. Identity matters. How we see ourselves and how others see us contribute to shaping what we believe we can and cannot do and influences who we believe we can and cannot be. We believe identity work is a starting point for all the other work. We must examine ourselves, face our biases, and understand the limitations of our perspectives before leading children to do the same.

In the conclusion, we invite you to engage in the process of creating your own unit of study using our critical comprehension framework. To do this we walk you through our process for creating one of the chapters in this book.

We hope you enjoy using the lessons we created for you as much as we enjoyed creating them. We look forward to hearing about the units and lessons that you create for your students.

Exploring Identities

2

Alyssa (Cameron) Likens read *Emmanuel's Dream* by Laurie Ann Thompson to her fifth-grade class (Figure 2.1). The story, based on the life of Emmanuel Ofosu Yeboah, includes both visible and invisible disabilities. Emmanuel was born with only one fully formed leg, but it didn't stop him from walking to school, playing soccer, and becoming a cyclist who advocated for others with disabilities. Jake (pseudonym), a student with a hearing impairment, instantly engaged with how Emmanuel viewed his disability as a difference, not as an inability. As the class talked through Emmanuel's view of a disability, there was a shift in the classroom tone. Other students who shared frequently, and sometimes dominated class discussions, made space for their classmates to share while they listened.

FIGURE 2.1   Ms. (Cameron) Likens's Class Discusses *Emmanuel's Dream*

© Lester Laminack

Stories offer opportunities to share, connect, and raise questions. Stories allow us to witness life from a different perspective. For Jake's classmates, *Emmanuel's Dream* served as a window (Bishop, 1990) to his experience that helped them to think about Jake as having a hearing difference rather than being disabled. For Jake, *Emmanuel's Dream* served as a mirror (Bishop, 1990) through which he was able to see himself and beyond his differences to imagine new possibilities. Stories situate us to recognize our common humanity while appreciating and celebrating the differences that make us who we are. Stories open the doorway into insight, questions, and conversation. Stories—something so simple—can have such a profound impact.

The focus on identity in this chapter is the bedrock for the work we invite you to do as you engage in reading, writing, and teaching with a critical lens. We contend that it is necessary for all of us as educators to examine our own social identities and how those identities influence our thinking and our teaching. As such we encourage you to do the work yourself by first examining your own identity and how it positions you in the world and in your teaching.

Who Is Teaching America's Children?

Although the demographics of K–12 students continue to become more diverse, teachers remain predominantly white and female. According to Pew Research data, 47 percent of students enrolled in K–12 schools in 2018–19 were white, and 79 percent of teachers identified as white in 2017–18.

When children of color have a teacher who looks like them, they are more likely to do better academically, graduate from high school, and have more positive feelings and attitudes toward school (Egalite & Kisida, 2017). So, it is imperative that school district teacher recruitment practices and hiring policies focus on hiring Black and Brown teachers who represent their students, especially in areas where there is a large percentage of children of color.

In addition to discrepancies in race and gender, there is an absence of gender nonbinary individuals in statistics representing the teacher workforce. Showing respect for gender identity and expression can be affirming for students who identify as nonbinary, gender nonconforming, and/or transgender, and creates a culture of inclusion and diversity in education (Roberts et al., 2020).

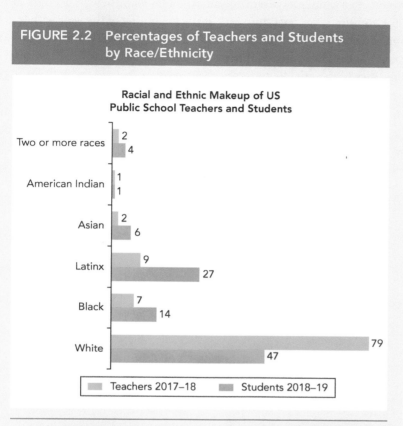

FIGURE 2.2   Percentages of Teachers and Students
by Race/Ethnicity

Racial and Ethnic Makeup of US
Public School Teachers and Students

Source: Adapted from Schaeffer, K. "America's public school teachers are far less racially and ethnically diverse than their students." Pew Research Center, Washington D.C. (2021) https://pewrsr.ch/3rSsNLB

Setting a Foundation for Exploring Identity

A strong foundation for learning begins by cultivating a community where all individuals feel visible and valued. Toward that goal, we provide a series of lessons featuring intentionally selected literature using the instructional framework (see Chapter 1) to spark conversations and exploration of our individual and social identities.

Young people are in a constant state of discovery—about themselves, others, the world, and their place in the world. Their thoughts and ideas are forming and reforming as they participate in the world and interact with others. Providing students with a safe space to explore identity is essential to help build a classroom community and help each child find their place within the larger society.

We can help students discover and celebrate who they are as individuals. Oftentimes we start this work at the beginning of the year with "getting to know you" and "all about me" activities. However, going beyond basic interests (e.g., liking dinosaurs) to learn about students' complex identities is essential to understanding them, connecting with them, and creating culturally relevant and sustaining student-centered learning opportunities. As Enriquez (2021) notes, "Identities never comprise single descriptors; a student's identity is a rich mosaic of experiences, values, perspectives, and cultural ways of knowing, being, doing, and communicating" (p. 104). Therefore, this work is ongoing, not limited to beginning-the-year "getting to know you" activities.

Critical Comprehension
Lesson Series
Exploring Identities

This lesson series begins with an exploration of identity in a broad sense, then explores more nuanced aspects that shape identity. Each lesson features one book, but also includes a list of alternatives for additional work to extend thought and insight. As is the case with all the lessons in this book, we offer these ideas as a starting point and encourage you to adapt them based on the interests and inquiries of students.

We encourage you to do the work alongside your students and to share your ideas and experiences regularly as a model of how thinking and insight evolve. Doing so will provide students with a window into your identity and help build classroom community as well.

Table of Lessons for Exploring Identities

LESSON FOCUS	ANCHOR TEXT
1. Exploring our identities	*I Am Every Good Thing* by Derrick Barnes
2. What is identity?	*Skin Again* by bell hooks
	This Book Is Anti-Racist by Tiffany Jewell
3. Hair and identity	*I Love My Hair* by Natasha Anastasia Tarpley
4. Telling our stories	*The Day You Begin* by Jacqueline Woodson
5. Being your truest self	*The Proudest Blue* by Ibtihaj Muhammad with S.K. Ali

Note: The blank spaces are an invitation for you to add your own related topics and texts.

Defining Identity

When introducing this lesson series, begin with an invitation for students to co-construct a definition of identity. Record their thinking on a chart or audit trail (see Figure 2.3) (Vasquez, 2014) and return to it over time to show how their thinking is changing and growing.

Second graders from Jessica Roberts's class defined identity as "what you look like or what you're known as" and "It's kind of like your history and your family and who you are" (Laminack & Kelly, 2019). Bryan Woods's kindergarten students shared examples of how other people's words and actions caused them to want to act and talk in certain ways (Vasquez et al., 2022). These students remind us that who we are, who we perceive ourselves to be, and how we move through the world are shaped by many factors including when we were born, where we live and with whom, our lived experiences with others, and events we see unfold in our social worlds.

FIGURE 2.3   Audit Trail

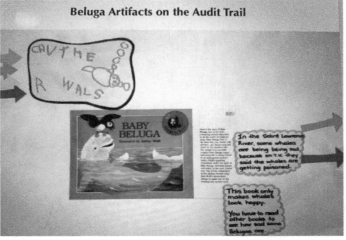

Beluga Artifacts on the Audit Trail

After constructing a definition of identity, have students engage in the following activity on identity and naming.

What Is an Audit Trail?

An audit trail is a visible articulation of learning over time (Vasquez, 2014). Instances of learning are captured and represented using various artifacts, including photographs, drawings, writing, and book covers (see Figure 2.3).

An audit trail is a powerful tool for showing the children's in-process thinking over time, generating topics for study, constructing meaning, and circulating meaning.

An audit trail is meant to be visible not only to the people in a classroom community but to others in the school community as well. This public visibility makes the audit trail a participatory site for becoming involved in the children's learning. Students and teachers research their world together and produce representations of that research, in the form of an audit trail displayed on a bulletin board, or another surface, covered with various artifacts of learning. Throughout the year, previous learning events can be revisited using the artifacts as trigger images that serve as reminders of work done and the learning that has taken place.

Hello My Names Are/Hello My Names Are Not

Vivian created this strategy after participating in a Podcaster conference where she noticed participants writing not only their real names but also their podcast names and social media names on their nametags. The strategy, therefore, creates space for children and adults to understand we don't have a single identity but rather multiple identities and that those identities are constructed in particular ways through our experiences and the situations we are in. It is also about helping learners to understand how their naming of others contributes to the identities of those individuals (Vasquez et al., 2022).

Hello, My Names Are . . .

To begin a conversation about names, **say to students:**

- *No matter what each of us believes, we must listen and respond to each other respectfully. So, we need guidelines to help us know what to do when we disagree or when we have hard conversations. To help us do so, we will create a class agreement together.*

- *Make a list of all the names you would respond to.*

- *Where do your names come from?*

- *Which names matter to you? Why do these names matter?*

- *Which names don't matter to you and why?*

- *Which names would you readily respond to?*

- *Which names would you not readily respond to?*

- *What effects do these names have on you?*

- *Do these names affect your actions or decisions in some way?*

Hello, My Names Are Not . . .

Next, **say to students:**

- *Make a list of names people call you that you ignore or that you find problematic.*

- *Where do these names come from?*

- *Are there any biases underlying these names?*

- *Are there any stereotypes underlying these names?*

- *How do you feel when you are called these names?*

- *What effects do these names have on you?*

- *Do these names affect your actions or decisions in some way?*

Names matter. Naming practices matter. These matter because they help shape who we see ourselves as being. Reflecting on your "namings" is a good first step in doing identity work and thinking about how our identities influence our thinking and our teaching. Muhammad (2020) reminds us that it is typically through our names that we are first introduced to the world and "they carry our cultures, values, traditions, and past" (p. 75).

For Younger Students

Rather than simply having students list their names, begin by giving them one name tag that has "Hello My Names Are" across the top. The children then write or draw their names using a variety of writing/ drawing tools. As a class, discuss the same sorts of questions as those listed above.

Following this, give students a second name tag with "Hello My Names Are Not" across the top. The children once again write and draw their names. This time, to ensure the children are not made vulnerable, give them a chance to think about those names on their own instead of sharing them aloud. To wrap up, students can engage in a general conversation about naming practices and the importance of names, including why names matter, the history of our names and the names we choose for others, and the positive and negative effects of names. Use this activity at the start of the year as one way to begin to establish what it means to be a classroom community.

For a name tag template, visit https://bit.ly/3A6XtfX.

Lesson 1: Exploring Our Identities
I Am Every Good Thing • by Derrick Barnes

FIGURE 2.4

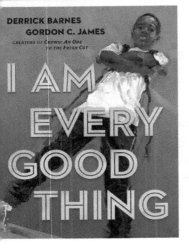

A teaching guide for *I Am Every Good Thing.*

 First Read: Movie Read

This first visit, the "movie read," focuses on taking in the story without interruption (see Chapter 1, p. 21). *I Am Every Good Thing* celebrates the wonders and genius of young Black boys in a playful but potent style. The young Black narrator is proud of the things that make him who he is, such as being creative, smart, and funny. Other times he's afraid of being misunderstood and called what he is not. The book creates space for engaging in important conversations about identity and how identity works to shape who we believe we can and cannot be and what we believe we can and cannot do.

Second Read: Reading With the Text

Before you begin the second read, display the cover and read the title.

Ask students: *What makes you feel happy, proud, seen, heard, and valued?*

As you read with the text, point out the repeating language "I am . . . I am every good thing."

Ask students: *Do you have any theories for why the author uses this repeating phrase?*

After reading, invite students to create a found poem. A found poem is a literary collage that consists of using words and phrases from existing texts and organizing them into a poem.

Begin by recording the student's favorite line or phrase on a sentence strip. Have them share why they selected that particular line. For example, "I am good to the core, like the center of a cinnamon roll" evokes sensory details, or "I am one eye open, one eye closed, peeking through a microscope, gazing through a telescope" is important because it highlights Black scientists and astronauts, such as Katherine Johnson, Ron McNair, and Mae Jemison.

Ask students:

- *Why did you choose that line?*

- *Did it remind you of something or someone?*

- *What is your connection to that line?*

- *Why did you choose that line over some of the other lines?*

Ideas come from somewhere. They are rooted in our past experiences and encounters. Asking questions like these helps students to reflect on where their ideas come from and what has influenced or shaped those ideas.

If multiple students select the same line, they could co-construct one sentence strip together to contribute to the found poem. Because it resonates with many, that line may become a refrain or repeating line in the poem. Read the poem aloud together.

Together with the students, begin to organize the sentence strips to create a poem. Read the poem aloud by having the students read their own sentence strips.

Ask students: *What effect did the combined sentences have?*

Alternative Second Read

If during the second read students begin sharing specific "I am" connections (e.g., a student shares something about being an avid reader), other students could be encouraged to add their own connections to their "I am" statements. Help students notice what they have in common with their peers and interesting things they learned about their peers. For instance, if Maxine likes to ride the skateboard, maybe she can teach Josh how to do an ollie.

Point out that learning more about each other helps us avoid making assumptions resulting from having a limited notion of one another. Students' "I am" statements could also be compiled into a poem or a class book or posted on a wall. This information could result in a class expert list, which may lead to informational writing to teach about various subjects (e.g., Maxine can create a multimodal informational piece about how to do an ollie, including writing, images, and maybe even video clips of her in action).

 ## Return Read: Reading Critically

Begin by reading aloud the dedication page and making note of the publication date. Pause and ask students to notice the names on the dedication page.

Ask students:

- *Why did the author Derrick Barnes deliberately choose to add a list of names?*

- *What effect does the listing of the names have on you as a reader?*

Ask if they recognize the names of Tamir Rice, Trayvon Martin, and others. You may pull up photos and provide some background information about the seven people whose names are included in the dedication.

Ask students:

- *Why do you think the author dedicated the book to these specific people?*

- *What might the author want you to know, think, feel, or wonder?*

- *Why is this important?*

Read the book, stopping in a few strategic places along the way to invite conversation. For example, pause when you get to "Although I am something like a superhero, every now and then, I am afraid. I am not what they might call me, and I will not answer to any name that is not my own. I am what I say I am."

Ask students:

- *Can you share connections?*

- *Do you have questions?*

- *What are you thinking or wondering?*

- *What do you think the author's message is?*

Write the following excerpt on chart paper:

I am afraid.

I am not what they might call me,

and I will not answer to any name that is not my own.

I am what I say I am.

Ask students:

- *If someone is afraid, then is there someone or something that they fear? Who or what is feared in the line "I am afraid"?*

- *Who are "they" in "I am not what they might call me"?*

- *What do you think "they" are calling the child narrator in the book?*

- *Why would someone call another person a name that is not their name? What effect does that have on a person?*

- *Why do you think the narrator in the book said, "I will not answer to any name that is not my own"? What did they mean by "I will not answer to any name"?*

- *What is the difference between saying "I am what I say I am" and "I am what they say I am"?*

Invite students to turn and talk if they need more time for conversation. After, give students the opportunity to reflect on the group discussion and their conversation with their peers. Ask students to write their own "I am/I am not" statements to reflect their identities (see Figures 2.5 and 2.6).

FIGURE 2.5 "I Am" Statement

I Am Equivalent to everyone like Fractions. I'm a Snowflake different from others I am Brave Like lions Protecting But Like a vase fragile I am Worthy of trust,

---

FIGURE 2.6 "I Am" Statement

I am a pusher I am the bird that is being held back by the wind but still manages to get somewhere

I am like a super hero. always has atleast 2 weakness.

I am a cricket who is small but can make a diffrence

I am worthy of good friendly realationship and friends of some kind.

Students could select a favorite line from their "I am" poem to contribute to a class poem, which could be posted in the classroom or the hallway. Invite each student to read their own line.

Additional Return Read Options

The return read options included in this chapter are additional experiences to explore identity, based on the students' responses and conversations. For each of these books, highlight how **who we are is shaped by those who come before us.**

Exploration of Stereotypes

A possible return read can engage students in various conversations, such as the importance of getting to know a person more fully by avoiding making decisions about them with limited information. This could lead to a powerful exploration of stereotypes. For example, Gordon James, the illustrator of *I Am Every Good Thing*, discusses the decision to include the illustration of the children swimming to dispel the stereotype that all Black people are afraid of the water. Further, it was important to acknowledge the history of access to swimming pools for Black people. If the conversation takes this direction, we invite you to explore the lessons featured in Chapter 4, "Examining Stereotypes."

Author's Craft

For another return read focused on the author's craft, invite students to examine the repetition of "I am." Ask students what the effect might be of the repeated use of "I." What difference does it make to use the sentence frame "I am" repeatedly? They may apply the technique to their own writing using the sentence frame "I am" to write affirmations about themselves.

Layering Texts

Looking Like Me by Walter Dean Myers is an excellent book to explore the author's craft and additional ideas related to identity. Myers's focus is embracing who you are, your strengths, and the qualities that make you uniquely yourself. *Looking Like Me* tells the story of a boy named Jeremy who comes across people and places in his life that remind him of who he is. Jeremy encounters his father, his sister, his brother, his teacher, and several others and realizes his relationship to each of them. For example, he is a brother to his sister, he is a son to his father, he is a writer to his teacher, and so on. Jeremy embodies the idea that no child should feel limited in any way and that they are much more valued and cherished than they imagine.

Older students can read the "I Am What I Am" essays from Romano's (2004) book, *Crafting Authentic Voice*, and craft their own "I Am What I Am" pieces: bit.ly/3GWS9PZ

Language for Liberation

Discuss how some words can be used to make people feel powerful while other words can be used to strip people of their identities and position them in inferior ways. Reclaiming who we are and who we come from is a way to position ourselves with love and liberation.

Read *The 1619 Project: Born on the Water* by Nikole Hannah-Jones and Renée Watson and make connections to the line "I am brave. I am hope. I am my ancestors' wildest dreams."

Read *The Year We Learned to Fly* by Jacqueline Woodson and compare and connect with the line "My grandmother had learned to fly from the people who came before. They were aunts and uncles and cousins who were brought here on huge ships, their wrists and ankles cuffed in iron, but, my grandmother said, nobody can ever cuff your beautiful and brilliant mind." Notice the illustration on the page and compare it with what students discussed in the book *Born on the Water* by Nikole Hannah-Jones and Renée Watson.

Scan here to access *An Educator's Guide to The 1619 Project: Born on the Water.*

Lesson 2: What Is Identity?
Skin Again • by bell hooks

FIGURE 2.7

 First Read: Movie Read

This first visit, the "movie read," focuses on taking in the story without interruption (see Chapter 1, p. 21). *Skin Again* makes the point that race matters, but what's most important is who we are on the inside and celebrating all that makes each individual unique and different.

 Second Read: Reading With the Text

After reading a second time, invite students to create self-portraits and sketch or list aspects of their identities around the drawing (see Figures 2.8 and 2.9). Note: You will be returning to these portraits. When finished, ask students to share with a partner and then invite those who wish to share with the whole group. This can be done during the lesson or during morning meeting time (see Chapter 1).

FIGURE 2.8   Identity Self-Portrait

Return Read: Reading Critically

For the return read, invite students to notice the illustrations in *Skin Again* and share thoughts about the illustrator's decisions.

Ask students:

- *What do you notice?*

- *Why do you think the illustrator included a snake and an onion in the illustrations?*

- *What might they symbolize?*

Discuss bell hooks's use of snakes and onions as a metaphor for talking about the skin we are in. The peeling of an onion or a snake's shedding of its skin are shown as ways for us to think about getting inside our skin to make our identities visible and how we shed the old as we grow and evolve into our new selves.

Reread the page:

If you want to know who I am

you have got to come inside.

Engage students in a discussion about how we have both outside and inside identities and have layers like an onion.

Have students return to their portraits and affix them to the center of a larger sheet of paper. Then ask them to list who they are on the inside and who they are on the outside (see Figure 2.9).

Post the revised portraits around the room. Have the students do a gallery walk to look closely at each other's portraits.

Ask students:

- *What have you learned about your peers after viewing their inside-outside portraits?*

- *Why is it important to get to know our peers, including their inside identities?*

Take this opportunity to reiterate that we do not have a single identity; rather we have multiple identities. Remind students that our identities have been shaped, and will continue to be shaped, by our participation

FIGURE 2.9   Revised Portrait

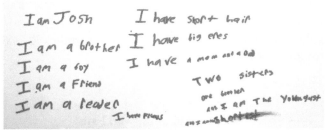

in the world through using words, being with people, going places, and interacting with things around us.

You might also discuss with students that in the same way that we are shaped by our participation in the world, we also contribute to shaping the world around us by our words and actions.

Layering Texts for Older Students

This Book Is Anti-Racist by Tiffany Jewell includes twenty lessons on how to take action and do anti-racism work with young people. Layering it with *Skin Again* can help students come to understand that their identity is multifaceted and influenced by many factors.

Revisit this excerpt from Chapter 1:

Your identity is what makes you, *YOU*: it's all the parts that make you unique. You are made up of your family, your friends, your neighborhood, your school, what you see on social media and read in books, what you hear and listen to, what you eat, what you wear, what you feel, your dreams, the stories you cannot wait to share and those you don't want to tell and everything in between and all around. YOU ARE EVERYTHING WITHIN YOU AND EVERYTHING THAT SURROUNDS YOU. You are all the ancestors who came before you: those you've never known, never heard of, never seen—and those you've passed on the street, sat next to, and snuggled near. (p. 10)

Highlight this statement:

YOU ARE EVERYTHING WITHIN YOU

AND EVERYTHING THAT SURROUNDS YOU.

Invite students to say something about this statement.

Ask students:

- *What does "You are everything within you" mean?*

- *What does "You are everything that surrounds you" mean?*

- *How does our environment at home, at school, in the community, and in the broader society affect who we are?*

Next, have students do a close read of their surroundings. Focus on the posters in the school hallways or classroom walls as well as advertisements in magazines, websites, and so on.

Ask students:

- *Do you see yourself in these posters?*

- *What do these posters say about you?*

- *In what ways do these posters tell you who you can and cannot be or what you can and cannot do?*

After some discussion, invite students to redesign the school posters in a way that makes their identity visible or that speaks to celebrating one's identity. Display posters for others in the school to see.

(Continued)

(Continued)

Re-create the following on chart paper and read with students.

YOU ARE EVERYTHING WITHIN YOU AND EVERYTHING THAT SURROUNDS YOU. (*This Book Is Anti-Racist* by Tiffany Jewell)	If you want to know who I am you have got to come inside. (*Skin Again* by bell hooks)

Ask students:

- *What do you think of these two definitions?*
- *How are they different?*
- *How are they the same?*
- *How does each define identity?*
- *How would you define identity, based on these quotes?*

Dominant Culture and Identities

When Beverly Tatum (2017) asks people to complete the statement "I am . . ." she finds that white people rarely mention race, men rarely mention gender, and heterosexuals rarely mention sexual orientation. That is because the categories with which these groups identify are dominant ways of being that position men, whites, and heterosexuals in privileged and powerful ways. These are categories that contribute to making up our identities. Kendi (2019) argues that it is incorrect to conceive of race as a social construct rather than as a power construct. The same can be said for being heterosexual and for being male. Dominance is about having power and influence over others. The flip side then is not having dominance, not having the same power and influence over others.

Jewell, in Chapter 2, p.18, of *This Book Is Anti-Racist*, states that these identities or categories have been created, named, framed, and defined by society for a very long time. As such, undoing these categories takes time. However, since these have been socially constructed, they can be deconstructed and reconstructed to create more equity-based categories.

For Older Students

Ask students to reflect on their "I am/I am not" statements, inside/outside identity maps, or self-portraits. Invite them to examine and name (e.g., race, ethnicity, gender, religion, sexual orientation, body size/shape) the aspects of their identity they included and those they excluded (whether intentional or unintentional). Make space for students to talk about what they notice.

Ask students:

- *How many of you noted race/gender/religion/etc.?*
- *Do the results align with Tatum's observations?*
- *What might have led you to include or exclude certain parts of your identities?*
- *How do certain parts of your identities afford you more (or less) privilege or opportunities?*

For Younger Students

To introduce the idea of power structures and identity to younger students, guide them through a series of picture books, such as those listed at the end of this lesson.

Ask students:

- *Which characters are the main characters in the story?*
- *What do they look like?*
- *Which characters have important roles in the story?*
- *Who are they and what roles do they play?*
- *Which characters don't have important roles in the story?*
- *Who are they and what roles do they play?*
- *Which characters do you see or hear a lot from in the story?*
- *Which characters do you rarely see in the story?*
- *What kind of characters do you think are missing from the story that should be added?*

Follow the children's lead, helping them to name issues (e.g., gender representation), and from there build on their understanding. You can do this by inviting them to come up with an alternate storyline that shifts the characters' roles or have them sketch and describe a character they think should be added to the story.

Pause to Reflect

We encourage you to engage in this work before you begin with students. Be attentive to aspects of identity you may want to layer into your list. Then examine what was NOT included. It is important for us, as adults, to acknowledge and understand our identities and to recognize how that shapes the way we move through the world and how it positions us in our spaces of teaching, learning, and life.

Consider the role of intersectionality (the way people's social identities can overlap) as you listen to Kimberlé Crenshaw's TED talk.

Additional Texts to Explore the Concept of Identity

- *A Place Inside Me* by Zetta Elliott
- *All Are Welcome Here* by Alexandra Penfold
- *Drawn Together* by Minh Le
- *Drum Dream Girl* by Margarita Engle
- *Eyes That Kiss in the Corners* by Joanna Ho
- *Let's Talk About Race* by Julius Lester
- *Our Skin: A First Conversation About Race* by Megan Madison, Jessica Ralli, and Isabel Roxas
- *The Colors of Us* by Karen Katz
- *The Day You Begin* by Jacqueline Woodson
- *Woke: A Young Poet's Call to Justice* by Mahogany L. Brown with Elizabeth Acevedo and Olivia Gatwood
- *Yo Soy Muslim* by Mark Gonzales
- *Maddie's Fridge* by Lois Brandt
- *Red: A Crayon's Story* by Michael Hall
- *Under My Hijab* by Hena Khan
- *When We Were Alone* by David Robertson

Lesson 3: Hair and Identity

I Love My Hair • by Natasha Anastasia Tarpley

 ### First Read: Movie Read

This first visit, the "movie read," focuses on taking in the story without interruption (see Chapter 1, p. 21). Keyana discovers the beauty of her hair and celebrates her hair as part of her heritage.

 ### Second Read: Reading With the Text

Begin the second read by reminding students about Keyana's nightly routine of Mama combing her hair. Her mom reminds Keyana how beautiful her hair is and how she can wear it in many styles.

Turn to the spread where Keyana describes why she loves her hair using a series of similes.

Ask students:

- *What is your favorite way to style your hair?*
- *Follow a similar structure to share or write about your hair: "I love my hair because . . ."*

FIGURE 2.10

For Younger Students

Invite students to sketch their favorite hairstyle. Ask what hairstyle makes them feel their best. They can respond using the sentence frame "My favorite hairstyle is . . . It makes me feel . . ." or "If I could wear my hair any way I like, I'd . . . because . . ."

Ask students:

- *What does your hair feel like?*
- *What does it look like?*
- *How does it make you feel?*

These descriptors could be developed into a collection of poems.

Return Read: Reading Critically

For this return read, focus on the way this book offers a tribute to the beauty of Black hair and how hair is part of our identity.

Ask students:

- *How does Keyana's mom influence Keyana's identity?*
- *What hairstyles come to mind when you think of your culture?*

When Keyana was teased for wearing her hair free in an afro, Keyana's teacher told her it is a way to demonstrate pride.

Ask students: *How does Keyana's teacher influence Keyana's identity?*

For Older Students

Before this return read, begin by sharing the following quote from *The Souls of Black Folk* by W. E. B. Du Bois with students and ask them to reflect on it as they read the story again.

> It is a peculiar sensation, this double-consciousness, this sense of always looking at one's self through the eyes of others, of measuring one's soul by the tape of a world that looks on in amused contempt and pity. One ever feels his two-ness . . .

After reading, ask students what they think Du Bois means by this statement and how it aligns with the book.

Layering Texts

Crown: An Ode to the Fresh Cut by Derrick Barnes focuses on Black boys' hair.

In the end pages, the author writes,

> The fresh cuts. That's where it all begins. It's how we develop swagger, and when we begin to care about how we present ourselves to the world. It's also the time when most of us become privy to the conversations and company of hardworking Black men from all walks of life. We learn to mimic their tone, inflections, sense of humor, and verbal

combative skills when discussing politics, women, sports, our community, and our future.

The book is a wonderful text that can serve as a mirror for Black boys to see themselves reflected in a story in a joyous way. The images and the words in combination are truly a celebration of Black boys as elucidated through barbershop culture.

Additional Books About Hair

- *Crown: An Ode to the Fresh Cut* by Derrick Barnes
- *Don't Touch My Hair!* by Sharee Miller
- *Hair Love* by Matthew Cherry
- *My Hair Is a Garden* by Cozbi A. Cabrera

Lesson 4: Telling or Sharing Your Stories
The Day You Begin • by Jacqueline Woodson

FIGURE 2.11

JACQUELINE WOODSON
illustrated by RAFAEL LÓPEZ

 First Read: Movie Read

This first visit, the "movie read," focuses on taking in the story without interruption (see Chapter 1, p. 21). *The Day You Begin* is a story about those times when you walk into a room and no one there is quite like you. In lyrical free verse, Woodson takes a moment of desolation as an opportunity to respond to the question "So what are you going to do?"

 Second Read: Reading With the Text

Read the first spread of the book:

> There will be times when you walk into a room
>
> and no one there is quite like you.

Ask students:

- *How do you think she is feeling?*
- *What might she be thinking?*
- *Do you have any connections?*

Alternatively, you could lay out art cards on a table (approximately five cards per student) and ask students to pick one that reflects what comes to mind when they hear or read the sentence. (Art cards are art-inspired postcards or cards that contain images of art pieces from around the world. You can purchase ready-made art cards from museums, art galleries, and shops. You can also use calendars with works of art on them in place of the postcard-type art cards.)

Using art cards allows students to represent their thinking about a topic or issue. As students share why they have selected a particular card, they inadvertently connect to the text. For some students using an art card to represent what is on their mind creates a space for them to get at more complex ideas that they are not able to articulate using words. In this case, the cards become a tool for articulating their thinking.

Have students share their chosen art card and explain why they selected it. You could also have the students create their own art cards to represent their learning as a culminating experience for the lesson. The art cards can be shared and then added to the class art card collection for future use.

Free Access Art Pieces for Art Cards

Rather than using paper-based art cards, you could have your students choose an art piece online. Following are online art sources.

Art Gallery of Ontario
bit.ly/3EPPRPN

Barcelona Museum: Fundació Joan Miró
bit.ly/3GWSAd5

MoMA: Jacob Lawrence
https://www.moma.org/artists/3418

McMichael Art Collection
http://collections.mcmichael.com/collections

NGAkids Art Zone
bit.ly/3ueOG7O

Saatchi Art
https://www.saatchiart.com/paintings

Tate Kids
https://www.tate.org.uk/kids/explore

Students can use art cards to

- introduce themselves

- share their opinion or understanding about a particular topic

- create space for conversation

- represent their understanding of a lesson or class conversation

- do some meta-analysis of their own thinking, reflecting on the process behind why they chose their card

- show teachers what's on their mind

(Vasquez et al., 2021, p. 34)

Return Read: Reading Critically

To read critically, begin by pointing out the various examples of ways we can differ from others (physical features, language, location, clothes, food, talents, etc.). Invite students to share other examples.

Read the fifth spread and look closely at what the children in the spread are doing:

> There will be times when the words don't come.

> Your own voice, once huge, now smaller

> When the teacher asks *What did you do last summer?*

> *Tell the class your story.*

Some students may have a clear understanding of what it means to have "voice" while others may need time to clarify their ideas. What follows is some language to engage students in a conversation about voice.

Explain that having voice is not just the sound you make through your vocal cords or the thoughts you communicate using gestures and signs or a communication board.

Having voice is

- when others respect your thoughts and ideas
- when others listen and value what you have to say
- when you can speak your mind
- when you have a say over matters that affect you in some way
- when you have opportunities to share your experiences, your questions, and your comments and ideas
- when you are not forced to say or believe things you do not want to say or believe
- when you can be you and not what others say you should be

Ask students:

- *What does it mean to have "voice" or for someone's voice to be heard?*
- *In the story, whose voice has gotten smaller?*

- *What or who caused that child's voice to become smaller?*

- *Why don't the words come? What does that mean? Where would the words come from?*

- *What or who caused the words not to come?*

The children may note that it was the question "What did you do last summer?" that contributed to the child feeling voiceless as if she had nothing to say. If they do not come to this conclusion, you could ask follow-up questions.

Ask students:

- *How did the question "What did you do last summer?" cause the child's voice to become smaller?*

- *How could the teacher and students create a space for everyone in the class to participate in the conversation?*

Reread and discuss the ninth spread where the boy feels left out at recess. This could connect with other books, such as *The Invisible Boy* by Trudy Ludwig or *Each Kindness* by Jacqueline Woodson.

Ask students:

- *How is the boy feeling in this scene? How do you know?*

- *Does this remind you of any other books you've read?*

Highlight the shift in the eleventh spread where the boy's reflection offers a glimpse at an alternate story. In his reflection, he is seen smiling with an open book with beauty and life depicted by the flowers pouring out of it.

Ask students:

- *What does this illustration suggest about how the boy has changed?*

- *What do you think has caused this change?*

Additional Return Read Option:
Tell Your Own Story

Invite students to craft the story they want to share as their truth. Ask, "What are the stories you want the world to know about you and people like you?" Consider the frame, "What others say . . . What I want the world to know . . ." When we empower students to tell the stories of their lives, they control the narrative and disrupt assumptions and stereotypes.

You could begin by modeling this with your own story. Think about something that would likely be of interest and easily relatable for children. For example, using the frame "What others say . . . What I want the world to know . . ." the teacher could model *I'm 45 and some people say that I'm too old to sled downhill, but I want the world to know that I am 45 and when it snows, I get out my sled and slide down the big hill in front of my house all afternoon.*

This lesson lends itself to narrative writing and/or storytelling. Once students have crafted their stories, invite them to share as a storyteller, as a writer, or in a multimodal presentation.

Additional Books for Telling/Sharing Our Stories

- *All Are Welcome* by Alexandra Penfold

- *All Because You Matter* by Tami Charles

- *Emmanuel's Dream: The True Story of Emmanuel Ofosu Yeboah* by Laurie Ann Thompson

- *I, Too, Am America* by Langston Hughes, illustrated by Bryan Collier

- *Island Born* by Junot Diaz

- *Mama, Where Are You From?* by Marie Bradby

Lesson 5: Being Your Truest Self

The Proudest Blue: A Story of Hijab and Family •
by Ibtihaj Muhammad with S.K. Ali

 First Read: Movie Read

This first visit, the "movie read," focuses on taking in the story without interruption (see Chapter 1, p. 21). Asiya selects a blue hijab to wear to school, and her sister Faizah thinks it is the most beautiful hijab, but children at school make fun of it. Faizah remains resilient, strong, and proud.

 Second Read: Reading With the Text

Before rereading the book, display the cover and discuss the illustration.

Ask students:

- *What is a hijab?*
- *What can you infer based on the illustration and the title?*

Students may recall that Asiya wears her blue hijab proudly and how it's like the ocean and the sky and that her younger sister Faizah admires her.

Begin rereading the book. From the beginning of the story, Faizah looks up to her big sister, Asiya. She calls her a princess, and she feels like one too. When a classmate asks Faizah what's on her sister's head, she whispers "a scarf." She then speaks up louder and names it as a "hijab."

Ask students: *Why did Faizah whisper and then speak up louder?*

Read the next page: "Asiya's hijab isn't a whisper. Asiya's hijab is like the sky on a sunny day. The sky isn't a whisper. It's always there, special *and* regular." Point out the seesaw structure of the language as well as the simile and record on an anchor chart.

Asiya's hijab isn't . . .	Asiya's hijab is like the . . .
The sky isn't . . .	It's always . . .

FIGURE 2.12

OLYMPIC MEDALLIST
Ibtihaj Muhammad
with S.K. Ali

ART BY
Hatem Aly

THE
PROUDEST
BLUE
A Story of Hijab and Family

The italicized print on the bottom right page reveals Mama's remind-ers that wearing the hijab for the first day is important and means being strong.

Continue reading and pause to discuss the page where a boy points and laughs at Asiya.

Ask students: *What do you notice about Faizah's reaction in the illustration?*

The next page compares Asiya's hijab to the ocean using another sim-ile: "Asiya's hijab is like the ocean waving to the sky. It's always there, strong and friendly." Notice the repeating phrase "It's always there" although the language shifts from "special and regular" to "strong and friendly" here.

Notice similar seesaw structure in the language in this spread.

Asiya's hijab isn't . . .	Asiya's hijab is like the . . .	It's always . . .

Read the italicized print of Mama reminding her that some people won't understand. "But if you understand who you are, one day they will too."

Ask students: *What do you think Mama means by this?*

Continue reading. At recess, she hears a boy tell Asiya he's "going to pull that tablecloth off [her] head!" Asiya runs off to play and we see Mama's words again in italics reminding her to drop hurtful words. *"They belong to only those who said them."*

After school, Asiya is waiting for Faizah and is a model for how to be strong in times of adversity. Discuss the notion of calling someone out or calling them in.

Ask students: *Why might it be important to speak out and speak up to the boy?*

The bond between the sisters is strong. They are always there just like the ocean and the sky with no line between them. Discuss the notion of barriers (connect with the lesson for *The Other Side* by Jacqueline Woodson in Chapter 3) and the use of blue as a symbol of connection, continuity, and unity.

Calling In and Calling Out

When someone says something harmful, it is important that we interrupt and have a brave conversation to avoid escalating conflict and offer opportunities for learning. Rather than calling someone out to shame them, we can call them in with love to foster deeper reflection and understanding. Begin by sharing the concern (e.g., I'd like to talk with you about what you just said . . .) and asking questions (e.g., What was your intention when saying/doing that? How might the impact of your words/action be different than your intention?). For example, if someone tells an offensive joke, you can interrupt by saying something like, "I'd like to talk about why that joke is not appropriate. I don't find that funny. Would you have said it if someone from that group were in the room? Have you considered the impact of your words on others?"

Find more suggestions in this article from Learning for Justice.

 Return Read: Reading Critically

Read the author's note at the back of the book. Ibtihaj Muhammad describes how she started wearing a hijab regularly at age twelve. She experienced bullying and a classmate asked why she was wearing a tablecloth on her head. She felt "othered" by her hijab as a child, an adolescent, and an adult.

Ask students:

- *What do you think the term "othering" means?*

- *What are some ways people might be "othered"? Or who else might experience being "othered"?*

Note: Responses could lead to further discussion and intentional selection of books. For instance, if a child responds that they feel othered for having two moms, you could read a book like *Heather Has Two Mommies* by Lesléa Newman.

The author says she wants the book to serve as a mirror for other girls to see how she and her sister took such great pride in the hijab. "So that children of color, Muslims, and those who are both (like me) know they aren't alone and that there are many out there who share our experience . . . My hijab is beautiful . . . so is yours."

Ask students: *How can we help everyone be welcomed and included for being who they are?*

Additional Books

- *Black Is Brown Is Tan* by Arnold Adoff
- *I Am Enough* by Grace Byers
- *Introducing Teddy* by Jessica Walton
- *Just Ask!* by Sonia Sotomayor
- *Marisol McDonald Doesn't Match* by Monica Brown
- *Red: A Crayon's Story* by Michael Hall
- *Stand Tall, Molly Lou Melon* by Patty Lovell
- *Spaghetti in a Hot Dog Bun* by Maria Dismondy
- *Sulwe* by Lupita Nyong'o
- *The Kindest Red* by Ibtihaj Muhammad and S.K. Ali
- *Three Hens and a Peacock* by Lester Laminack
- *Under My Hijab* by Hena Khan

Additional Resources

- "My Identity is A Superpower" TED talk
  bbit.ly/3XJ2epz
- Learning for Justice's Social Justice Standards: Unpacking Identity

READING FOR ACTION

After reading a collection of texts focused on exploring individual and collective identities, invite students to reflect on what they have learned and how their thinking has changed.

Ask students: *What will we do with this new insight? How can we take action?*

SOME IDEAS/SUGGESTIONS

- Connect with a peer they don't know as well to learn more about them.

- Research to learn more about different identities they are less familiar with.

- Explore stories of those who have been historically marginalized or silenced. Whose stories do we need to learn more about? How will we collect and share those stories with others?

- Brainstorm ways to honor students' names and others' names and identities. Commit to pronouncing others' names correctly and explore how to help others when they mispronounce names.

Examining Perspective

3

//

Our prior knowledge and lived experiences shape our perspectives and how we approach text as readers. When reading the book *Visiting Day* by Jacqueline Woodson, this sentence can elicit different predictions from students: "Only on Visiting Day is there chicken frying in the kitchen at 6 A.M. and Grandma humming soft and low, smiling her secret just-for-Daddy-and-me smile and me lying in bed, smiling my just-for-Grandma-and-Daddy smile." Alyssa (Cameron) Likens's fifth-grade students predicted that the girl's parents were divorced, that she lived with her Grandma, and they were going to visit her daddy (Figure 3.1). In contrast, students in Reilly Mahan's fourth-grade class quickly determined that the girl's father was in jail. Although both classes heard the same book read aloud, their interpretations were very different based on their prior knowledge and lived experiences.

Several students in Ms. (Cameron) Likens's class have parents who are divorced, and their prediction was made from the perspective of their lived experiences. Ms. Mahan's students determined that the girl was visiting her father in jail because several of them know someone who is incarcerated. Again, children's personal experiences offered a perspective that shaped their expectations as many of them know only men who are incarcerated.

Ms. Mahan's students also discussed police brutality, and the disproportionate rate of incarceration of Black and Brown people, after someone in the group commented, "Well, aren't mostly Black people in jail? That's what my grandma said. And a lot of the time they are in there for no good reason."

FIGURE 3.1   Ms. Cameron Likens's Class Discusses
Visiting Day

Pairing Fiction and Nonfiction Text

As mentioned previously, children's books can serve as windows into worlds we do not fully understand. Sometimes pairing other types of nonfiction texts with fiction is one way to offer a more in-depth perspective on an issue. The question raised by one of Ms. Mahan's students regarding the disproportionate rate of incarceration of Black people is the kind of moment that could be enriched by pairing children's books with nonfiction texts, such as statistical information.

It is important to note that Black Americans are incarcerated at five times the rate of white Americans. Black men account for 6.5 percent of the US population but 40.2 percent of the prison population (Duvernay & Moran, 2016). The mass incarceration of Black men began after the Civil War with the imprisonment of freed people for minor crimes to provide the labor needed to rebuild the economy of the South after the war and to uphold white supremacy.

Although more men are in prison than women, the growth of female imprisonment far surpasses men. Approximately 75 percent to 80 percent of incarcerated women are mothers with minors. The number of parents of minor children incarcerated increased by 79 percent between

1991 and 2007 (Glaze & Maruschak, 2010). According to the Annie E. Casey Foundation (n.d.), more than 5 million children have had a parent incarcerated. Incarcerating parents results in single-parent households, damages family ties, and exacerbates chronic childhood poverty.

The prison population has drastically increased through the years because of the criminalization and vilification of Black People as dangerous drug users and distributors. The for-profit prison industrial complex has resulted in the United States having the highest rate of incarceration in the world. "More African American adults are under correctional control today—in prison or jail, on probation or parole—than were enslaved in 1850, a decade before the Civil War began" (Alexander, 2010, p. 180).

Additional resources:

- *13th* documentary by Ava Duvernay

- *Just Mercy* by Bryan Stevenson

- The Sentencing Project's "The Color of Justice: Racial and Ethnic Disparity in State Prisons" report: bit.ly/3ATqqvJ

- National Institute of Corrections' Children of Incarcerated Parents Project: bit.ly/3UjH7Ht

What Is Perspective?

Perspective is the capacity to view things in their true relations or relative importance (trying to maintain my perspective), the interrelation in which a subject or its parts are mentally viewed (placing the issue in proper perspective), a mental view or prospect (to gain a broader perspective on the international scene), a standpoint, or a position from which something is considered or evaluated.

We think of perspective as the eyes, ears, heart, mind, and mouth of the story. Whose eyes are we seeing through? Whose ears are we hearing with? Whose heart is feeling and experiencing the emotions? Whose mind is making sense of events and offering us thoughts? Whose mouth is speaking all this to us and other characters?

Perspective is also whose eyes we are not seeing through. Whose ears we are not listening with? Whose feelings are not considered? Whose ideas are not included? Whose voices are silenced?

Perspective is interpretation, opinions, attitudes, beliefs, thoughts, actions, and reactions filtered through experience, language, culture, history, physical traits, and so forth. Perspective is also about whose interpretations, opinions, thoughts, actions, and reactions are privileged and whose are not. It is a window into how the character makes sense of the world and forms decisions about how to navigate through it. Perspective enables us to have a glimpse into events, ideas, attitudes, and interpretations that may reflect or challenge our own.

Readers must come to understand that all writing comes from a particular perspective. No text is neutral. We must recognize that all stories and information are presented through a perspective and, therefore, represent a limited view. We must learn to name the perspective, unearth the influences of that perspective, and question whose perspectives are missing and how these missing perspectives could provide alternate views that help us to better understand people and events in the past, present, and future.

An exploration of perspective in story offers readers an opportunity to examine how a character's choices, actions, and reactions are the result of their personal histories, identities, and biases. When we examine how a change in perspective can result in a shift in thought, language, and actions we can begin to recognize the importance of seeking various perspectives on any topic.

In this chapter, we have selected a collection of books for the specific exploration of perspective. Each book offers an opportunity to zoom in and examine how the character's perspective limits interpretation and how gaining a new or broader perspective offers an opportunity to reexamine choices, attitudes, or beliefs that may result in a change in thought, language, and behaviors.

> When we recognize the idea that perspective fronts one set of ideas presented through filters specific to the character, we are in a better position to explore the idea that other perspectives would most likely provide variants of the same story.

Understanding the concept of perspective is an essential beginning step toward learning to critically examine a text. Readers and writers must first understand how perspective influences the whole of the story. When we recognize the idea that perspective fronts one set of ideas presented through filters specific to the character, we are in a better position to explore the idea that other perspectives would most likely provide variants of the same story. From this vantage point we are positioned to take a deeper look into the impact of perspective in our reading, our writing, and in our lives.

Reading to Make a Difference: Using Literature to Help Children Think Deeply, Speak Freely, and Take Action (Laminack & Kelly, 2019), explores the notion of books as bridges. "When the reader stands in [their] own worldview, unable to see or conceive of any other perspective, a book can be a bridge" (Laminack & Kelly, 2019, p. xiii). Books help us expand our understanding and perspective. They help us consider alternate experiences, views, and ideas. They help us peel back the blinders of our own biases. However, for many, this work does not come easily. When selecting books for our classroom libraries and read alouds, we want to not only ensure all students can see themselves but also provide opportunities for students to read about lives unlike their own. Yet we must be critical when examining these texts to ensure accurate and authentic representations. We also want to lead children (and ourselves) through critical disruption of the word and the world (Freire, 2000). We can do this by questioning:

- Whose perspective is included and whose is excluded? Why?
- How does this perspective position the reader?
- How do our own assumptions position us to interact with the text?
- How does that compare with the way in which others interact with the text?

Creating a space for children to engage in critical conversations as they construct and deconstruct meaning from texts is essential to helping children move beyond a one-dimensional view of themselves and the world. Helping children to examine multiple perspectives supports the development of empathy and advocacy.

Helping children to examine multiple perspectives supports the development of empathy and advocacy.

Critical Comprehension
Lesson Series

Examining Perspective

These lessons are designed to launch the exploration of perspective. The lesson series begins with the exploration of perspective using a wordless picture book to show how more information can be revealed when we broaden our view to gain new insight and a lesson to acknowledge that there are multiple ways of viewing something. The lessons then move to more complex concepts around perspective, including the role of power in decision making and considering other perspectives.

Table of Lessons for Examining Perspective

LESSON FOCUS	ANCHOR TEXT
1. Widening the lens to reveal more	*Zoom* by Istvan Banyai
2. What do you see? Realizing there are multiple ways to view things	*Duck! Rabbit!* by Amy Krouse Rosenthal
3. Examining power and perspective	*The True Story of the Three Little Pigs!* by Jon Scieszka
4. Understanding power and the choices we make	*Hey, Little Ant* by Phillip and Hannah Hoose
5. Discovering the power of recognizing another perspective	*Jamaica's Find* by Juanita Havill
6. How others can influence our perspective	*Last Stop on Market Street* by Matt de la Peña
7. Exploring multiple perspectives	*The Other Side* by Jacqueline Woodson

Note: The blank spaces are an invitation for you to add your own related topics and texts.

Lesson 1: Widening the Lens to Reveal More
Zoom • by Istvan Banyai

 First Read: Movie Read

This first visit, the "movie read," focuses on taking in the story without interruption (see Chapter 1, p. 21). This wordless picture book, *Zoom*, offers an opportunity to view an object from different perspectives by first offering a glimpse of the object through a narrow focus and then widening the lens with each turn of the page to provide additional context. The book creates a space for discussing how things are not always as they seem and that looking at things from different perspectives allows us to engage in more meaningful or informed readings of the text.

 Second Read: Reading With the Text

When reading *Zoom*, show students one page at a time and give them ample opportunity to discuss their thinking with each illustration. During this second read, students should have an opportunity to freely interpret each image.

Ask students:

- *What do you see?*
- *What do you not see?*
- *What are you thinking?*
- *What are you wondering?*

FIGURE 3.2

For Younger Students

To help younger students understand the concept of zooming in or out, or looking through a lens then widening it, have them use their hands or cardboard paper towel or toilet paper tubes to make a spyglass to look through. Ask them to focus on an object in the room.

Ask students: *Can you describe what you see?*

Then have them look at the object again without looking through their spyglass.

(Continued)

(Continued)

Ask students: *How does the object look different when you look at it without the spyglass?*

Discuss how there is so much more when they expand their perspective or view. Invite students to make their own Zoom books to widen and narrow the focus on a particular object or scene.

 Return Read: Reading Critically

For the return read, highlight some of the differences in students' responses during the first read. For instance, while viewing the first image someone may have described what they saw as a painting, while someone else might have said the image was a red mountain range.

Ask students:

- *Why do you think different people had different ideas about what the images represent?*

- *Where do you think those ideas came from?*

- *What would lead different people to interpret the images differently?*

- *Who do you think would have an advantage in interpreting the images as farm scenes? As a magazine cover?*

- *Who do you think might find it hard to imagine the images as farm scenes or as a scene on a magazine cover?*

- *How did the different perspectives in each image influence your interpretation of the images?*

- *What difference does it make to read an image or a text from different perspectives?*

For Older Students

As a follow-up lesson, share with students the *Guardian*'s 1986 "Points of View" short video clip on YouTube (see the QR code). Before watching, set a viewing purpose by asking students to pay close attention to the man in the video. Stop the video after each of the three perspectives to discuss.

Ask students:

- *What is happening in the scene?*

- *What clues led you to think that?*

Video of the *Guardian's* "Points of View."

After the third and final perspective is viewed, engage children in a discussion about how our perspective can sometimes be limited unless we widen the lens to include the full story.

Ask students:

- *What surprised you after viewing the third perspective?*

- *How did your interpretation of what the main character was doing change from one scene to the next?*

- *What helped shape your interpretations?*

- *What other perspectives could be added to the video?*

Tip on Using Drama in Critical Comprehension

Children could be invited to dramatize their alternate perspectives. Doing so could help them better visualize and experience the different perspectives they are considering. They could then talk about why they chose to move their bodies in a certain way and why they chose to use certain words. They could also talk about how moving their bodies differently and choosing different words could lead viewers of their dramatization to different interpretations.

Additional Wordless Books to Widen the Lens

- *Across Town* by Sara

- *Flotsam* by David Wiesner

- *ReZoom* by Istvan Banyai

- *The Other Side* by Istvan Banyai

- *The Red Book* by Barbara Lehman

- *They All Saw a Cat* by Brendan Wenzel

Examining Perspective

Lesson 2: What Do You See?
Duck! Rabbit! • by Amy Krouse Rosenthal

FIGURE 3.3

 First Read: Movie Read

This first visit, the "movie read," focuses on taking in the story without interruption (see Chapter 1, p. 21). *Duck! Rabbit! is a* clever take on the age-old optical illusion: Is it a duck or a rabbit? The book readily lends itself to exploring how our experiences and encounters with the world around us help shape our readings of the word and the world.

 Second Read: Reading With the Text

Revisit the book *Duck! Rabbit!* by Amy Krouse Rosenthal.

Ask students:

- *What was the story about?*
- *What are you thinking now?*

Have your students create an image that represents their understanding of the text.

 Return Read: Reading Critically

Revisit and reread the book *Duck! Rabbit!* by Amy Krouse Rosenthal.

Ask students:

- *Why is it important to see things from multiple perspectives?*
- *Why is it essential to respect other people's interpretations and views?*
- *What are your experiences with changing your perspective or opinion after hearing someone else's perspective or opinion?*
- *Have you ever felt like you were being forced in some way to adopt someone else's opinion, perspective, or belief? How did that go? What did you do to resist or what convinced you to change your mind?*

- *How does hearing multiple perspectives help you to make an informed decision about what to believe?*

- *What are ways that people, groups, or the media might influence you to change your opinion or belief about something?*

For Younger Students

It is important to introduce younger children to more challenging academic words, such as those used in the list of questions above. As such, consider integrating some of those words (e.g., multiple perspectives) into your conversation with younger children.

Ask students:

- *Why do you think it is important to be able to see things in different ways?*

- *Why do you think it is important to listen to other people's ideas even if they are not like yours?*

- *Have you ever felt like someone forced you to change your mind? What was that like?*

- *What are some ways that you think people could try to get you to change your mind?*

- *What are some things you can do to stop people from trying to make you change your mind if you don't believe that you should?*

Additional Books to Explore Perspective

- *Ish* by Peter H. Reynolds
- *Not a Box* by Antoinette Portis
- *Not a Stick* by Antoinette Portis
- *Out of My Mind* by Sharon Draper (chapter book)

Lesson 3: Examining Power and Perspective

The True Story of the Three Little Pigs! • by Jon Scieszka

FIGURE 3.4

Note: If your students are unfamiliar with the original version of this folktale, take the time to share that story as a point of reference before you read *The True Story of the Three Little Pigs!*

 First Read: Movie Read

This first visit, the "movie read," focuses on taking in the story without interruption (see Chapter 1, p. 21). *The True Story of the Three Little Pigs!* offers a counternarrative to the traditional story "The Three Little Pigs." This version of the story positions the wolf as the narrator and invites readers to consider the story from his perspective. The wolf claims to be innocent—merely borrowing a cup of sugar from his neighbors (the pigs) to make his grandma a cake for her birthday. This humanizes the wolf and portrays him as caring and thoughtful. He claims to have accidentally blown down the pigs' homes due to his nagging cold that results in a powerful sneeze.

Counternarrative Texts

A counternarrative text disputes commonly held beliefs or truths. These texts are often told through the vantage point of those who have been historically marginalized.

Second Read: Reading With the Text

The story begins, "You thought you knew the story of 'The Three Little Pigs' . . . You thought wrong." Right away the readers are confronted with disrupting their notion of what they believed to be true. At first, we may feel a sense of discomfort because none of us likes to be wrong. Yet, it is this type of disruption that moves our thinking forward and deepens our understanding.

Revisit the story to engage children in a discussion about perspective. You might initially frame this work-around by comparing and contrasting with the traditional tale. However, we invite you to go deeper with the conversation to examine perspective.

Ask students:

- *What do you notice about the book?*

- *Who is telling the story?*
- *Who tells the story in other versions of "The Three Little Pigs" that you have read or heard?*

After reading, invite students to debate about whether they believe the wolf or not.

 ## Return Read: Reading Critically

For this return read, invite students to read other versions of the story of "The Three Little Pigs" and "Little Red Riding Hood" to explore how the wolf is portrayed in those stories as well as what we know about real wolves through a study of informational texts. Provide each group with a different book to read and analyze the ways in which the wolf is portrayed.

- *Imagine a Wolf* by Lucky Platt (see the lesson in Chapter 4: "Examining Stereotypes")
- *Lon Po: A Red Riding Hood Story From China* by Ed Young
- *National Geographic Readers: Wolves* by Laura Marsh
- *The Fourth Pig* by Teresa Celsi
- *The Three Little Wolves and the Big Bad Pig* by Eugene Trivizas
- *The Three Pigs* by David Wiesner
- *Wolf!* by Becky Bloom
- *Wolves* by Seymor Simon

Record students' discoveries on an anchor chart.

TITLE/ AUTHOR	WHO IS TELLING THE STORY?	HOW IS THE WOLF PORTRAYED?	WHAT ARE WE THINKING NOW?

Ask students:

- *How does who is telling the story affect the message conveyed to the reader?*
- *In what ways do our feelings about the wolf change depending on how the wolf is portrayed or the perspective from which the wolf is portrayed?*
- *What new thoughts or ideas do you now have about wolves based on the different perspectives or ways they are portrayed in the different books?*

Examining Perspective

Lesson 4: Understanding Power and the Choices We Make

Hey, Little Ant • by Phillip and Hannah Hoose

 First Read: Movie Read

This first visit, the "movie read," focuses on taking in the story without interruption (see Chapter 1, p. 21). *Hey, Little Ant* is a conversation between a boy and an ant presented in the format of a theater script. The boy, part of a group of children who squish ants each day, finds himself engaged in a conversation with an ant that presents the world through the perspective of ants. The conversation gives the boy (and the reader) an opportunity to examine a different perspective and leaves the more informed reader with a decision to make.

 Second Read: Reading With the Text

Before you return to *Hey, Little Ant* take a moment to review insights about what perspective is and how viewing something from a different perspective can give us new ideas and understanding. You may want to connect these insights to the books *Zoom* and *Duck! Rabbit!*

Open the book to the spread where the ant is depicted on the left page lying on a blade of grass and the boy is on the right page lying in the grass.

Ask students:

- *Why do you suppose the illustrator chose to show the ant and the boy doing the same thing?*

- *Why is the ant shown up close on one blade of grass while the boy is lying in a patch of grass?*

- *What does this prompt you to consider?*

Turn to the full title page where we see the ant carrying two bags of groceries.

Ask students:

- *Why would the illustrator choose to depict the ant carrying grocery bags?*

- *How does this image help us consider an idea from a different perspective?*

Return Read: Reading Critically

As you begin the critical read, display the cover and read the title.

Begin reading and pause after the scene where the ant says, "Come down close, I think you'll see that you are very much like me." Point out that each time you turn the page the perspective shifts back and forth between the boy and the ant. Note that each time the boy makes an assertion about ants, the ant has a response to provide a different perspective.

Ask students:

- *How does hearing a different perspective influence our thinking?*
- *Does the conversation between the boy and the ant give either of them new things to think about?*

Continue reading and pause after the page where the ant explains, "One little chip can feed my town . . ."

Ask students:

- *Each time the boy shares his perspective about an ant's life, the ant responds with more information. How does this exchange affect your thinking about ants?*
- *Does it cause you to have new questions?*
- *Does it change your thoughts or feelings about ants?*

Read the next two spreads and pause on the page where the ant asks, "What would you want me to do?" Turn the book lengthwise for the full impact of the image. Point out that the ant has offered an alternative perspective and now the boy has new information that enables him to make more informed decisions.

Ask students:

- *What is the impact of the illustrator's decision to switch the perspective, making the ant the "giant" and making the boy a "tiny speck"?*
- *How does this illustration help you understand what the ant has been saying?*

Explore the role of power. For example, the boy is so much bigger than the ant. His power is in the advantage he has in size, and he uses that power to attempt to intimidate the ant. Yet, the ant holds power in its knowledge and words. It speaks up and asks the kid to listen to its perspective. The ant acknowledges the kid's strength and points out their similarities in an appeal to the boy. Explore the ant's arguments and consider the connections it is trying to make between the boy and ants. Note how these connections give the boy more to consider in that they challenge his notions about the value of an ant.

Take a close look at the final page.

Ask students: *How does gaining insight into someone else's perspective give you additional information, fresh ways to think about a situation, and an opportunity to change your behavior?*

Engage students in a debate to discuss the ending of the story. They could write/act out a new ending. Or they could write out an argument for the ant, using evidence from the text and outside resources to support their claims. You may also invite students to analyze the information by looking first at what beliefs the boy held about all ants and how those beliefs have been informed through personal interaction with an ant. What did he know in the beginning compared to what new insights he gained by the end of the story? Then have a conversation about how additional information and new perspectives inform us and may leave us feeling unsettled and in need of more information before we make decisions.

Additional Resources to Learn More About Ants

- *Ant Cities* by Arthur Dorros
- *Ants* (*National Geographic Kids*) by Melissa Stewart

Lesson 5: Discovering the Power of Recognizing Another Perspective

Jamaica's Find • by Juanita Havill

 First Read: Movie Read

This first visit, the "movie read," focuses on taking in the story without interruption (see Chapter 1, p. 21). Jamaica finds two things at the park when she stops to play for a few minutes on her way home. She returns one item to the park attendant but puts the other in her bicycle basket to take home. At home, Jamaica's mom gently leads her to consider the newly found treasure from a different perspective.

 Second Read: Reading With the Text

For the second read, remind students that Jamaica found two things at the park, a hat and a stuffed dog. She took the hat to the lost and found but she took the dog home with her. Then, something caused her to change her mind and she returned the dog to the park attendant the next morning.

Before you begin reading, take a moment to think about losing things, finding things that someone else has lost, and the purpose of a "lost and found" space.

Ask students:

- *How does it feel when you lose something that is important to you?*

- *How would you feel if you found something that you really liked even though you know that someone else lost it?*

- *Why do places like the park have a space for lost and found things?*

Record a summary of their thoughts on a chart.

As you read with the text, point out that the story is told from Jamaica's perspective. Begin rereading and pause at the scene where Jamaica finds the hat and the dog. Read the description of the dog again.

FIGURE 3.6

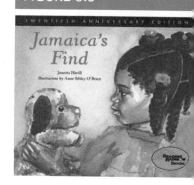

Ask students:

- *What can you infer about this dog?*

- *What do all these details let us know?*

Read the next page and pause after Jamaica puts the dog in her bicycle basket.

Ask students:

- *Why did she take the dog?*

- *What do you suppose she was thinking?*

You may want to make connections between students' earlier comments about finding and losing things and Jamaica's thoughts and feelings.

Read the next page and pause. Point out that she keeps the dog but not the hat.

Ask students:

- *When Jamaica takes the hat to the lost and found what does that show us about what she understands?*

- *Why would she keep the dog and not the hat? Whose perspective is she considering?*

Read on and pause after Jamaica's mother says, "It probably belongs to a girl just like Jamaica." Invite students to reflect on what Jamaica is thinking as she talks with her mom.

Ask students:

- *How is Jamaica feeling about the dog at this moment?*

- *Do you think her mother intended for Jamaica to hear that comment? Why? Why not?*

- *How would it change things if Jamaica had not heard her mother's comment?*

Read on and pause after, "Mother, I want to take the dog back to the park . . . We'll go first thing in the morning." Point out that we see a change in Jamaica's behavior and demeanor.

Ask students:

- *What do the changes in Jamaica's behavior reveal about changes in her feelings?*

- *What is she thinking about now that she had not considered before?*

- *What has caused this change in her thinking and her feelings?*

 ## Return Read: Reading Critically

For this return read, recap the comments and insights from previous discussions.

Ask students:

- *How does a person's perspective influence their thinking, their comments, and their actions?*

- *Why is it important to look at things from different perspectives?*

- *How can a person change their perspective?*

- *How can a change of perspective make a difference in how we think, what we say, and how we act?*

Additional Books to Explore Perspective

- *Love That Dog* by Sharon Creech (poetry)

- *One Crazy Summer* by Rita Garcia Williams (chapter book)

Examining Perspective

Lesson 6: How Others Can Influence Our Perspective

Last Stop on Market Street • by Matt de la Peña

FIGURE 3.7

LAST STOP ON MARKET STREET

WORDS BY
MATT DE LA PEÑA
PICTURES BY
CHRISTIAN ROBINSON

 First Read: Movie Read

This first visit, the "movie read," focuses on taking in the story without interruption (see Chapter 1, p. 21). CJ and his nana ride the bus to serve others at a soup kitchen. Throughout their journey, CJ questions his life circumstances and poses several questions, such as why they must wait for the bus in the rain and why they do not have a car. Nana encourages CJ to look at the world around him through a new perspective.

 Second Read: Reading With the Text

For the second read, invite the students to pay particular attention to what CJ says and does and how Nana responds to him. Create an anchor chart to record students' noticings during reading.

WHAT CJ SAYS/DOES	HOW NANA RESPONDS

Ask students:

- *What do CJ's questions suggest about him and his thinking?*
- *How do Nana's responses influence his thinking?*
- *How does the visit to the soup kitchen with Nana change CJ's thinking and perspective on the world around him?*

Return to the anchor chart and add a third column ("Now I'm thinking . . .") to record the exploration of these questions.

WHAT CJ SAYS/DOES	HOW NANA RESPONDS	NOW I'M THINKING . . .
CJ asks why the man can't see.	Nana tells him, "Some people watch the world with their ears."	
CJ is envious when he sees two kids listening to music with earbuds.	Nana points out the live music right across the bus as the man plays the guitar.	

Guide students to notice how Nana responds to CJ with a focus on what is good and valued. She sees others and the world around her in a positive way. For instance, when CJ asks Nana why they must wait for the bus in the rain, she helps him see how the trees are like straws drinking the rain.

Note: In the clip below, author Matt de la Peña tells the children on the bus that if they understand the page where Nana tells CJ that the trees drink the rain like straws then they will understand the rest of the book.

Author Matt de la Peña brings the story to life in this video.

While on the bus, CJ asks why they must go to the soup kitchen.

Ask students: *Why does CJ ask Nana why they don't have a car like his friends?*

With each spread, the reader is introduced to new people on the bus. The people on the bus are all unique and offer a gift whether music, the celebration of life with butterflies, or the gift of smell and sound even when one is visually impaired.

Ask students:

- *What does CJ learn from being on the bus?*

- *How do we know that he has learned those things?*

- *In what way does being on the bus change CJ?*

 Return Read: Reading Critically

Engage students in a discussion about how people can influence our thinking and our perspective. Nana helps CJ to see the beauty in the world around him rather than feeling sorry for himself and focusing on what he does not have. In fact, even though CJ and his Nana don't have a lot, they still give back to others. (If you have read *Jamaica's Find* together [see p. 91 for this lesson], remind students of the way Jamaica's mom helped her reconsider the stuffed dog she found in the park. When Jamaica's mom suggested that the stuffed dog might belong to someone else, Jamaica considered someone else's perspective and decided she wanted to return it to the lost and found.)

Examining
Perspective

When CJ and Nana get off the bus on Market Street, they see crumbling sidewalks, broken-down doors, and graffiti. The colors shift to drab and gray tones compared to the beginning of the book when they leave for the journey. CJ asks Nana why it's so dirty. She responds, "Sometimes when you're surrounded by dirt, CJ, you're a better witness for what's beautiful." Then he sees the perfect rainbow over the soup kitchen.

Read the page where "He wondered how Nana always found beautiful where he never even thought to look."

Ask students:

- *What is the difference between how Nana sees the world and how CJ sees the world?*

- *Nana always found beauty where CJ never even thought to look. Do you know someone who helps you find the beauty and the good where you don't even think to look?*

- *Who or what has influenced your perspective and the way you see the world?*

- *What happened?*

- *What did that person say or do that influenced your thinking?*

- *How can we reimagine someone, something, or someplace through a different lens?*

- *Why is it important to consider other perspectives?*

Additional Books to Explore the Perspective of Finding Beauty

- *Beautifully Me* by Nabela Noor

- *Beautiful Oops* by Barney Saltzberg

- *Maybe Something Beautiful: How Art Transformed a Neighborhood* by F. Isabel Campoy

- *Something Beautiful* by Sharon Dennis Wyeth

- *The Day You Begin* by Jacqueline Woodson

- *The Day You Learned to Fly* by Jacqueline Woodson

- *Crenshaw* by Katherine Applegate (chapter book)

Lesson 7: Exploring Multiple Perspectives
The Other Side • by Jacqueline Woodson

 First Read: Movie Read

This first visit, the "movie read," focuses on taking in the story without interruption (see Chapter 1, p. 21). In *The Other Side* two girls, one white and one Black, live on opposite sides of a fence. Clover, the Black girl, is told by her mother to never climb the fence because it is not safe on the other side.

 Second Read: Reading With the Text

For the second read, focus on the perspective of the girls and the adults, as well as the perspective in the illustrations to convey meaning. Remind students that considering the perspective of a character who is like you may be less challenging than thinking through the perspective of a character who may be different from you. It will also be helpful to consider the setting (the geography and time period) as a contextual frame when delving into perspectives.

Begin by exploring perspective through examination of the illustration on the first few pages. Point out how the house is on one side of the page and the fence on the other side of the page (where we learn it wasn't safe on the other side).

On the next page, Clover is on one side and Annie is on the other page separated by the page gutter (the place in the book where the binding meets).

Ask students: *Why do you think the illustrator made these decisions?*

Continue reading and engage students in discussion of perspective through examination of illustration as well as characters and story events.

Ask students:

- *What do you notice?*
- *What are you thinking?*

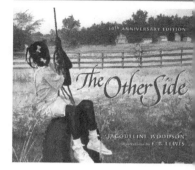

FIGURE 3.8

Continue reading to the page where Annie asks to play when the girls are jumping rope and one of the girls immediately responds no.

Ask students:

- *Why do you think she responded this way?*
- *What reasons can you offer to explain why she responds so quickly?*

Point out how Annie, the white girl, is on one side of the fence and the Black girls are on the other side divided by the page gutter.

Ask students:

- *Do you think the illustrator did this intentionally?*
- *If so, what are your thoughts about why this decision was made?*
- *What does this suggest?*

Continue reading where the girls are in town with their mothers.

Ask students: *Why do you think they look at each other but don't speak?*

(Note: This could be a place to discuss how Black people may have felt silenced or "kept in their place" due to the long history of oppression. As the book says, "because that's the way things have always been.")

The girls continue to be separated by the page gutter when Annie introduces herself as well as on the following page when Annie tells Clover that "it's nice up on this fence" and "A fence like this was made for sitting on." Clover touches the fence.

Ask students: *How does this part of the story shift or reposition the fence from a force of separation to the possibility of a shared space?*

On the next page, they are no longer separated by the fence or the page gutter. They sit on the fence together all summer long.

Ask students:

- *What does this suggest?*
- *How have their perspectives changed?*

On the spread where the two girls are sitting together and Clover's mom is watching them, Clover's mom is on the other side of the gutter.

Ask students:

- *What does this suggest?*

- *Has the mom's perspective changed?*

On the page where Sandra and the other girls jump rope with Clover and Annie, notice that Sandra is on the same page as Clover and Annie.

Ask students:

- *What does this suggest about how Sandra's perspective may have changed?*

- *What influenced her shift?*

 ## Return Read: Reading Critically

Prior to the return read of *The Other Side*, revisit the page in *Last Stop on Market Street* where CJ and Nana first get on the bus. Read the sentence at the top of the page: "They sat right up front."

Ask students: *Why is this an important line in the story?*

If the students do not offer responses, explain to them that people of color were not always allowed to sit at the front of the bus. (They may be familiar with the story of Rosa Parks; see the next box for resources.) Explain that in the book *The Other Side*, they met two little girls, one white and one Black, who live on opposite sides of a fence. Clover, the Black girl, is told by her mother to never climb the fence because it is not safe on the other side. The story is told from Clover's perspective.

Ask students: *What are possible connections between people of color not being allowed to sit at the front of the bus and Clover's mom telling her to never climb the fence because it isn't safe on the other side?*

Return to the end of the book and reread the line where all the girls are sitting on the fence. "Someday somebody's going to come along and knock this old fence down."

Ask students:

- *How is the fence a metaphor for racism in the United States both past and present?*

- *What are other examples of fences that create barriers for some?*

- *How can we mend or take down those fences?*

Invite students to create an artist's representation of the fence as a symbol for barriers or inequities.

Here are some resources you can use to provide background knowledge about Rosa Parks, if necessary:

- *Rosa* by Nikki Giovanni

- *Rosa Parks: My Story* by Rosa Parks and Jim Haskins

- Rosa Parks interview (1995): bit.ly/3XFjplJ

- Rosa Parks interview (1956): bit.ly/3ivy7la

Return Read Extension

On the page where Clover's mom tells her to play with rainy-day toys instead of going outside to play, there is a white doll sitting in the chair (note its location on the other side of the page gutter). This could lead to a discussion about diversity in toys and the famous Clark doll study. This experiment asked both Black and white children to look at two dolls, one Black and one white, and to answer a series of questions, including Which one is the pretty doll? The nice doll? The good doll? The bad doll? Both groups showed a preference for the white doll, revealing anti-Black bias for both groups. This is significant because it suggests the need to create affirming spaces for and representations of BIPOC children. See Chapters 4 and 5 for more information about addressing stereotypes and bias and Chapter 7 for information on critically consuming.

The 1940 Clark doll study found that when given a choice between Black dolls and white dolls, white dolls were preferred and viewed as smarter, more beautiful, and good by both Black and white children. The results suggest that children notice race and display racial preferences. The findings were used to support the need for desegregation in schools. However, half a century later, when the study was replicated by Toni Sturdivant the findings revealed that anti-Black bias persists even in integrated spaces (read more about Sturdivant's findings here: bit.ly/3UhD5zj).

Additional Books to Examine Multiple Perspectives

- *Follow Follow: A Book of Reverso Poems* by Marilyn Singer

- *Mirror Mirror: A Book of Reverso Poems* by Marilyn Singer

- *The Wall in the Middle of the Book* by Jon Agee

Video with author Jacqueline Woodson.

- *A Long Walk to Water* by Linda Sue Park (chapter book)

- *Rules* by Cynthia Lord (chapter book)

Examining Perspective

READING FOR ACTION

After reading with and reading against a collection of texts focused on examining perspective, invite students to reflect on what they learned and how their thinking has changed.

Ask students: *What will we do with this new insight? How can we take action, or do something to help?*

SOME IDEAS/SUGGESTIONS

- Explore a story from a perspective that is missing from the text and reconstruct the narrative.

Ask students:

- *Whose perspective is missing and should be told?*

- *What might the new version sound like? For instance, what would grandma's version of "The True Story of the Three Little Pigs!" be? What would the police officers say?*

- *Share examples of a time when your perspective changed. Discuss the factors that led to that change.*

Ask students:

- *How can we actively remember to consider other perspectives and invite others to do the same?*

- *How can we help others to expand their perspectives to consider things in different ways? For instance, if you had an argument with a friend or a sibling, how can you work to see their perspective and help them to see yours?*

- *How can we engage in civil discourse when examining conflicting opinions and ideas?*

- *Invite students to brainstorm ways they can take action to find and celebrate the beauty in places that don't seem beautiful at first glance.*

Ask students: *For instance, how can a run-down park be transformed into a useful space for people in a community?*

Brainstorm various metaphorical fences that work to divide people and create inequities.

Ask students: *How do fences that keep people in or keep people out contribute to creating inequities?*

Engage in collaborative inquiry as a whole group or in small groups to explore ways to remove the metaphorical fences and foster greater equity and inclusion.

- Reconstruct a text by crafting poetry for two voices. One side of the poem is told through one perspective (e.g., Rosie, the hen), while the other side of the poem is told through another perspective (e.g., the fox). Common experiences, thoughts, or comments are included in the middle of the poem. For an example of a two-voice poem about Malala Yousafzai and Rosa Parks, see Chapter 5 in Laminack and Kelly (2019). Additionally, students can create two-voice poems with their peers to explore their similarities and celebrate their differences.

Examining Stereotypes

4

Before reading *Milo Imagines the World* by Matt de la Peña, fifth grad-ers in Daniel Hoilett and Alyssa (Cameron) Likens's classrooms used the Talking Drawings strategy (Wood et al., 2016) to sketch what they imagined about things like family, royalty (kings/queens), home, and dancers (Figure 4.1). They displayed their sketches and conducted a gallery walk to view their peers' drawings. When they returned to their seats, they engaged in a discussion based on their observations.

It had not occurred to them that a princess would be anyone other than someone who wore pink and jewels or that a family could consist of dynamics other than a heteronormative family structure. Many of

FIGURE 4.1   Ms. (Cameron) Likens's Class Discusses *Milo Imagines the World*

© Lester Laminack

Ms. (Cameron) Likens's students tapped into their knowledge of princesses based on popular culture. Specifically, they considered Disney princesses and Queen Elizabeth from what they've seen in the news and on shows like *The Crown*.

When asked to sketch dancers, most drew ballerinas with pink tutus. Even two girls in the class who are step dancers drew female ballerinas (see Figure 4.2). The students were surprised to see the dancers in the book were break dancers. Their construct of dancers did not include break dancers as valid "dancers."

FIGURE 4.2   Ms. (Cameron) Likens's Talking Drawing

Pause to Reflect

Pause and consider what the students' construct of dancers suggests about societal values and the messages it sends to young people. The world around us shapes our thinking and our perceptions of self and others.

After reading, students returned to their initial Talking Drawings (Wood et al., 2016) to reimagine them. For example, one of the students who drew a ballerina updated it to include hip-hop and TikTok dances. Ms. (Cameron) Likens noticed that the students had yet to consider family structures beyond heteronormative families, so she decided to include additional read alouds featuring diverse families.

Books on Diverse Family Structures

View the article linked from this QR code for a thorough, recent list of suggested books focused on diverse family structures (Kelly et al., 2021).

When noticing the way Milo reimagined the woman in the wedding dress, students in Mr. Hoilett's and Reilly Mahan's classes reacted similarly. When one fourth grader in Ms. Mahan's class asked, "Are they both girls?," referring to the same-sex marriage, many of their classmates looked shocked and impish. One of the fifth graders in Mr. Hoilett's class laughed when seeing the illustration.

This led to critical conversations to disrupt heteronormativity. When asked if they'd ever seen same-sex couples in their community or on TV, several nodded and others said they'd seen people holding hands walking downtown. Some made their disapproval clear, citing religious and parents' views. Yet they agreed that, regardless of belief systems, we should treat others with respect and kindness. They listened respectfully, disagreed civilly, and found common ground. One student shyly and nervously shared that his uncle has a boyfriend.

In these classes, this initial discussion broke the ice for future conversations about the LGBTQ+ community where it became more normalized. For example, when reading *Imagine a Wolf* by Lucky Platt, students noticed the wolf dressed in women's clothing and wondered what gender pronouns were used in the book to know if it was "a boy wolf or a girl wolf."

Ms. Mahan asked them to consider if knowing the gender of the wolf would change the story.

Marco:	"If it's a boy wolf who likes to knit and wear a dress, then maybe the author wants us to know that boys can do those things too."
Emma:	"If it's a transgender wolf, people still see a boy wolf in a dress when they should just see a girl wolf."
Ms. Mahan:	"So which is the focus, the wolf's identity, or the assumptions of the people around the wolf?"

| Jordan: | "The theme is to not judge a book by its cover." |
| Darius: | "Can we just keep reading? It's about not judging people so why do we even care so much if the wolf is a boy or a girl or whatever?" |

They ultimately agreed that the way we treat people shouldn't depend on what they look like.

Children regularly collect information from the world around them to shape their beliefs. For instance, they may believe that only men can be president of the United States. The portrayal of gender in media also sends messages that may influence children's understanding of social norms (see Chapter 7: "Consuming Critically"). Further, when we say seemingly innocuous things like "boys and girls," young children infer that gender is an important social category (Winkler, 2009). They then begin to attach meaning and beliefs to gender categories. Instead, we suggest greetings such as "class," "friends," or "students." Gendered notions of intelligence develop at an early age as well. Bian and others (2017) found that by age six, girls began to view boys as "really, really smart." The stereotype that males are more intelligent shapes children's interests and narrows their future career aspirations (e.g., women are underrepresented in fields such as science and math; see Corbett & Hill, 2015).

Pause to Reflect

Before reading further, pause and jot your own definition of a stereotype. What is a stereotype and what are examples of stereotypes? After reading more about stereotypes in this chapter, revisit your definition and examples. Consider using a similar pre- and post-reflection with your own students.

STEREOTYPES	
Before reading, I think . . .	After reading, I am thinking . . .

What Is a Stereotype?

The dictionary definition of *stereotype* is the unfair belief that all people or things with a particular characteristic are the same.

We can look deeper at stereotypes through critical comprehension. According to Chimamanda Adichie, the "problem with stereotypes is not that they are untrue, but that they are incomplete. They make one story become the only story." In her TED talk, Adichie (2009) warns that if we are only exposed to a single story then we risk critical misunderstanding and develop stereotypes. Therefore, it is necessary to ensure we move beyond a single story when discussing representation of people whether from a historical or a more contemporary lens. Further, we want to avoid stereotypes and tropes and teach children how to recognize and confront them.

Scan the QR code to watch Chimamanda Ngozi Adichie's TED talk "The Danger of a Single Story."

Stereotypes, or generalizations, are problematic because they lead people to believe something as true for an entire group. Rather than generalizations, specific language can help avoid the development of these assumptions (Rhodes, 2017). For example, when discussing racial stereotypes, Mr. Hoilett explained that although he does not like to swim, that does not mean that is true for all Black individuals. He reminded students of the book *Jabari Jumps* by Gaia Cornwall and then returned to the illustration of Black children swimming in the book *I Am Every Good Thing* by Derrick Barnes. One Black student remarked, "I love to swim too!" Seeing these images and hearing first-hand accounts help dispel the stereotype that Black people don't like to swim and repositions it as individual and more nuanced.

Helping children to recognize stereotypes in the world around them helps them recognize stereotypes in texts, images, and other representations. For example, the popular *Skippy Jon Jones* book series by Judith Bryon Schachner is often included in classrooms and libraries for the silly language and fun character of a Siamese cat who dresses up as a Chihuahua named El Skippito. However, a critical examination reveals stereotypes of Mexican culture and Spanish speakers. For example, adding "o" to the end of words is inaccurate and offensive for Spanish speakers and perpetuates the stereotype with another generation of readers.

A Hispanic student in Mr. Hoilett's fifth-grade class shared about a time in the cafeteria when a volunteer server from the community acted surprised when she did not want guacamole with her lunch. "You should like it!" the server said, and her friends erupted in laughter. More than a year later, she still remembered this experience and connected it to Milo's initial assumptions of the people on the train in the book *Milo Imagines the World*. When asked how this experience made her feel, she stumbled to find the words and then bravely responded, "Shame." She said she felt like she had done something wrong. She knew the adult's comment and her peers' reaction were not appropriate, yet she felt that she was the one who had done something wrong.

Examining
Stereotypes

When the comments or actions of others arising from long-held stereotypes leave a child feeling embarrassed and ashamed, we must intervene. When Mr. Hoilett asked what she thought could be done to address this, she suggested a need for more books to help people dispel stereotypes about Hispanics, commenting, "Not all Hispanics speak Spanish and eat guacamole."

Stereotypes are dehumanizing and can cause harm. The introduction to different perspectives, viewpoints, and lifestyles through books and conversation can help dismantle harmful stereotypes and build relationships (Norris, 2020). When selecting books, we must be conscious of the portrayal of individuals and groups. Reading books that only reflect a singular way of being can be limiting, result in stereotypes, and create a sense of superiority. If the representations are close approximations, they become "foggy mirrors that reflect only vague contours of the identities and lived experiences that comprise a child's reality" (Enriquez, 2021, p. 104). The overrepresentation of texts featuring one perspective or way of being perpetuates the "danger of the single story" (Adichie, 2009). For example, in one scene in the Newbery Award–winning graphic novel *The New Kid* by Jerry Craft, the teacher, Miss Brickner, assumes that Maury, a Black student, would love to read a book about the survival of a boy who grew up in poverty without a father. Maury rejects the book and responds, "Ummm . . . thanks, Miss Brickner, but my dad is the CEO of a Fortune 500 company" (Craft, 2019, p. 129). Therefore, we must critically examine texts and our social worlds for the presence of stereotypes and disrupt them just like Maury does in *The New Kid*.

Evaluating Your Classroom Library for Stereotypes

Knowing that each of us comes to texts with the limitations of our own narrow lens means we may miss something others may notice. Consider working with a group of colleagues to curate a collection of texts that will offer a well-rounded and more accurate representation of individuals and groups. As you build the collection, consider the need for mirrors that will allow children to see themselves reflected in ways that celebrate their genius and joy (Bishop, 1990; Muhammad, 2020). Consider the need for windows that will allow children to see into the brilliance of the lives of others who are different from themselves. And consider the need for sliding glass doors that allow children to step into the world of others in story (Bishop, 1990; Laminack & Kelly, 2019).

In an interview with Reading Rockets (2015), Rudine Sims Bishop says, "Diversity needs to go both ways. I mean it's not just children who have been underrepresented and marginalized who need these books. It's also the children who always find their mirrors in the books and, therefore, get an exaggerated sense of their own self-worth and a false sense of what the world is like." The inclusion of texts that serve as mirrors, windows, and sliding glass doors for students is essential to dismantling the stereotypes they may already hold or develop. (For more, refer to Chapter 1 of this book.)

When evaluating books and other forms of text, consider the following list of common harmful and undermining stereotypes from Social Justice Books.

Scan the QR code to access Social Justice Books' Common Harmful/ Undermining Stereotypes list.

Critical Comprehension
Lesson Series
Examining Stereotypes

The lesson series begins with a foundational lesson as an introduction to the concept of stereotypes using the book *Milo Imagines the World* by Matt de la Peña. The lessons then move to the exploration of different ways stereotypes may shape our thinking and understanding. The lessons included in this series provide a foundation for understanding the concepts presented in the lessons in Chapter 5 focused on bias.

Each lesson features one book, but also includes a list of alternatives for additional work to extend thought and insight. As is the case with all the lessons in this book, we offer these ideas as a starting point and encourage you to adapt them based on the interests and inquiries of students.

Table of Lessons for Examining Stereotypes

LESSON FOCUS	ANCHOR TEXT
1. Introducing stereotypes	*Milo Imagines the World* by Matt de la Peña
2. Exploring gender stereotypes	*Bunny Cakes* by Rosemary Wells
3. Understanding microaggressions	*Where Are You From?* by Yamile Saied Méndez
4. Examining the good vs. bad trope	*Imagine a Wolf* by Lucky Platt
5. Defining beauty	*Beautifully Me* by Nabela Noor
6. Celebrating all kinds of minds	*The Girl Who Thought in Pictures: The Story of Dr. Temple Grandin* by Julia Finley Mosca
7. Disrupting notions of normalcy	*A Normal Pig* by K-Fai Steele

Note: The blank spaces are an invitation for you to add your own related topics and texts.

Lesson 1: Examining Stereotypes
Milo Imagines the World • by Matt de la Peña

 ## First Read: Movie Read

This first visit, the "movie read," focuses on taking in the story without interruption (see Chapter 1, p. 21). Milo, in *Milo Imagines the World*, is a writer and an artist who is observant about his world. While traveling on the subway, he notices the people around him and imagines (then reimagines) their stories.

 ## Second Read: Reading With the Text

Throughout this reading, students will record responses in chart form, which you can create ahead of time, such as the one shown in Figure 4.4.

Before reading, display the cover of the book. Invite students to retell the story. Then reread the book, pausing to stop and discuss along the way.

Read the first spread.

Ask students to visualize the setting of the subway. Invite them to pay attention to the way the author describes the setting of the book in the subway station to help bring the readers right into the story.

Read the second spread. Note the character descriptions (whiskered man, businessman, wedding-dressed woman, etc.) and add to the first and second columns of the *Milo Imagines the World* chart.

Ask students:

- *What are you thinking?*
- *What are you wondering?*

Read the third spread, stopping after the first sentence: "These monthly Sunday subway rides are never ending, and as usual, Milo is a shook-up soda."

Ask students: *Where do you think they might be going on the subway one Sunday a month?*

FIGURE 4.3

FIGURE 4.4 Examining Stereotypes Student Response Chart

CHARACTER	CHARACTER DESCRIPTION (BASED ON TEXT AND ILLUSTRATION CLUES)	WHAT ARE YOU THINKING OR WONDERING ABOUT THIS CHARACTER?	HOW MILO IMAGINES THE CHARACTER	WHY DO YOU THINK HE IMAGINED THEM THIS WAY?	HOW MILO REIMAGINES THE CHARACTER	WHAT I'M THINKING NOW
Whiskered man						
The boy						
Wedding-dressed woman						
Break dancers	Girls are walking up the walls, whirling around poles, backflipping over shopping bags.	Wow, they are so talented and athletic!	People watch them perform but when they go to the store or into a fancy neighborhood, people watch them in a different way as if they don't belong.	Some people might judge others as being "bad" or "troublemakers" based on their appearances.	Smiling and being welcomed into the apartment building in the fancy neighborhood.	The break dancers deserve to be given a chance without judgment.

Reread the sentence "Milo is a shook-up soda."

Ask students:

- *What happens when you shake a soda?*

- *Why do you think the author chose to describe Milo in this way?*

You might use the language "I infer . . ." as you respond. (Students may infer that he is excited or nervous about where he is going.)

Read the third spread (left), stopping after the second sentence: "Excitement stacked on top of worry on top of confusion on top of love." Confirm that Milo is excited but note that he is experiencing other emotions as well (e.g., confusion, love). Again, **ask students** to consider where he is going. Notice how the author stacked the sentence and consider the effect.

As you read each of the spreads aloud, focusing on the different characters Milo encounters, fill in the columns on the chart for each character, noting students' wonderings, how Milo imagines the character and why, then how Milo reimagines the character.

Read the third and fourth spreads.

Ask students:

- *Why do you think Milo envisioned the whiskered man's life in that way?*

- *What factors could have influenced Milo's drawing?*

Record the students' responses on the chart.

Read the fifth spread (left).

Ask students: *Why do you think the author chose to describe Milo's sister as ". . . a shook-up soda, too"?*

Encourage students to continue to refine their predictions about where Milo and his sister are going.

Read the fifth spread (right). Note the character description of the boy who entered the train and add to the *Milo Imagines the World* chart (see Figure 4.4).

Ask students:

- *What are you thinking?*

- *What are you wondering?*

Update the chart with students' thinking.

Read the sixth spread.

Ask students:

- *Why do you think Milo envisioned the boy's life in that way?*
- *What factors might have influenced Milo's drawing?*

Record the students' responses on the chart.

Read the seventh and eighth spreads where the wedding-dressed woman gets off the train followed by Milo's drawing of the woman.

Ask students:

- *Why do you think Milo envisioned the woman's life in that way?*
- *What factors might have influenced Milo's drawing?*

Record the students' responses on the chart.

Read the ninth spread.

Ask students: *Why did Milo feel like the walls were closing in around him when he locked eyes with the other boy?*

Read the tenth spread when the break dancers enter the train and the eleventh spread where Milo imagines their story. Point out the use of the word "but" to indicate a change or a problem.

Ask students:

- *Why do you think Milo envisioned the dancers' lives in that way?*
- *What factors might have influenced Milo's drawing?*
- *Why do you think Milo doesn't like this picture?*
- *What do you believe Milo is thinking as he looks at his reflection in the window?*

Record the students' responses on the chart.

Read the twelfth spread where Milo wonders what people imagine about *his* face.

Ask students: *Why do you think he suddenly shifts to wondering what people think about him?*

Read the thirteenth spread (left) where Milo and his sister get off the train.

Ask students: *Why would Milo have butterflies in his stomach?*

Read the thirteenth spread (right) where they are street level and he sees the boy in the suit. Point out the police car and officers.

Ask students:

- *What do you notice about this page?*
- *Where do you think they are?*
- *Why would he be surprised to see the boy in the suit at this place?*

Read the fourteenth spread where they are in line for the metal detector.

Ask students:

- *What do you notice in the art and in the details?*
- *What do you think they are thinking about?*
- *Where do you think they are?*
- *If necessary, draw their attention to the textual clues, including Milo's feelings leading up to this part. Point out the other boy in line too.*

Read the fifteenth spread where Milo reimagines the stories.

Ask students:

- *What do you notice?*
- *Why do you think Milo is reimagining the stories in this way?*

Add to a new column in the chart labeled "What I'm thinking now." Return to the earlier conversations and revisit students' thinking about the factors that influenced Milo's first drawings. Think of these as before and the reimagined sketches as after. Compare/contrast the factors influencing his drawings before and after.

Read the sixteenth spread when Milo sees his mom. Remind students to pay attention to the illustrations as well as the text.

Ask students: *Now do we have more clues about where Milo and his sister are?*

Students may respond by suggesting that they are visiting their mom. They may also notice that they are in jail based on the orange jumpsuits.

Ask students: *Do you think Milo and his sister still feel like a shook-up soda? How are they feeling now?*

If students do not notice the boy with the Nikes at another table, point out this detail in the illustration.

Ask students: *Why do you think Milo was surprised to see the boy outside the building, waiting in line for the metal detector, and now inside the jail?*

Read the seventeenth spread where Milo shows his mom the drawing he made. Then show the final spread with his drawing.

Ask students:

- *How do the characters (Milo, his sister, and his mom) feel?*
- *What is your reaction to the events in the story? What are you thinking and wondering now?*

Return to the chart and complete the last column (What I'm thinking now) for each character together. Use this column as a springboard for the next read and a deeper, more critical conversation about stereotypes.

 ## Return Read: Reading Critically

Begin the return read by reviewing the anchor chart from the second read. Focus specifically on the final two columns: (1) how Milo changed the way he imagined the people's stories after he looked at his own reflection in the window and (2) What I'm thinking now.

Introduce the concept of stereotypes: the unfair belief that all people or things with a particular characteristic are the same, often based on assumptions, incomplete information, or lack of experience with people from different backgrounds than oneself.

Ask students: *Can you think of a few examples of stereotypes in Milo's original drawings?*

Together, discuss how just like Milo, we can make assumptions about people based on limited information.

Ask students: *What are some examples of stereotypes?*

These can be recorded on chart paper (e.g., Asian Americans are good at math, Black people are dangerous, girls like to play with dolls, people in poverty don't work hard, boys like sports, Native Americans wear moccasins and carry bows and arrows, etc.) Refer to Chapter 1 for suggestions for preparing students for conversations such as these.

Review the list of stereotypes.

Ask students: *What factors influence or form the stereotypes we have toward others? In other words, where do we get these ideas from?*

Discuss how we receive subtle messages from the information all around even if someone isn't directly teaching us or telling us to believe something (e.g., TV, media, advertisements, books, other people).

Ask students: *What are some examples of subtle messages that may influence what we think or believe (e.g., stores being divided into girls' sections and boys' sections, couples on TV)?*

Reread the book, pausing to stop and discuss how Milo made assumptions but changed his thinking after reflecting and wondering how others view *him.*

Ask students:

- *Can you recall some of the assumptions Milo made about people?*

- *What changed his thinking?*

- *Why was that a turning point for Milo?*

Pause and engage in a brief conversation about the idea that we can grow and change and develop new ideas and perspectives.

Finish reading the book.

Ask students:

- *What are you thinking now after seeing the ways in which Milo reimagines the people's lives?*

- *Have you ever discovered that you believed something about a person without really getting to know them or hearing their story?*

- *Are there opportunities for you to reimagine how you see someone?*

- *How can you know when you are thinking about someone or something as a stereotype?*

Give students an opportunity to stop and jot or quickly sketch here using a before/after format. Give them an opportunity to share if they so choose.

First I thought (or assumed) . . .	Now I'm thinking . . .

Ask students:

- *Can you think of times in the community or the world around us when people have made assumptions about someone without knowing their story? What happened?*

- *How can we work to understand someone and avoid making assumptions about them?*

Additional Texts for Examining Stereotypes

- *Far Apart, Close in Heart: Being a Family When a Loved One Is Incarcerated* by Becky Birtha

- *Knock Knock: My Dad's Dream for Me* by Daniel Beaty

- *Our Moms* by Q. Futrell

- Chimamanda Adichie's TED talk, "The Danger of a Single Story"

- *Visiting Day* by Jacqueline Woodson

Examining
Stereotypes

Lesson 2: Exploring Gender Stereotypes
Bunny Cakes • by Rosemary Wells

 ### First Read: Movie Read

This first visit, the "movie read," focuses on taking in the story without interruption (see Chapter 1, p. 21). In *Bunny Cakes*, Max and Ruby want to make Grandma a cake for her birthday, but they each have different ideas about the type of cake to make.

 ### Second Read: Reading With the Text

Before reading, set a reading purpose by asking students to pay attention to how the author developed the characters of Max and Ruby.

Ask students: *As we read, consider what the author wants us to know or think about Max and Ruby.*

Read the first page.

Ask students: *What do you think about Max and Ruby after just meeting them?*

Continue reading.

Ask students: *How has your thinking about Max and Ruby changed or stayed the same?*

Record students' responses on a two-column character analysis anchor chart, like the one in Figure 4.6.

Invite students to share their thinking and generalizations about each character. This may lead, for example, to discussions about the notion of good versus bad, the role of writing well, or gender norms.

FIGURE 4.5

FIGURE 4.6   Sample Character Analysis Chart

Use a different color marker/font or add another column to provide evidence from the text as support. See examples noted in parentheses.

Bunny Cakes by Rosemary Wells

Character Analysis

MAX	RUBY
• Likes to play in the dirt	• Seems bossy
• Cares about his grandmother	• Cares about her grandmother
• Wants to help	• Good writing
• Clumsy	• Sets boundaries/rules for Max
• Doesn't listen to Ruby	• Kicks Max out of the kitchen ("The kitchen is no place for you.")
• Focused on his dirt cake	
• Bad writing	• Focused on making the cake
• Persistent (keeps trying to help and to get his marshmallow squirters from the grocer)	• Good
	• Wants the cake to be perfect
• Always thinking/creative (tries drawing instead of writing to communicate with grocer)	
• Doesn't follow the rules ("he crossed the line," licks the spoon through the window)	
• Bad	
• Persists and is proud of his earthworm cake	

 Return Read: Reading Critically

Before reading, **ask students** what comes to mind when they think of gender.

Record their responses on chart paper.

> **Gender:** The social construction of characteristics associated with what is masculine and feminine (not defined by the sex assigned at birth).

Ask students:

- *Are there certain ways or expectations that the world suggests are for boys or girls? (Invite students to share examples.)*

- *Are there things people expect of boys that we don't expect of girls?*

- *Are there things people think only girls should do? Are there things people expect only boys should do?*

After this discussion, reread the book.

Ask students:

- *What messages does the book suggest about gender?*

- *How are the characters positioned in terms of gender norms?*

When we think of stereotypical gender roles, females are often portrayed as doing domestic chores like cooking and cleaning, and males are often depicted as the ones working at a job, doing hard labor, or working outside in the dirt. Girls may be portrayed as neat, tidy, organized, and thoughtful while boys are often portrayed as messy, careless, and disobedient. We may also see stereotypical portrayals of children's independence based on age. Older children are portrayed as more capable and self-sufficient while younger children are portrayed as needing more supervision. This may be seen with the characters of Max and Ruby in *Bunny Cakes*.

Ask students:

- *What message does the line "The kitchen is no place for you" send to Max as well as to readers of the book?*

- *What other messages could be implied based on Max's character? What other messages could be implied based on Ruby's character?*

- *What are you thinking now after reading this book through the lens of gender?*

For Younger Students and/or SEL Connection

Read the book *Tough Boris* by Mem Fox. Boris is all the things people expect a pirate to be: tough, fearsome, and scary. When his pet parrot dies, he is sad and cries. Explain to students that even though Boris is tough, it is okay for him to cry and express his feelings when he is sad. The stereotype that boys and men should be tough can be harmful because it prevents some people from being comfortable when expressing their feelings.

Show the cover of the book.

Ask students: *What do you think this pirate will do in the story?*

(Continued)

(Continued)

Read the book.

Ask students:

- *What surprised you?*

- *What was the author trying to convey by having Tough Boris cry?*

- *Why is it important to see images of all sorts of people experiencing all sorts of emotions?*

Extend the Reading: Curating a Collection of Text to Examine Gender Stereotypes

These books can be used to think about gender beyond traditional gender norms.

- *Amazing Grace* by Mary Hoffman (Note: We recommend the twenty-fifth-anniversary edition of this book because the stereotypical image of Grace pretending to be a Native American was removed.)
- *Do Princesses Wear Hiking Boots?* by Carmela Coyle
- *Introducing Teddy* by Jessica Walton
- *Morris Micklewhite and the Tangerine Dress* by Christine Baldacchino
- *My Princess Boy* by Cheryl Kilodavis
- *My Shadow Is Pink* by Scott Stuart
- *Oliver Button Is a Sissy* by Tomie dePaola
- *Pink Is for Boys* by Robb Perlman
- *Red: A Crayon's Story* by Michael Hall
- *Sissy Duckling* by Harvey Fierstein
- *The Boy with the Pink Hair* by Pérez Hilton
- *The Paperbag Princess* by Robert Munsch
- *Tough Boris* by Mem Fox
- *Want to Play Trucks?* by Ann Stott
- *William's Doll* by Charlotte Zolotow
- *Worm Loves Worm* by J.J. Austrian

Lesson 3: Understanding Microaggressions
Where Are You From? • by Yamile Saied Méndez

 First Read: Movie Read

FIGURE 4.7

This first visit, the "movie read," focuses on taking in the story without interruption (see Chapter 1, p. 21). *Where Are You From?* is the question at the center of this book by Yamile Saied Méndez. The text answers this simple question by examining our relationships with other people and how our lives are intertwined in the world around us. This book could also be a springboard for discussions about how asking where someone is from can be a microaggression.

> Microaggressions are subtle negative comments or actions that can be intentional or unintentional toward a member of a historically marginalized group.

 Second Read: Reading With the Text

Return to the book for a second read.

Ask students to notice and list all the answers given by Abuelo when asked, "Where are you from?"

After reading, unpack the list by grouping the words and finding categories (e.g., biosphere—parts of the earth where life exists, land masses, geographic locations, people).

Ask students: *How do the descriptions give you a way to think about where the child and Abuelo are from and how integral they are to the world around them?*

Invite students to brainstorm about where they are from. They can create a graphic organizer with "Where I Am From" in the center and spokes to list/draw various aspects about their home. For instance, they can sketch their home, family members, favorite meals, or activities. They might add speech bubbles to illustrate the types of things being spoken by various family members.

Alternatively, you can provide a handout, such as the one in Figure 4.8, which students can fill in to help them start thinking about where they are from. Invite students to share their organizers but respect the rights of those who choose not to share.

FIGURE 4.8 Where I Am From Organizer	
Who are the people/pets who are important to you?	What do your home and neighborhood look like?
What foods make you think of home?	What are common activities or things you and your family do in your home and neighborhood?
What do you hear at your home and in your neighborhood?	What smells remind you of your home and neighborhood?

Adapted from Laminack and Kelly (2019).

Doing this activity yourself would be a powerful demonstration for your students and also help them learn more about you while building classroom community.

Avoiding Harm

Asking students to explore where they are from may cause harm for some students. For instance, children who have immigrated to the United States may have experienced trauma in their journeys and may not be ready to recount where they're from. Likewise, Native American students whose origin stories involve a history of genocide, and African American students whose origin stories may involve enslavement, may not be ready to share.

Thus, we should be mindful of their personal experiences and circumstances. Reflect on the identity work from Chapter 2 and remember that there are parts of our identities that we intentionally keep close and don't invite others into until we are ready to do so. Remember that home, family, and culture are parts of our identity and the choice of what to share with others should always be the individual's. Let students share what they are comfortable sharing without pushing or prying.

Alternate Activity: Where We're From Collaboration

Read other texts that explore the idea of where I'm from. George Ella Lyon's poem "Where I'm From" and Renée Watson's "Where I'm From" poem are accessible examples that could be revisited as mentor texts for students to write their own poems.

Renée Watson recites her "Where I'm From" poem at the International Literacy Association conference.

"Where I'm From" by George Ella Lyon

http://www.georgeellalyon.com/where.html

"Where I'm From" by Renée Watson

bit.ly/3udY23z

Invite students to share their poems with the class. After sharing, ask them to select a favorite line from their poem and record it on a sentence strip. Then in small groups have students collaborate by contributing their favorite line sentence strip to a group poem titled "Where We're From." This can also be done with a broader audience, including family and community members (see Laminack & Kelly, 2019, p. 39).

Alternatively, students can post their poems and record themselves reading their poems aloud using various digital tools. Read students' poems and make note of the overlaps and differences. Then use notes to create a community poem alternating between overlap and difference. For example,

> We are from (common items), From (contrasting items),
> . . . etc.

> (e.g., We are from backpacks filled with books and homework, from writers' workshops and . . . from walkers and car riders and big yellow school buses. We are from . . .)

 ## Return Read: Reading Critically

Reread the first few pages of the book. When the young, brown-skinned girl is asked, "Where are you from? Is your mom from here? Is your dad from there?" she replies, "I'm from here, from today, same as everyone else." They counter with "No, where are you really from?"

Ask students:

- *What does this question mean?*
- *Why do the other kids say, "No, where are you really from?"*
- *Why do they use the word "really"?*

Continue reading. The girl asks Abuelo to help her understand where she is from. Discuss the sentence "Unlike me, he looks like he doesn't belong."

Ask students:

- *What does it mean to look like you belong or not belong?*

- *Who determines who belongs and who doesn't belong?*

Explain that we all come from somewhere but not all of us are asked where we are from.

Ask students: *Have you ever heard someone ask the question "Where are you from?"*

Pause and explain that this is an example of a microaggression. Define microaggression.

For Younger Students

Explain that microaggressions are negative and hurtful things we say and do against someone's race or culture.

Continue the discussion using the following questions as a guide.

Ask students:

- *Who was asked this question and by whom?*

- *Why do you suppose they asked the question?*

- *What do you think the person who asked the question meant?*

- *What do you think "from" refers to? A kind of house? A street? A specific neighborhood? A town, region, or country?*

- *Do you think everyone gets asked where they are from? Why or why not?*

- *Who do you think gets asked that question most often? Why?*

- *Who do you think asks that question?*

- *How might asking the question "where are you from" be hurtful to someone?*

- *What can be said or done instead?*

Emphasize the question "How might asking the question 'Where are you from' be hurtful to someone?" to help students better understand everyday microaggressions.

Provide additional examples of microaggressions and invite students to brainstorm others. For example,

- an Asian American being complimented for how well they speak English, or a Black person being told they are articulate

- a woman clutching her purse and/or crossing the street when she sees a Black man

- calling someone by another name because theirs is "too difficult" to pronounce

- laughing at someone's name

- catcalls or whistles at women

Ask students:

- *Why are microaggressions problematic? (Discuss how they can result in feelings of inferiority and self-doubt.)*

- *How do microaggressions reinforce stereotypes?*

- *What messages do the microaggressions convey?*

Ask students: *How could we intervene if we came across these situations?*

Help students to identify microaggressions and develop the language necessary to respond. For example, you might ask the person if you can talk about what just happened or ask them to say more about what they mean by what they said. Additionally, microaggressions are often said in a lighthearted, joking manner. Explain that it wasn't funny and why. You might also offer them another way to think about what they just said or did. Follow up this discussion by emphasizing the question "What can be said or done instead of . . . [the microaggression]?"

For example, they could redirect by asking the person what they meant by their comment. Practice by role-playing.

Christensen (n.d.) teaches her students how to navigate an unjust world—and how to change it. While discussing instances of injustice, she has her students create a chart with four categories: Ally, Target, Perpetrator, and Bystander. She then has them fill in the chart to identify the positions they and others have taken as the instance of injustice was unfolding. The activity could help students to understand how they may have been complicit,

(Continued)

(Continued)

what to do about changing their own behaviors, and how the behaviors of others contribute to sustaining or disrupting microaggressions. Manvell (2022) added two additional categories—Audience and Cheerleader—to further help students understand the roles they and others play in problematic situations.

Ally:	The defender
Target:	The victim of the microaggression
Perpetrator:	The individual or group engaging in the microaggression
Bystander:	Someone who is aware of what is happening
Audience:	Individual or group that watches but does nothing to stop the microaggression
Cheerleader:	Individual who encourages the perpetrator

For Younger Students

To introduce microaggressions to his class, Mr. Hoilett held up a character he sketched and told the students it was his new friend. Some students laughed, called the sketch ugly, questioned why it looks like that, and asked why Mr. Hoilett wanted to be friends with him. Some students caught on quickly and immediately pulled back as they heard the kinds of things their peers said or gently defended them. Yet others continued with mean comments (proving the point of the activity). Mr. Hoilett used this to drive the conversation.

With each negative comment, Mr. Hoilett crinkled his sketch with the face of his "friend." For particularly mean comments, he ripped the paper. When the paper was unfurled and whole again, the lines were still visible. Mr. Hoilett theatrically and frantically attempts to smooth the paper out and fix his "friend," but the sketch never returns to its original smooth, flawless form. He then invited the students to engage in a conversation. This visual activity demonstrated how our words can be harmful and leave scars. Mr. Hoilett posted the sketch of his "friend" on the board as a reminder of the impact our words can have on others.

As a follow-up to this demonstration, teachers can engage students in a conversation to distinguish the difference between hurt feelings (e.g., telling someone their shirt is ugly or calling them stupid) and microaggressions (e.g., telling someone they run like a girl or asking to touch a Black person's hair). Encourage students to consider the conversations focused on identity (see Chapter 2) and reflect on whether the comments were identity-based, in particular around a part of their identity that is marginalized.

Additional Texts to Explore Microaggressions

10,000 Dresses by Marcus Ewert	Bailey, a trans girl, loves dresses despite her father's and brother's attempts to dissuade her by saying "you're a boy" and "That's gross. You're a boy . . . Get out of here before I kick you."
Amazing Grace by Mary Hoffman (Note: We recommend the twenty-fifth-anniversary edition of this book because the stereotypical image of Grace pretending to be a Native American was removed.)	Grace is told she can't play Peter in the play *Peter Pan* because she is Black.
A Different Pond by Bao Phi	A classmate tells the boy his Vietnamese father's English "sounds like a thick, dirty river." But to the little boy, his father's English sounds like "gentle rain."
Don't Touch My Hair by Sharee Miller	Hair shouldn't be treated as a curiosity.
The Name Jar by Yangsook Choi	Unhei's classmates laugh at her name and refuse to learn the correct pronunciation.

Resources

- "Teaching First-Graders About Microaggressions" from Learning for Justice

  bit.ly/3XOfY2g

- "Microaggressions: More Than Just Race" by Derald Wing Sue

  bit.ly/3AYu0EF

Examining Stereotypes

Lesson 4: Examining the Good vs. Bad Trope
Imagine a Wolf • by Lucky Platt

Imagine a
WOLF

What do you see?

Lucky Platt

Tropes can be character types, such as the damsel in distress or the mad scientist. When characters are oversimplified, such as the "bad guy" always dressed in black, stereotypes can develop.

 ## First Read: Movie Read

This first visit, the "movie read," focuses on taking in the story without interruption (see Chapter 1, p. 21). *Imagine a Wolf* invites the reader to look beyond the surface to reimagine their preconceived ideas about wolves.

Prior to reading *Imagine a Wolf*, engage students in Talking Drawings (Wood et al., 2016) by asking them to fold a paper in half and label the top "before" and the bottom "after." (Note: This can also be preprinted on a handout for younger students. See Figure 4.10.) Before reading, ask students to draw a picture of a wolf in the "before" space. Invite them to use labels and/or sentences to describe their drawing. Next, ask students to share their drawing with a peer followed by whole-group sharing.

FIGURE 4.10 Before and After Reading Talking Drawing Template	
Before	After

Most likely students will draw versions of a wolf from familiar stories, such as "Little Red Riding Hood" or "The Three Little Pigs," or wolves in nature. Collect the Talking Drawings and set them aside for the second read, then read the story without interruption.

Second Read: Reading With the Text

For the second read, pause throughout the book for each question posed to the reader and invite students to respond. Record their responses on a chart like the one in Figure 4.11.

IMAGINE A WOLF	WE SAY (PREDICT)	TEXT SAYS
FIGURE 4.11 Imagine a Wolf Chart		
Teeth	To eat you!	"The better to hold the wool while my paws spin the wheel."
Eyes	To hunt for food.	"The better to enjoy all of the colors around me."
Ears	To listen to music.	"The better to pick up a faraway cry for help."

Ask students:

- *How does what the text says compare with your prediction?*

- *Were you surprised the wolf uses its teeth to help him knit?*

Continue reading. Pause and discuss the page that reads, "There's always someone who cries wolf."

Ask students:

- *Have you heard that expression before? What do you think it means?*

- *How do you think that affects the wolf?*

Read the speech bubbles on the following page: "Because everywhere I go, I try to be me."

Ask students: *What are you learning about the wolf?*

On the page where the reader is prompted to close their eyes and picture a wolf, provide students with the Talking Drawings from the first read.

Ask students: *What are you currently thinking about a wolf?*

Ask students to sketch a new drawing of their current thinking on the side of the Talking Drawing labeled "after." Direct them to use labels and/or sentences to describe their drawing.

When students are finished, ask them to turn and share their drawings with a peer. Then read the last page of the book and ask students to compare their drawings.

Ask students:

- *How has your thinking changed about wolves?*

- *What is the author's message?*

- *What do you think the author's intentions were for writing this book?*

 Return Read: Reading Critically

Before reading critically, ask students to think about good versus bad and share ideas that come to mind. Record their ideas on a good/bad chart like the one in Figure 4.12. Explore the characteristics, traits, or behaviors that result in this characterization.

FIGURE 4.12   Sample Good/Bad Chart

GOOD	CHARACTERISTICS, TRAITS, BEHAVIORS	BAD	CHARACTERISTICS, TRAITS, BEHAVIORS
Batman	Helps people	Joker	Hurts people
Fairy Godmother	Grants wishes	Wolf	Eats three little pigs

With the notion of good and bad at the forefront of their minds, invite students to consider this binary when revisiting the book *Imagine a Wolf*.

Ask students:

- *How is the wolf depicted in the beginning and in familiar stories, such as "Little Red Riding Hood" and "The Three Little Pigs"?*

- *What are possible consequences for the portrayal of the wolf with the stereotype as bad?*

- *How has your thinking about the wolf changed after reading Imagine a Wolf?*

- *How does the book compare to The True Story of the Three Little Pigs! by Jon Scieszka? (see Chapter 3: "Examining Perspective")*

- *Why is it important to have alternate versions of stories to help disrupt stereotypes?*

- *What are some examples of characters portrayed as good or bad? How can we disrupt those stereotypes?*

Examining Good vs. Bad in Fairy Tales

Extend the conversation of the good and bad (or right or wrong) binary in other familiar books and fairy tales.

Ask students:

- *Why are stepmothers and stepsisters in stories like "Cinderella" typically viewed as bad?*

- *How does this compare with the portrayal of the stepmother in the book The Memory String by Eve Bunting?*

- *Why does the "good" handsome prince have to kiss Sleeping Beauty to wake her up?*

- *Why does the damsel in distress need to be rescued by the knight in shining armor?*

- *Why is the witch typically bad and ugly?*

- *How do you think the witch feels?*

- *Why is the troll in "Three Billy Goats Gruff" so mean?*

- *Why are the goats in "Three Billy Goats Gruff" considered the good guys?*

- *How do you think the troll feels?*

- *Could Jack from "Jack and the Beanstalk" be considered bad? Good? Explain.*

- *How do you think the giant felt when Jack took his belongings?*

- *Did the giant in "Jack and the Beanstalk" have a right to protect his property?*

- *How do you think the three bears reacted when they found Goldilocks in their home?*

- *Did Goldilocks have a right to enter their home without permission?*

- *What if Goldilocks was not a girl with blond hair? Would it change the way you feel about the character's actions?*

- *How is color used to create good/bad binaries in traditional tales? For example, consider the dark forest in "Little Red Riding Hood" or "Hansel and Gretel" as a scary and dangerous place. Or the way the fairy godmother in stories like "Cinderella" is dressed in white clothing.*

Examining
Stereotypes

Examining the Good and Bad Binary with *Bunny Cakes* (from Lesson 2)

Remind students of the book *Bunny Cakes* from Lesson 2.

Ask students: *How are Max and Ruby portrayed as good or bad?*

They might note that Max is bad because he doesn't follow the rules and is kicked out of the kitchen.

Max does not speak at all in the story and has difficulty communicating in writing until he draws a picture. Ask students to consider how the story might be different if told from Max's perspective just like the way *The True Story of the Three Little Pigs!* changed when told from the wolf's perspective.

Ask students: *How does hearing a story from the perspective of the character who is portrayed as bad change our opinions of the character and the way the character is perceived?*

Pause to Reflect

- Consider how the notion of good and bad writing transfers to what students come to believe matters in school writing.

- What do our comments and actions communicate about what is valued in writing?

- Consider how our own stereotypes of "good" students versus "bad" students may already position some students with advantages or disadvantages. What are some harmful practices that could be reimagined to disrupt the good/bad binary in our classrooms? For instance, punitive disciplinary practices, such as referrals and suspensions, contribute to the school-to-prison pipeline.

When considering the role of good and bad stereotypes in our lives and the broader world, an example might include that if someone doesn't follow the rules at school, they might be kicked out just like Max was kicked out of the kitchen. Students may discuss the harassment, arrest, or even shooting of unarmed Black men. Discuss whether this is fair or just and what factors lead society to view people in these ways. Explain that this is a result of bias or prejudice (see Chapter 5: "Confronting Bias"). Define these terms. Lead students in a discussion around how to unpack our biases and reposition our views of good and bad.

Additional Texts to Examine Good vs. Bad

- *The Bad Seed* by Jory John

- *Wolf!* by Becky Bloom (Compare the portrayal of the wolf in this story to traditional notions of the wolf in familiar stories and in the book *Imagine a Wolf*.)

Lesson 5: Defining Beauty
Beautifully Me • by Nabela Noor

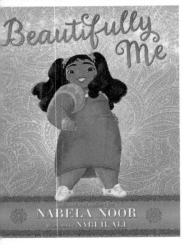

FIGURE 4.13

 First Read: Movie Read

This first visit, the "movie read," focuses on taking in the story without interruption (see Chapter 1, p. 21). Zubi, a Bangladeshi girl, is excited for her first day of school. But when she starts to notice the way her family members talk about their bodies and when a peer at school is teased about being overweight, she starts to question her own body.

Before reading *Beautifully Me*, have students take a moment and individually consider the meaning of the word "beautiful."

Ask students: *What does the word "beautiful" mean to you?*

They can write a definition of beauty, list examples of what they deem beautiful, or even illustrate examples. After a few minutes, invite students to share their ideas about beauty with the group and record them on a chart.

 Second Read: Reading With the Text

As you return for another read, stop along the way to discuss ideas and concepts being presented. Explain the meaning of "Salaam!" on the first spread. This is an Arabic greeting meaning peace. Throughout the reading, stop and encourage students to use context clues to determine the meaning of words such as Amma (mother), Baba (father), sari, lassis, and parathas.

On the page where Zubi goes to her parents' room to show off her first-day outfit, notice the way she admires Amma's beauty in the sari.

Ask students: *How might Amma's comment about her tummy looking big influence Zubi?*

On the next spread when they are in the kitchen, Dani Ma reminds them to practice speaking Bangla. Think aloud about how you can infer this is the language of the people from Bangladesh and perhaps the family has moved to a new country and Dani Ma doesn't want them to forget the language.

On the same page, Zubi's sister, Naya, requests oatmeal for breakfast instead of the traditional parathas (even though she hates oatmeal!).

Ask students: *Why do you think she'd ask for a food she doesn't even like?*

Continue reading and confirm any predictions that she is on a diet and wants to lose weight. Naya says she's on a diet and wants to lose weight to look pretty for the school dance.

Ask students: *What are you thinking or wondering?*

Encourage students to examine how Naya's remarks and behavior influence Zubi. Begin to explore the notion that our ideas about body size and shape are influenced by social factors, including other people such as our family.

Ask students:

- *What other factors could influence our beliefs about body image?*
- *How is your thinking about the notion of beauty evolving from your initial writing or drawing?*

Continue reading. Baba tells Dadi Ma that he hasn't worn the shirt she bought him for Eid (a Muslim holiday) because he's gained weight and is now a size large. He adds, "Not good." Zubi wonders why wearing a size large is not good. Think aloud about how yet another person in Zubi's life is sending her messages about size.

Ask students:

- *How does this influence Zubi?*
- *Why is it problematic?*
- *What do you think will happen next?*

Continue reading. Pause when Zubi observes a child telling a peer they look fat in their dress.

Ask students: *How does this event influence Zubi's view of herself as well as her ideas of what beauty is?*

Continue reading. At dinner, Naya doesn't eat the rice (even though she loves it) because she's on a diet. When Amma asks if she wants any rice, Zubi declines and states that she is on a diet.

On the next spread, she says, "Naya said you have to be on a diet to be pretty . . . and I want to be pretty." She then lists all the factors that influenced her thinking and her decision (including her family and the teasing at school) and said she doesn't "want kids to make fun of [her], too!" Pause here and allow for open-ended discussion and reaction.

Ask students: *What are you thinking now?*

Continue reading. Baba comes to Zubi's room and consoles her. He explains that sometimes people say hurtful things to others when they are hurting inside. He goes on to say that sometimes we can also be mean to ourselves without even realizing it and this can also hurt those we love, which is what they did to Zubi today. Pause here and allow for open-ended discussion and reaction.

Ask students: *What are you thinking or wondering now?*

Continue reading. Each family member apologizes and shows gratitude for their bodies and each other. Amma tells her she was named "Zubi because it means loving and understanding." And she will "make the world more beautiful just by being Zubi." Zubi responds by saying that she doesn't even know what "beautiful" means anymore.

Amma explains what beauty means.

Ask students:

- *Has your initial idea about beauty evolved or changed? If so, in what way?*

- *How do you define beauty after reading the book?*

 ## Return Read: Reading Critically

For the return read, remind students of the previous conversation about their evolving notions of beauty.

Ask students: *What is body image?*

> Body image refers to how someone thinks about their body and how others perceive their body. Another way to think about body image is how we think about our physical appearance.

Ask students: *Where do we get ideas about (positive or negative) body image from?*

Explain to students that body image is something that is socially constructed. In other words, we construct or create ideas based on messages in the world around us. That is just like the way Zubi started developing her ideas about body image based on comments from her family and classmates.

Provide students with an image, such as one from the Learning for Justice handout titled "Different Images of Beauty," which you can view and download from the QR code in the margin.

"Different Images of Beauty" from Learning for Justice.

Ask students:

- *What does this image make you think about in terms of beauty?*

- *How do you think someone in the same racial, ethnic, historical, gender, or age group as the person or people in the picture might be affected by this image?*

- *How do you think someone in a different racial, ethnic, historical, gender, or age group might be affected by this image?*

- *What does this image try to teach you about what is beautiful?*

(Note: These questions have been adapted from Learning for Justice, where you can find a different lesson about beauty:bit.ly/3Vpfiz0)

Explain that just like these photographs send us messages about body image, so do the books we read, including *Beautifully Me*. Reread the book and ask students to think about the author's message.

Ask students:

- *What is the author's message in the book?*

- *Why do you think she wrote this book?*

Pause when you read "You get to define what is beautiful. Whatever your body looks like. Beauty is how you make people feel and the kinds of things you do."

Ask students: *How does this influence the way you think about your own ideas about beauty?*

Return to their drawings/definitions from the second read. Provide students with an opportunity to update the document with their evolving understanding.

Read the following sentence: "A beautiful person is someone who embraces who they are and helps others do the same."

Ask students:

- *In what ways do you embrace who you are?*

- *In what ways do you embrace who others are?*

- *How can you help others to embrace who they are?*

- *Who else do you think should read this book?*

Revisit the end of the book and highlight the idea that we are all beautiful just the way we are.

Use the following excerpt from *Beautifully Me* as a sentence frame for students to write about their own bodies. Each page can be collected and compiled into a class book. Students can illustrate their self-portraits or include photographs.

My name is . . .

I am beautiful because . . .

We are one of a kind, and that makes us beautifully us.

"There is only one you, and that makes you beautifully you."

Cultural Extensions

Encourage students to learn more about the Muslim holiday of Eid and Ramadan. Read books such as *Lailah's Lunchbox* by Reem Faruqi and *Night of the Moon* by Hena Khan.

Additional Resources

You might also read the book *The Best Part of Me* by Wendy Ewald and invite students to share gratitude for their bodies by creating photo essays of the best parts of them. This can also be compiled into a class book.

Books to explore the notion of beauty and body positivity:

- *Abigail the Whale* by Davide Cali

- *Fry Bread* by Kevin Noble Malliard

- *Her Body Can* by Katie Crenshaw and Ady Meschke

- *His Body Can* by Katie Crenshaw and Ady Meschke

- *Not Quite Snow White* by Ashley Franklin

- *Starfish* by Lisa Fipps (chapter book)

- *Sulwe* by Lupita Nyong'o

- *What Is Beautiful* by Abbie Sprunger

Books to explore the notion of beauty in the world around us:

- *Something Beautiful* by Sharon Dennis Wyeth

- *Maybe Something Beautiful* by Isabel Campoy

- *Last Stop on Market Street* by Matt de la Peña

According to Dr. Kendrin Sonneville (Cully, 2022), most children ages five through eight are dissatisfied with their bodies. Body dissatisfaction increases as children age. To help develop a healthy body image, it is important to help children separate their sense of self-worth from their bodies.

Dear Highlights podcast, "How Can Kids Develop a Healthy Body Image?"

Allow children to have agency over the language and words they find comfortable or stigmatizing. For instance, by using language such as larger bodies and fat (like the way we use short and tall) we reclaim pejorative terms to use as a description of the body in a neutral way. Terms such as *overweight* and *obese* are not recommended because they are pathologizing and stigmatizing as diseased or unhealthy.

For more on helping kids to develop a healthy body image, listen to the podcast linked from the QR code.

Lesson 6: Celebrating All Kinds of Minds
The Girl Who Thought in Pictures: The Story of Dr. Temple Grandin • by Julia Finley Mosca

Before beginning this lesson with *The Girl Who Thought in Pictures*, read *My Brother Charlie* and/or *Ian's Walk* to build students' background about autism. As you consider ways to introduce this topic in sensitive, developmentally appropriate ways, you might invite parents/caregivers of a child on the autism spectrum, or a child if they are comfortable, to talk with the class about their neurodiversity.

First Read: Movie Read

This first visit, the "movie read," focuses on taking in the story without interruption (see Chapter 1, p. 21). This true story of renowned scientist Dr. Temple Grandin celebrates neurodiversity. As a child, Temple Grandin was nonverbal. She loved spinning and twirls, but hated loud noises, crowded places, large cities, itchy clothing, and hugs most of all. Despite being shy and preferring to be alone, Temple could not control her tantrums when something frustrated her. Later she was diagnosed with autism. She went to college and became a successful scientist whose inventions changed the livestock industry. Dr. Grandin now speaks around the world to advocate for more humane farming practices.

Language Is Evolving

Language and its use are constantly evolving as we come to new understandings. The word "crazy" (included in the book) can be harmful because it draws on stereotypes and perpetuates mental health stigmas. One in five Americans lives with a mental illness. Thus, we should consider reframing language to bring more dignity to people with mental illness.

Second Read: Reading With the Text

Read the book a second time.

Ask students:

- *What did you learn about Temple Grandin? (Allow for discussion and time for students to jot their responses on chart paper.)*

- *What surprised you?*

Allow students' responses to determine the direction of the conversation. For instance, if students note they are surprised to learn that Temple went to college, became a doctor, or now speaks around the world, pause and explain that there are common stereotypes of people with autism (e.g., aggressive, obsessive, highly intelligent or unintelligent, limited communication skills, emotionless).

Return to the beginning of the book and discuss how Temple did not like loud noises, scratchy clothes, or hugs; didn't speak; and sometimes had temper tantrums. Continue reading to the part where she was removed from school for throwing a book. Explain to students that sometimes we make assumptions about people based on their behaviors. A commonly held stereotype of people with autism is that they are aggressive or violent. However, these outbursts are often a result of a trigger, which might include a break in routine, lack of sleep, or jarring sensory stimuli (Wallace, 2018).

Ask students:

- *Can you find evidence in the text that reveals how Temple was triggered?*

- *How might knowing this affect the way we interact with others who have autism?*

As a young person, Temple was nonverbal and communicated better through pictures and art. Yet today she speaks around the world to teach others how to build better farms and to teach people about autism.

Explain that another common stereotype of individuals with autism is that they are unintelligent. In the book, we learned that the way Temple thought was "different, not less" (return to this page in the book).

Ask students: *What do you think the author means by the notion of being "different, not less"?*

Examining Stereotypes

Continue reading, highlighting Temple's accomplishments.

Ask students: *What factors or changes led to Temple's success?*

Continue reading and pause at the line "it takes brains of all kinds."

Ask students: *What do you think the author means by this?*

For Younger Students

Draw students' attention to the rhyming words in the book. Record lists of rhyming words on an anchor chart and invite students to add additional words following each rhyming pattern.

 Return Read: Reading Critically

Return to the page where people said, "She'll never be normal" and her mom "must send her away." Explain that in 1947 when Temple was born, there was little understanding of autism and people with disabilities or neurodiversity. They were often viewed as different and sometimes were even sent away to live in special homes or facilities.

Ask students:

- *Do you think it's fair to send people away because they aren't considered "normal"?*
- *What does it mean to be normal?*
- *Who is considered normal? Why?*
- *Who decides what normal is?*
- *How might the idea of normalcy be problematic or even dangerous?*

Temple Grandin has autism, and she is very smart. Her important work has contributed to making the world a better place for both people and animals.

Ask students:

- *How can we disrupt stereotypes of people with autism or other neurodiversity?*
- *How can we celebrate all kinds of minds and ways of learning?*
- *What makes it easier for you to learn?*

Additional Books and Resources

- *Ian's Walk* by Laurie Lears

- *My Brother Charlie* by Holly Robinson Peete

- *Rules* by Cynthia Lord (chapter book)

- "Debunking 8 Common Stereotypes of Individuals With Autism" from Autism Learning Partners:
  bit.ly/3Umwd3V

- "The World Needs All Kinds of Minds" by Temple Grandin (a TED talk):
  bit.ly/3uevGGo

- Temple Grandin explains sensory issues on PBS:
  bit.ly/3VyszVG

Lesson 7: Disrupting Notions of Normalcy
A Normal Pig • by K-Fai Steele

First Read: Movie Read

This first visit, the "movie read," focuses on taking in the story without interruption (see Chapter 1, p. 21). Pip is a normal pig whose life changes when a new student teases her for being different. Pip no longer wants any of the things she used to like until her interaction with another pig changes her perception of normalcy.

Second Read: Reading With the Text

Before reading, ask students to define "normal" on an index card. Collect for use in the return read.

Next, draw students' attention to the cover of the book.

Ask students: *What do you notice?*

They may point out how the pig in the center has spots. They may recall this is Pip.

Read the first page.

Ask students:

- *What do you think the author means by "normal stuff"?*
- *What do you do that you consider to be normal?*
- *What do you think is normal about you?*

Read the next page and compare the "normal" things Pip does to the types of things students shared. Notice any similarities and differences.

Continue reading and pause on the page when the other pigs said "eww!!" and "it stinks" about Pip's lunch. Discuss how "Pip didn't know how to respond [because] it was just her normal lunch."

Ask students: *What is a normal lunch for you?*

Point out the varied responses and how what is normal can be different for each of us. You may also reference the book *The*

Sandwich Swap by Kelly DiPucchio and Rania Al Abdullah, if previously read.

Ask students: *How could Pip respond to the other pigs when they make those negative remarks about her food?*

Continue reading to the page where Pip is at band practice. Draw students' attention to the illustration.

Ask students: *Why do you think the new pig asked Pip if her mom was the babysitter?*

(Notice how mom is gray and the baby also has spots. This could inform a discussion about multiracial families.)

> ## Multiracial Families in the United States
>
> Did you know the number of people who identify as multiracial has increased by 276 percent between 2010 and 2020? Census data shows that families in the United States are becoming more diverse. However, it wasn't always legal for people of different races to marry. Interracial marriage was illegal until the 1967 Supreme Court case *Loving v. Virginia*. To learn more about this case, read *A Case for Loving: The Fight for Interracial Marriage* by Selina Alko.

Continue reading and point out how Pip seems sad and angry at home. She snaps, "Why can't you make me a normal lunch?!" to her parents.

Ask students: *What else could she have done or said instead?*

Continue reading about how Pip and her family go to the city.

Ask students: *What happens when Pip and her family go to the city?*

Discuss Pip's interaction with the striped pig she meets. Specifically, when she asks if there's anything on the menu that's not weird, the pig replies, "Maybe it's weird for you, but not for me. I like it." Continue reading the next page.

Ask students:

- *How did the striped pig's response affect Pip when she returned home?*

- *How does Pip respond when the other pigs continue to tease her about her "weird" lunch at school?*

- *What happened next?*

- *What lessons did Pip learn?*

- *How can we apply these lessons to our own lives?*

 ## Return Read: Reading Critically

Before the return read, provide students with the index cards from the second read with their definitions of "normal." Set a reading purpose for the return read.

Ask students: *How is your understanding of what is "normal" evolving?*

Engage in a discussion to disrupt the notion of normalcy.

Ask students:

- *How did reading the book help you disrupt the notion of normalcy?*

- *How might the idea of normalcy be problematic or even dangerous?*

- *How does this connect to the book The Girl Who Thought in Pictures?*

- *What connections can you make to other books, people, or situations?*

READING FOR ACTION

After reading with and reading critically a collection of texts focused on examining stereotypes, invite students to reflect on what they have learned and how their thinking has changed.

Ask students: *What will we do with this new insight? How can we take action?*

SOME IDEAS/SUGGESTIONS

- Evaluate books for stereotypes. Write to the publishers to request a change.

- Examine product and sports logos for stereotypes. For example, explore recent changes to brands such as Land O'Lakes and Aunt Jemima. Write to the companies or create petitions to recommend changes.

- Create a public service announcement (PSA).

- Create opportunities at the beginning or ending of each day to write notes of affirmation to classmates, family members, or other individuals. (See example from Chapter 1 and "Sharing When You Have Little to Give" from *Reading to Make a Difference* by Laminack & Kelly [2019].) Note: This can also be done verbally during morning meeting (see Chapter 1).

Additional Resources

- Teaching About Stereotypes 2.0
  bit.ly/3Fe3Q3w

- Let's Talk!
  bit.ly/3OR5ivQ

Confronting Bias

5

The children in Hannah Reyes's kindergarten classroom were talking about the book *Something from Nothing* by Phoebe Gilman when they had the following conversation.

Ebeth: When I get married, I will get a girl to sew me a dress.

Maddy: Why?

Victor: Girls sew dresses, right, Ebeth?

Ebeth: Uh huh. Good dresses.

Maddy: That's a boy sewing things in the story.

Ebeth: It's a story.

Maddy: My brother sews costumes all the time. He's a boy like the grandpa in the story.

Victor: Your brother sews?

Ebeth: Oh [pauses]. I don't know why I think that. I just think that. What does your brother sew?

Maddy: He sewed a vest and a shirt and he sewed patches on his shirt and . . .

Victor: He sewed a vest?! I wanna sew a pirate vest.

These three kindergarten children are engaged in a discussion that centers on the issue of gender, specifically who is a good sewer—girls or boys? Ebeth states that when she gets married, she will have a girl sew her a dress because girls sew good dresses. Maddy presents an alternate perspective when she refers to the text *Something from Nothing* and notes that in the story it is a boy who is doing the sewing. When Ebeth argues that the boy is sewing because "it's a story," meaning it's not real, Maddy offers real-world evidence when she shares, "My brother sews costumes all the time." Maddy then goes further by relating her real-world experience to the story when she says, "He's a boy like the grandpa in the story." This comment refutes Ebeth's earlier comment that the only reason there was a boy sewing in the book is because it was a story and therefore not real. In the end, Ebeth begins to come around to the idea that maybe boys can sew after all when she states, "I really don't know why I think that. I just do," and then follows this up by asking what Maddy's brother sews. Victor agreed with Ebeth until he heard about Maddy's brother sewing costumes, at which time he also shifted his position and decided he wanted to sew a pirate vest.

Saad (2020) suggests, "You cannot dismantle what you cannot see" (p. 38). By the end of the conversation, Ebeth and Victor started to see differently. At first, these two children were biased toward girls as good sewers, then Maddy's sharing her brother's experience as a sewer offered a different perspective and helped Ebeth and Victor to shift their biased opinion and recognize that boys can also be good sewers.

What Is a Bias?

We are all biased (yes, even you). We learn biased ways of being early on in childhood from the world around us, the communities in which we live, and the societies we encounter (Bian et al., 2018). As adults, we bring our biases to our teaching whether consciously or unintentionally (Yates & Marcelo, 2014). These personal biases can influence what we teach and don't teach our students about valuing difference. So, it is important for us to reflect on, understand, and dismantle our own biases.

A bias is a preconceived opinion or prejudice, preference, or tendency that results in unconscious and automatic judgment in favor of or against an individual or group. As such, biases are often unfair and make it hard for one to be impartial. In the opening exchange, for example, Ebeth had a preconceived opinion that favored girls as good sewers. Her position is unfounded and not based in reason or experience. This is made clear when Ebeth says, "I don't know why I think that. I just think that."

Davis (2022) argues that if "girls don't see themselves on screen as STEM professionals, they're less likely to pursue those career paths." Ebeth's comment is an example of gender bias that can result when girls and boys don't see themselves represented in particular professions on screen or in books and other texts. A study by Davis (2019), for instance, shows that 63 percent of STEM characters in film and television are male in comparison to 37 percent of STEM characters who are female.

Examples of Bias

Following are other examples of bias that are not addressed in this chapter but are important to recognize. These biases become especially problematic when they happen at the expense of others or when such preferences or tendencies are unfair to some and can potentially cause harm to others.

Affinity bias	Preference or tendency to connect with others who share similar interests, experiences, or backgrounds
Attribution bias	Tendency to judge a person based solely on prior observations and interactions
Conformity bias	Tendency to act like people around you, regardless of your own personal beliefs
The halo effect	Tendency to place someone on a pedestal after learning something impressive about them without really understanding why
The horns effect	Tendency to view someone in a negative way after learning something unpleasant about them without fully understanding why
Gender bias	Preference or tendency to prefer one gender over another without reason
Ageism	Preference or tendency to have negative feelings about another person or group based solely on their age
Beauty bias	Tendency to believe that attractive people are or can be more successful, competent, and qualified
Height bias	Tendency to view someone in a negative way solely because of their height
Nonverbal bias	Tendency to analyze nonverbal communication attributes and let it affect a decision or opinion (particularly problematic across cultures due to the diverse ways that body language is used and interpreted in different places and locations)
Authority bias	Preference or tendency to support the opinion of someone solely because they are in a position of authority

Pause to Reflect on Our Own Biases

When was the first time you became aware of differences? What situation led to that awareness? What role did you play in that situation? Would you consider yourself to be a target, perpetrator, bystander, or other participant of some sort?

Finish the following sentences and reflect on your responses.

I feel *most* comfortable when I am around people who do/who are . . .

- Why are you most comfortable around those people?
- Where do the feelings of comfort come from?
- What experiences led to those feelings?

I feel *least* comfortable when I am around people who do/who are . . .

- Why are you least comfortable around those people?
- Where do the feelings of discomfort come from?
- What experiences led to those feelings?

Tips for Choosing Books for Teaching From an Antibias Lens

Children's books are a mainstay in classrooms and therefore are instrumental as a source of information and values. Books often "reflect the attitudes in our society about diversity, power relationships among different groups of people, and various social identities (e.g., racial, ethnic, gender, economic class, sexual orientation, and disability)" (Derman-Sparks, 2016). The images and text young children see, read, and hear from books (and other media) can influence their ideas about themselves and others regarding who they can be, who they cannot be, and what they can and cannot do. As such, it is important to carefully choose the children's books you use to best support the needs of your students from an antibias lens.

The following questions and things to avoid when choosing books are adapted from Louise Derman-Sparks's *Guide for Selecting Anti-Bias Children's Books* located at socialjusticebooks.org.

Questions to ask when choosing books:

- Are the messages conveyed in the book accurate?
- What identity groups (e.g., gender, race, ethnicity, ability/disability) are visible? Invisible?

- Does the story line carry biases regarding how it treats power relationships between the characters from different identity groups? For example, are people of color supporting characters or central characters? Does a character with a disability have to do something extraordinary to gain acceptance?

- Are there negative value judgments associated with characters who don't fit a dominant way of being?

- Does the story reflect current life or problematic assumptions about life in the past?

- What is the background of the author and/or illustrator? What is their experience with the topic of the book?

- Does the book have any words that are demeaning to some identity groups (e.g., fireman vs. firefighter, brotherhood vs. community)?

Things to avoid when choosing books:

- Oversimplified generalizations about a particular identity (e.g., gender, race, ethnicity, ability/disability) group

- Derogatory language against a particular identity group

- Tokenism, or seeing only one person of an identity group fulfill the diversity role

- Unfavorable contrasts between the lives of people of color or those living in poverty and white suburban life

- Implied value judgments about ways of life that are not from the dominant culture or economic class

- Oversimplification of important issues

Confronting
Bias

Pause to Reflect: Examining
My Classroom Library

Now that you have had a chance to engage with books from an antibias lens, have a look at your own classroom library. As you do, ask yourself some of the questions and consider the things to think about in the "Tips for Choosing Books for Teaching From an Antibias Lens" section of this chapter.

Classroom Library Analysis Book Sorting Activity
bit.ly/3Fd2dTF

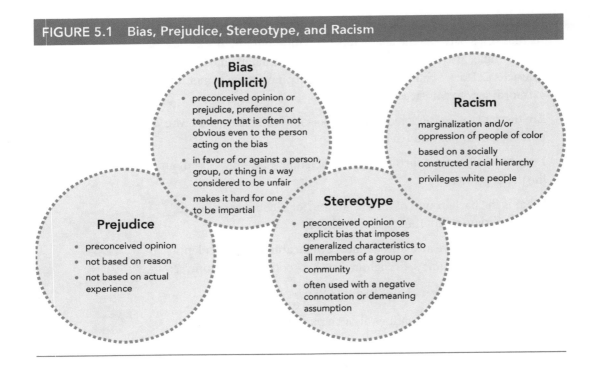

FIGURE 5.1   Bias, Prejudice, Stereotype, and Racism

Bias (Implicit)
- preconceived opinion or prejudice, preference or tendency that is often not obvious even to the person acting on the bias
- in favor of or against a person, group, or thing in a way considered to be unfair
- makes it hard for one to be impartial

Racism
- marginalization and/or oppression of people of color
- based on a socially constructed racial hierarchy
- privileges white people

Prejudice
- preconceived opinion
- not based on reason
- not based on actual experience

Stereotype
- preconceived opinion or explicit bias that imposes generalized characteristics to all members of a group or community
- often used with a negative connotation or demeaning assumption

Confronting Bias

Figure 5.1 outlines the relationship between bias, prejudice, stereotype, and racism. The terms *bias*, *prejudice*, *stereotype*, and *racism* are often used as if these words all mean the same thing—yet they have slightly different meanings. It is also important to note that prejudice can lead to bias. In turn, biases readily circulate and can lead to problematic generalized ideas that contribute to the construction of stereotypes. Subsequently, prejudices, biases, and stereotypes can contribute to racist ways of being, doing, and thinking.

Figure 5.2 demonstrates each term in Figure 5.1 using the discussion from the opening of the chapter. In Figure 5.2, we have imagined what could have been said during the children's discussion, to offer examples of problematic comments from a prejudiced position, a biased position, a stereotypical position, and a racist position.

FIGURE 5.2   Recasting the Children's Conversation

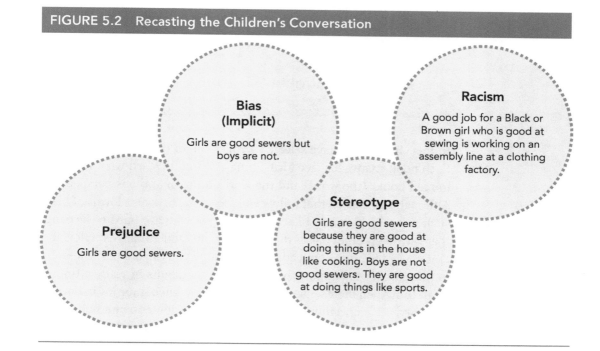

Bias (Implicit)

Girls are good sewers but boys are not.

Racism

A good job for a Black or Brown girl who is good at sewing is working on an assembly line at a clothing factory.

Prejudice

Girls are good sewers.

Stereotype

Girls are good sewers because they are good at doing things in the house like cooking. Boys are not good sewers. They are good at doing things like sports.

Critical Comprehension
Lesson Series

Confronting Bias

In this chapter, we have selected a collection of books to explore bias. Each book creates a space for helping children to learn what it means to read books (the word) and the world from an antibias perspective. Although the lessons that follow will focus on particular forms of bias, such as racial bias and bias against people who are hard of hearing, there are likely other biases that you and your students are experiencing that you could and should address. We hope you can adapt the lessons in this chapter to support the needs of the students in your setting to help strengthen their sense of self and identity, encourage joy in human diversity, recognize hurtful behavior, and contribute to building inclusive and fair ways of being. As noted by Derman-Sparks and Olsen Edwards (2020), "When children notice and address unfairness, even very young children are able to be strong and clear in standing up for themselves and others" (p. 6).

Table of Lessons for Confronting Bias	
LESSON FOCUS	**ANCHOR TEXT**
1. Encouraging joy in human diversity	*Crow Boy* by Taro Yashima
2. Racial bias through naming practices	*Alma and How She Got Her Name* by Juana Martinez-Neal
3. Avoiding audism	*Listen: How Evelyn Glennie, a Deaf Girl, Changed Percussion* by Shannon Stocker
4. Identity bias	*Jingle Dancer* by Cynthia Leitich Smith (citizen of the Muscogee Nation)
5. Building inclusive and fair ways of being	*Missing Daddy* by Mariame Kaba

Note: The blank spaces are an invitation for you to add your own related topics and texts.

Types of Biases Explored in These Lessons

Racial Bias Through Naming Practices

One thing we all share is the fact that we each have a name. Some of us have the same name as another person. Some of us have a name no one in our class has ever heard before. Some of our names derive from our loved ones or hold a special meaning in our cultures. Each of us has our own story about our name.

Some of us like our names. Others do not. Yet, this may change with time and the shifting nature of our identities as we navigate through the world. Names have more power than we realize. Conaway and Bethune (2015) note that as children we likely never considered that our social status could have been influenced by our names. According to Dr. Ronda Taylor Bullock (n.d.), the lead curator of *We Are* (www.weare-nc.org), a nonprofit organization that provides antiracism training for children, explicit name bias is one of the earliest types of racism kids face. This is evident in earlier studies (McDavid & Harari, 1966), which show that popularity status in elementary-school children was "highly correlated with the social-desirability value of the individual's first name" (p. 454), and more recent studies (Erwin, 2006) that show common or more familiar names were viewed more positively than unique or unusual names. These studies support the idea that people tend to judge others by their labels (names).

It is therefore important that we honor students' names, including learning to pronounce them correctly. It is also essential for children to understand the long-lasting harm that can be caused by name bias. Bullock (2021) states, "Children are not too young to have these conversations because they are not too young to cause the harm."

To find out more about ways to explore each other's name stories, visit My Name, My Identity at https://www.mynamemyidentity.org/, and take a pledge to pronounce students' names correctly.

Audism

Audism is a belief that the ability to hear makes one superior to those with hearing loss. Those who engage in audism bias are known as audists; see Figure 5.3 for more examples of audism and how to avoid audism bias. In the lesson on audism, we focus on understanding how to respect, honor, and better support the needs of people who are deaf and hard of hearing to disrupt bias against them.

The term *audism* was coined by Humphries (1977) in their dissertation study on communicating across deaf-hearing cultures. For the most part, the term remained unused until Lane's (1992) book, *The Mask of Benevolence: Disabling the Deaf Community*, which is said to be the most extensive published survey and discussion of audism. More recently, the word appears on the Gallaudet University web page on audism. The web page offers various definitions including the following:

> Audism is a bias toward the belief that life without hearing is futile and miserable, that hearing loss is a tragedy and the "scour-age of mankind" and that deaf people should struggle to be as much like hearing people as possible.

> Audists are biased against and shun Deaf culture and the use of sign language, and have an obsession with the use of residual hearing, speech, and lip-reading by deaf people.

> "Audism is the hearing way of dominating, restructuring, and exercising authority over the deaf community. It includes such professional people as administrators of schools for deaf children and of training programs for deaf adults, interpreters, and some audiologists, speech therapists, otologists, psychologists, psychiatrists, librarians, researchers, social workers, and hearing aid specialists." (Lane, 1992, p. 43)

FIGURE 5.3   Examples of Audism and How to Avoid Audism Bias

EXAMPLES OF AUDISM NOTED BY WAECH AND HOOG (2014)	HOW TO AVOID AUDISM BIAS
Jumping in, without being asked, to help a deaf person communicate	Wait until the deaf or hard of hearing person asks before jumping in to help them. Or wait until they signal in some way that they need help. Don't just assume.
Asking a deaf person to read your lips or write when they have indicated this isn't preferred	Follow the deaf or hard of hearing person's lead in terms of how they would like to communicate with you.
Making phone calls for a deaf person, without being asked, since they "can't"	Don't assume that a deaf or hard of hearing person can't make a phone call. Wait for them to ask you for help.
Refusing to call an interpreter when one is requested	Never refuse to call an interpreter if one is requested.
Assuming that those with better speech/English skills are superior	There are many ways to effectively communicate thoughts and ideas beyond spoken English. Never assume superiority.

EXAMPLES OF AUDISM NOTED BY WAECH AND HOOG (2014)	HOW TO AVOID AUDISM BIAS
Asking a deaf person to "tone down" their facial expressions because they are making others uncomfortable	In American Sign Language, facial expressions are an important part of communication that affects the meaning of that sign. Read facial expressions as one way to make sense of what a deaf or hard of hearing person is telling you through signing. Teach others through your demonstration.
Refusing to explain to a deaf person why everyone around them is laughing ("never mind, I'll tell you later, it doesn't matter")	Deaf and hard of hearing people have every right to engage in a conversation in real time. They should never be made to wait for an explanation. Making them do so is both rude and condescending.
Devoting a significant amount of instructional time for a deaf child to learn lipreading and for speech therapy, rather than educational subjects	Mandated mask-wearing during the pandemic is a good demonstration of why devoting a significant amount of instructional time on lipreading is problematic. Deaf and hard of hearing children should be given opportunities to engage with educational subjects in other ways that make sense for them without relying on lipreading.

Gallaudet University

According to the Gallaudet website, theirs is the only university in the world where students live and learn using American Sign Language (ASL) and English.

It was in 1864 when President Abraham Lincoln signed legislation to authorize the establishment of a college for deaf and hard of hearing students in Washington, D.C. Since then, for more than 150 years, Gallaudet has been the political, social, and economic engine of the signing community. To date, the university remains the world's only liberal arts institution for deaf and hard of hearing students.

For further information regarding significant moments for the deaf and hard of hearing community and Gallaudet University, go to bit.ly/3isp3NY

Identity Bias

Identity bias happens when individuals see themselves and others as members of specific social groups in ways that influence their beliefs and emotions. These biases are often implicit, which means they affect our understanding, actions, and decisions in an unconscious manner. They may be based on any aspect of a person's social identity, from race or ethnicity to sexuality or nationality, or even arbitrary categories, such as categorizing someone who dyes their hair blue as "emo" (Greenwald & Banaji, 2017). It is likely that implicit biases reflect a combination of one's own beliefs and the information we absorb over a lifetime regarding how people from different groups should be treated and how groups of people interact with each other (Amodio & Devine, 2006).

We develop attitudes about differences beginning at a very early age. We begin to form racial biases as early as toddlers (Winkler, 2009). However, as Lipkin (2018) notes, "engaging students in a conversation about identity and bias is challenging" (p. 3). This challenge is compounded by the fact that we may or may not have awareness of our implicit biases. As a result, these biases can be expressed indirectly (i.e., implied in one's actions). Lipkin (2018) suggests that in order "to approach these topics, we, as educators, must establish learning environments where students feel that these conversations are not something to be ashamed of or had in hushed tones. Rather, we should be facilitating that dialogue with our students directly" (p. 3). The identity bias lesson is one way to facilitate that dialogue regarding identity bias and Indigenous peoples.

Confronting Bias

Lesson 1: Encouraging Joy in Human Diversity
Crow Boy • by Taro Yashima

First Read: Movie Read

This first visit, the "movie read," focuses on reading aloud the story without interruption (see Chapter 1, p. 21). *Crow Boy* was first published in 1955 and was a recipient of a 1956 Caldecott Honor for its illustrations. The book focuses on a shy Japanese boy named Chibi who is judged unfairly by the other children until a new teacher takes notice of him. The book readily lends itself to conversations and lessons about bias and stereotypes.

FIGURE 5.4

Taro Yashima Bio-Note

Taro Yashima, the author of *Crow Boy* and other children's stories, is the pseudonym of Atsushi Iwamatsu, a Japanese artist who lived in the United States during World War II. Iwamatsu was born September 21, 1908, in Nejima, Kimotsuki District, Kagoshima, in Japan. His father collected art from the area and encouraged Iwamatsu's interest in art. Iwamatsu studied at the Imperial Art Academy in Tokyo and became a successful illustrator and cartoonist. At one point in time, both he and his wife, Tomoe, went to jail for opposing the militaristic government.

In 1939, Iwamatsu and his wife went to the United States to study art, leaving behind their son, Mako. After Pearl Harbor, Iwamatsu joined the US Army and went to work as an artist for the Office of Strategic Services. It was at that time that he first began using the pseudonym Taro Yashima. He did this fearing repercussions for Mako and other family members if the Japanese government knew of his employment with the army. Iwamatsu died in 1994.

For more about Taro Yashima, we recommend these resources:

- Taro Yashima, Children's Book Art—Online Exhibits
  http://gallery.lib.umn.edu
- *Crow Boy* by Taro Yashima, Penguin Random House
  https://www.penguinrandomhouse.com

Confronting Bias

Second Read: Reading With the Text

After reading the book a second time, focus on the students' overall responses and reactions to the story.

Ask students:

- *What is the book about?*
- *What message do you take away from the story of Chibi?*
- *What comments do you have about the book?*
- *What connections can you make to Chibi's experience?*
- *What questions do you have after hearing the story?*

Record the responses on a chart paper.

Extension for Older Students

Share with the students Taro Yashima's bio-note.

Ask students:

- *What are your thoughts about the author?*
- *What can you say about the story Crow Boy after reading Yashima's bio-note?*
- *What new questions do you have about the story after reading Yashima's bio-note?*

 Return Read: Reading Critically

Begin by revisiting the comments on the chart paper from the second reading of the book.

Ask students:

- *How did the children treat Chibi before the talent show?*
- *What are some of the words used to describe Chibi?*
- *Why did the children treat Chibi the way they did?*
- *What do you think they believed about Chibi?*

Record the responses on a chart paper. Invite students to turn and talk, and then have them share highlights with the large group.

Share with the children what bias means (see Figure 5.2 or use the definition below).

> **Bias**: A bias is when you have opinions about someone or something even before you have a chance to get to know them or before you have a chance to learn about that thing. Sometimes we don't realize that we are acting in a biased way. This means biases can be implicit causing us to behave or act in a certain way without really understanding why. Biases are often unfair and can cause us to treat someone unfairly.

Invite students to return to their earlier comments recorded on chart paper about how the children treated Chibi before the talent show and why.

Ask students:

- *Where do you think the children's beliefs about Chibi came from?*

- *How was Chibi treated in a biased way in the story?*

- *What were the children biased against?*

- *If the children showed bias against a certain way of being, it means they have a positive view of something else. What ways of being did the children see in a positive light? What does this mean for children like Chibi?*

- *What caused the children to change their minds about Chibi?*

- *Would the children have treated Chibi differently if they had known about his gifts and talents when they first met him?*

As a final activity for this lesson, have students use art cards (see Chapter 2) or do a sketch to represent a time when they experienced bias in some way. Have students pair up to say something about the art card they chose, or the sketch they created, to represent their experience with bias. Their experience could be one where they felt someone was biased against them or it could be one where they felt they treated someone in a biased way.

Give students an opportunity to share highlights from their conversations with the large group.

Ask students: *Does anyone have any other comments, connections, or questions about bias that you would like to share?*

Lesson 2: Racial Bias Through Naming Practices
Alma and How She Got Her Name • by Juana Martinez-Neal

FIGURE 5.5

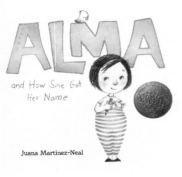

Juana Martinez-Neal

Confronting
Bias

 First Read: Movie Read

This first visit, the "movie read," focuses on taking in the story without interruption (see Chapter 1, p. 21). *Alma and How She Got Her Name* is a story about Alma Sofia Esperanza Jose Pura Candela who at first thinks she has too many names, so she goes to her father and tells him her name is so long. She tells him "it never fits." As her father shares with her the history of each part of her name, Alma begins to see how well her name fits her after all.

 Second Read: Reading With the Text

Before engaging in the second read, have students create a staple-free mini notebook (see Figure 5.6). While listening to a read aloud of the story for a second time, ask students to listen with a pencil and use the pages in the mini notebook to either write words or phrases or draw images that represent things in the story that stand out for them.

Ask students to work in small groups of four to six children.

Ask students: *What are some things that you wrote or drew in your mini notebook? Talk to the people in your group about the thoughts or drawings you added to your notebook or pass them around to see what others in your group have written or drawn.*

 Return Read: Reading Critically

The focus of the return read will be unpacking one's name and on bias as it relates to naming practices.

In preparation for the return read, have students create a second staple-free book. This time they take the mini book home to do some research on the history of their name(s). They can do this by reaching out to friends and relatives. They can jot down their findings to questions, such as the ones below, in their mini books to share with others in the classroom.

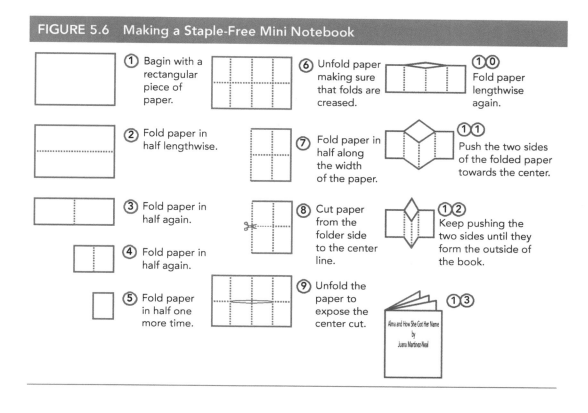

FIGURE 5.6   Making a Staple-Free Mini Notebook

① Begin with a rectangular piece of paper.

② Fold paper in half lengthwise.

③ Fold paper in half again.

④ Fold paper in half again.

⑤ Fold paper in half one more time.

⑥ Unfold paper making sure that folds are creased.

⑦ Fold paper in half along the width of the paper.

⑧ Cut paper from the folder side to the center line.

⑨ Unfold the paper to expose the center cut.

⑩ Fold paper lengthwise again.

⑪ Push the two sides of the folded paper towards the center.

⑫ Keep pushing the two sides until they form the outside of the book.

⑬ Alma and How She Got Her Name by Juana Martinez-Neal

- Who selected your name?

- How was your name chosen?

- Are you named for someone? Some place? Something?

- Was your name created just for you? Who created it? How did they decide?

- Does your name have a significant meaning?

Give the students an opportunity to share their findings, but only if they wish to do so.

Ask students:

- *Do you like your name(s)? Why or why not?*

- *What are things you like about your name(s)?*

- *What are things you don't like about your name(s)?*

- *If you could change your name, would you? If yes, why? If no, why not?*

- *If yes, what name would you choose and why? If not, what names would you find hurtful?*

Note: When asking students these questions, expect that some of them may not be comfortable sharing their responses aloud. Some students may prefer to write down responses for themselves, while other students may choose to reflect on their own while listening to others' responses.

Highlight for students the comments that speak to the importance of naming practices, such as names that are tributes to relatives, or names that signify a special memory, occasion, or moment in time.

Return Read Extension

Show students the book *Your Name Is a Song* by Jamilah Thompkins-Bigelow.

Summarize the book for the students and read a few pages aloud, such as the page where the girl says, "What about the kids at recess who says my name sounds made up?" and the following page where her mom says, "Made up names come from dreamers. Their real names were stolen long ago so they made up new ones. They make a way out of no way, make names out of no names—pull them from the sky!"

Ask students:

- *How would you feel if someone changed your name without asking you?*

- *Why is it important to pronounce names correctly?*

- *How would you feel if someone continued to mispronounce your name even after you have told them the correct way to pronounce it?*

- *Why is it harmful to mistreat someone's name?*

- *Do you think people are treated differently because of their names? If so, how?*

- *Are some names more valued than others?*

- *What can we do to make sure that we don't take part in name bias?*

- *What can we do to honor every person's name(s)?*

To end the lesson, create a name mural, to be posted inside the classroom or the hallway, where each person in the class can write or draw their name along with a graphic or image that represents something about their name that they feel is important for others to know.

Additional Books to Explore Name Stories

- *A Moon for Moe and Mo* by Jane Breskin Zalben

- *Chrysanthemum* by Kevin Henkes

- "My Name" from *The House on Mango Street* by Sandra Cisneros

- *My Name Is Bilal* by Asma Mobin-Uddin

- *My Name Is Sangoel* by Karen Williams and Khadra Mohammed

- *My Name Is Yoon* by Helen Recorvits

- *Sumi's First Day of School, Ever* by Soyung Pak

- *The Name Jar* by Yangsook Choi

In 2005, Figlio published a study showing that teachers had lower expectations for children with Black-sounding names, such as Da'Quan, in comparison to children with names that are less Black-sounding, like Mark. This is a clear example of bias against particular kinds of names. It is no surprise that in some cases Black naming practices that are often questioned in mainstream society have themselves become acts of resistance (Hannah-Jones, 2021).

According to Pulitzer Prize–winning journalist Hannah-Jones, "Our last names often derive from the white people who once owned us" (2021, p. 35). She notes that this is why Black Americans, particularly those who have been marginalized deliberately, choose names for their children that they create, that are not European, and that are not from Africa, a place that many Black Americans have never been.

Lesson 3: Avoiding Audism

Listen: How Evelyn Glennie, a Deaf Girl,
Changed Percussion • by Shannon Stocker

FIGURE 5.7

 First Read: Movie Read

This first visit, the "movie read," focuses on taking in the story without interruption (see Chapter 1, p. 21). *Listen: How Evelyn Glennie, a Deaf Girl, Changed Percussion* is a story about the life of Evelyn Glennie who was the first full-time solo percussionist in the world. The book tells the story of her hearing loss and the journey Evelyn took to feel and "hear" the music with every part of her being.

 Second Read: Reading With the Text

After reading the book a second time, ask students to use items in the classroom to create "music" that represents their thoughts regarding the story. Ask student volunteers to play their "music" while others listen.

Ask students:

- *What does [student's name] music tell you about how they feel about the story?*

- *What is it about [student's name] music that leads you to think that?*

After student listeners have had a chance to say something about the music they heard, have the student performer share the message behind their music.

 Return Read: Reading Critically

Now read the first third of the book aloud. Turn the book's pages away from the students and mouth the words throughout the second third of the book without making a sound. Read the last part of the book out loud.

Ask students:

- *What did it feel like for you to experience the story this way?*

- *What went through your mind?*

- *What surprised you?*
- *What do you know now that you didn't know before reading the book?*

Revisit the following passage from the book:

> Every first year student was tested for musical ability. Questions quietly crackled through a tape recorder. Evelyn strained to hear. She scored poorly. They tested only her ears' ability to listen. Not her heart's. And not her body's.

Ask students:

- *What difference would it make for Evelyn's "heart" and "body" to be tested instead of just her ears?*
- *What other parts of the school day would be hard for someone who is deaf or hard of hearing?*
- *What can schools do to make sure that deaf and hard of hearing students are able to do what all other students are able to do in school?*

Talk to the children about bias and audism bias.

Ask students:

- *What is an example of bias in the story?*
- *What did the teacher do to disrupt the bias experienced by Evelyn?*
- *What are some things you might do to avoid audism bias if you were to meet someone who is deaf or hard of hearing?*

Confronting
Bias

Additional Books

- *El Deafo* by Cece Bell
- *Freddie and the Fairy* by Julia Donaldson
- *Just Ask!* by Sonia Sotomayor
- *Moses Goes to a Concert* by Isaac Millman

Lesson 4: Identity Bias

Jingle Dancer • by Cynthia Leitich Smith
(citizen of the Muscogee Nation)

FIGURE 5.8

 First Read: Movie Read

This first visit, the "movie read," focuses on taking in the story without interruption (see Chapter 1, p. 21). *Jingle Dancer* is a story told from the perspective of Jenna, a young contemporary Muscogee (Creek) girl in Oklahoma who wants to honor a family tradition by jingle dancing at the next powwow.

 Second Read: Reading With the Text

Read the book a second time.

Ask students: *What stuck with you from the story?*

To help facilitate the conversation, you could give students the option of writing or drawing their thoughts and ideas in a staple-free mini book (refer to Lesson 2 in this chapter) or on a graffiti board.

Graffiti Board

A graffiti board is a shared writing space that is accessible to all the students at the same time (e.g., a large sheet of paper, blackboard, or whiteboard). It is a way for students to see and then hear about each other's thoughts and ideas. It also provides a record of those thoughts and ideas.

Students are invited to draw or write thoughts using various writing tools anywhere on the "board." We suggest using different color writing tools so that students can use color to further represent their thinking. For some students, drawing may help them sort out what they are thinking (e.g., regarding a text).

Once all who want to contribute have had a chance to do so, ask students to peruse the board overall before beginning a conversation based on what is represented on the board.

Confronting Bias

> **Ask students:**
>
> - *What do you see on the board as overall ideas?*
> - *What patterns do you notice?*
> - *What things do you see that don't fit a pattern?*

Return Read: Reading Critically

Search for portrayals of Indigenous people in famous paintings, such as John Hauser's *Plains Indians Hunting in Winter Landscape,* or other portrayals in movies, such as Disney's *Pocahontas.*

Ask students:

- *What is different between the images of Indigenous people in the painting/movie and the illustrations in* Jingle Dancer?
- *Why is it wrong to continue to portray images of Indigenous people in books and movies that are set in modern times in the same way that they do in the painting/movie?*
- *What do those kinds of portrayals lead us to believe about Indigenous people?*
- *How does* Jingle Dancer *present a different version of life as an Indigenous person?*

Return Read Extension

Jingle Dancer's author, Cynthia Leitich Smith, shared in an interview that Cousin Elizabeth's character as someone who is both Black and Indigenous generated conversation. (Scan the QR code in the margin to view this interview.) The illustrators, Cornelius Van Wright and Ying-Hwa Hu, told Cynthia that they had never illustrated a book that was not reflective of either of their heritages, so she sent them as many resources as possible, including family photographs and a video. She also told them that Muscogee people are both Black and Muscogee and that it was very important to her that all Indigenous children feel that they are reflected in Jenna's world.

Cynthia Leitich Smith interview.

Ask students:

- *What can you say about the illustrator's use of color in creating skin tones and hair texture for the characters in the book?*
- *What different skin tones and hair textures do you notice?*

Confronting Bias

Why is it important to portray differences in characters' skin tones and hair texture? For whom do you think this is important and why?

The First Nations Development Institute (2016) commented, "The story [*Jingle Dancer*], set in the present day, dispels the idea that Native people no longer exist. It also demonstrates that Native ways of being are part of the lives of Native children, families, and their nations, today."

Ask students:

- *What could you say in response to this statement?*
- *Who would be advantaged by seeing Native people depicted in present-day settings in various texts?*

Do an image search for the words "Native people." How many images do you see on the first page of your search? Of those images, how many depict Native people in present-day settings? What surprised you about the images that came up in your search?

Confronting Bias

For Older Students

Share with the students that in an interview with Colorín Colorado, Cynthia Leitich Smith (2021) talked about an incident with an editor with whom she shared the manuscript for *Jingle Dancer*. The editor told her that the character of Cousin Elizabeth as a Native woman attorney is not realistic. As a follow-up to this, have students fill out the speech bubble image in Figure 5.9.

Ask students:

- *Why would the editor say that portraying a Native woman as an attorney is not realistic?*
- *What do you think the editor was seeing in their mind's eye when they made that comment? If they don't think it is realistic to see Native women as attorneys or lawyers, then what do you think they are imagining as realistic roles for Native women? Why?*

Before discussing responses to this question, enlarge the image in Figure 5.9. Have students fill out the thought bubble using words or images. Have students say something about the things they added to the thought bubble.

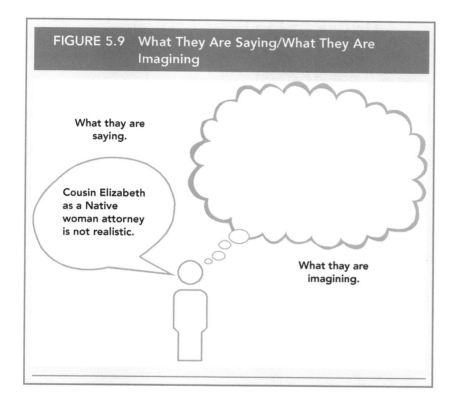

FIGURE 5.9   What They Are Saying/What They Are Imagining

Lesson 5: Building Inclusive and Fair Ways of Being

Missing Daddy • by Mariame Kaba

FIGURE 5.10

 ## First Read: Movie Read

This first visit, the "movie read," focuses on taking in the story without interruption (see Chapter 1, p. 21). *Missing Daddy* is a candid story about a young Black girl whose father is incarcerated, as told from her perspective. In the story, we become privy to the emotional rollercoaster experienced by the girl as she deals with such things as her love for her father and her classmates' bias against her because of him.

The focal story in this lesson centers on a Black child whose father is incarcerated. As we learn in the book, "There are 2.7 million children under 18 who have an incarcerated parent and over 5 million have experienced the incarceration of a parent at some point in their lives. In other words, 1 in 28 American children (3.6%) has an incarcerated parent. Thirty years ago, the number was 1 in 25. About 1 in 9 Black children and 1 in 28 Latino children have an incarcerated parent" (p. 32). These children have stories to tell and yet we rarely create spaces for their voices to be heard. This lesson focuses on ways to avoid bias against such children and on the need to avoid negatively biased attitudes and ways of being in general toward building inclusive and fair ways of being.

 ## Second Read: Reading With the Text

After the second read, have the students choose an art card (see Chapter 2) that represents a connection to the text. Using art cards can create a space for students to talk about a challenging topic that most of them have probably not had a chance to talk about.

Ask students: *What are the connections you see between the art card you chose and the story?*

 ## Return Read: Reading Critically

Before engaging in the return read, revisit past conversations and definitions of bias that you have had with your students in the previous lessons.

Biases result in our tendency to come to a conclusion about a situation or person based on personal desires and beliefs that make it difficult to be impartial and is therefore unfair. Such biases can lead us to make problematic decisions because it distorts the reality or information we use to make decisions about someone or about a group of people. These individual effects can have social implications when members of a group have a biased tendency to favor information that confirms their shared beliefs while ignoring other perspectives.

Share the following quote from the book:

"Each and every family is unique. From its people, to its food, to the words that we speak. Related or chosen, large or small, We can feel loved, even when the world puts up a wall."

Ask students:

- *What does this quote mean to you? What does it mean for the world to put up a wall?*

- *What is the wall that is put up in the story? How is the wall put up?*

- *Who is on either side of the wall? How do they end up on those sides of the wall?*

- *What are some things we can do to take down the wall?*

Revisit the page that reads,

Sometimes my classmates

laugh and make fun.

They say, "You know, your daddy's

a criminal so that makes you one."

Ask the students:

- *What do the girl's classmates mean when they say, "You know, your daddy's a criminal so that makes you one"?*

- *Where does this attitude of showing bias against a person because of someone they are associated with come from?*

- *Have you ever experienced such bias?*

- *Have you ever witnessed such bias? If so, what did you do? Would you do something different now?*

- *What are some things we can do to avoid such bias in the future?*

- *How can we help others to avoid such biased ways of being?*

Return Read Extensions

To extend the conversation about diverse family structures, we recommend reading a book such as *Stella Brings the Family* by Miriam B. Schiffer. When the teacher tells the class to bring a guest for Mother's Day, she creates stress and worry for Stella who has two dads and no mom to invite. Together, discuss how sometimes well-meaning intentions can be biased and cause harm.

Other books with diverse family structures include the following:

- *Heather Has Two Mommies* by Lesléa Newman
- *The Case for Loving: The Fight for Interracial Marriage* by Selina Alko
- *Mango, Abuela, and Me* by Meg Medina
- *My Man Blue* by Nikki Grimes
- *The Memory String* by Eve Bunting
- *Night Job* by Karen Hess
- *Monday, Wednesday, and Every Other Weekend* by Karen Stanton
- *The Red Blanket* by Eliza Thomas
- *Jin Woo* by Eve Bunting
- *Knock Knock: My Dad's Dream for Me* by Daniel Beatty

Confronting Bias

Additional Resources

Antibias Education for Young Children and Ourselves
bit.ly/3OP4Xts

Creating an Antibias Library
bit.ly/3AZhDIE

Early Childhood Antibias Education Booklists
bit.ly/3EUzXDQ

Freedom Reads: Antibias Book Talk Series
https://socialjusticebooks.org/freedom-reads/

Guide for Selecting Antibias Children's Books
bit.ly/3VnWobu

Carefully Selected Lists of Multicultural and Social Justice Books
https://socialjusticebooks.org/booklists/

READING FOR ACTION

After reading with and reading critically a collection of texts focused on bias, invite students to reflect on what they have learned and how their thinking has changed.

Ask students: *What will we do with our new insights? How can we take action?*

SOME IDEAS/SUGGESTIONS

- Never assume things about a person's actions and treat them badly based on that action; always give them a chance to explain themselves.

- Always look beyond boy/girl gender identities and instead consider what someone can do, regardless of their gender identity.

- If you are unsure as to how to pronounce someone's name, make sure to ask them rather than mispronouncing their name or calling them by a name that isn't theirs.

- Always look beyond a person's physical differences and focus instead on their abilities, strengths, and what they can contribute.

- Avoid praising someone or agreeing with someone, at the expense of another individual or group, simply because they are an authority figure or someone you feel is important.

- Avoid disregarding or ignoring someone simply because you believe they are inferior in some way. Instead, give them a chance to show you what they can contribute.

- Avoid biased attitudes or biased ways of being against someone just because of who they are related to or who they associate with. Get to know that person and who they are.

Additional Books for Exploring Bias

- *Africa Is Not a Country* by Margy Burns Knight and Mark Melnicove

- *Drum Dream Girl* by Margarita Engle

- *Gathering the Sun* by Alma Flor Ada

- *Keep Climbing Girls* by Beah E. Richards

- *Sulwe* by Lupita Nyong'o

- *Those Shoes* by Marybeth Boelts

- *The Upside Down Boy* by Juan Felipe Herrera

- *The Sandwich Swap* by Queen Rania Al Abdullah and Kelly DiPucchio

- *The Wall in the Middle of the Book* by John Agee

Confronting Bias

Interrogating the Past and the Present

6

When reading Amanda Gorman's poem "The Hill We Climb," fourth graders in Reilly Mahan's class (Figure 6.1) made connections between our country's past and present. Specifically, they discussed how effects of slavery remain today, although slavery is part of our country's dark history.

They reflected on the line "the norms and notions of what just *is*, isn't always justice."

Jasmine:	Racism just is.
Aubrey:	The police sometimes blame innocent Black men and they get hurt.
Malcolm:	My papa tells me things because he was born during the Civil Rights. Racism has been happening since the 1860s.
Jasmine:	[Returned to the poem and highlighted the line, "quiet isn't always peace."]
	Even though things may be quiet, it doesn't mean bad stuff isn't happening.

The students then discussed a popular YouTube video where a young Black girl (who turns out to be the police captain's daughter) is wrongly arrested by a racist cop named Officer "Karen" for riding her scooter (scan the QR code in the margin to view this video). Ms. Mahan brought the conversation back to the poem and invited students to reflect on the following lines: "That even as we grieved, we grew/That even as we hurt, we hoped/That even as we tired, we tried." Jasmine reflected, "I think Amanda Gorman is telling us we must learn from the past."

Video depicting a police officer arresting a Black girl riding her scooter.

Interrogating the
Past and the Present

> **FIGURE 6.1   Reading "The Hill We Climb"**

When children have opportunities to connect the past to the present, history becomes more relatable and relevant. Yet oftentimes history is taught through memorization of a series of events with key dates and names of historical figures. Because it's learned primarily through textbooks (Brophy & Alleman, 2009), history tends to be oversimplified and told through the dominant narrative that omits the voices and stories of marginalized groups. The consequences result in a narrow, biased, whitewashed curriculum (see Chapter 4 for more information about examining stereotypes). The result is a sanitized version of history that evokes a sense of patriotism while ignoring the complicated past and present (Demoiny & Ferraras-Stone, 2018). Thus, there is a need for history to be explored through multiple perspectives to provide a more complete and accurate presentation of history, allowing learners to construct a more complete truth. For instance, from an American perspective, Malcolm's comment about racism occurring since the 1860s omits the enslavement of Africans beginning in 1619 and the history of racism and genocide of Indigenous people since colonization. In reality, forms of bias, prejudice, and oppression have existed in some ways as long as there have been humans.

For example, stories of Indigenous people are often limited to the traditional Thanksgiving tale where Natives sit gleefully around a table with the Pilgrims sharing a feast; teaching young children about Thanksgiving often omits the historical and present-day mistreatment of Native Americans (Demoiny & Ferraras-Stone, 2018). Some children learn about the Trail of Tears, but few learn about the genocide of Native Americans throughout history, including their forced removal from their land and the stripping of their identity and culture at boarding schools in many places in Canada and the United States, including the Carlisle School in Pennsylvania (Dunbar-Ortiz et al., 2019). Further, widely read books denoted as classics, such as the *Little House on the Prairie* series by Laura Ingalls Wilder, inaccurately portray Native Americans. These books have been challenged for being culturally insensitive and racist in their depiction of Indigenous people (McLemore, 2018; Reese, 2019a).

So, what can we do? We must seek to unlearn and relearn by questioning what we once accepted as truth or the only truth. One way to do this is by reading broadly, including counternarratives.

Some example counternarratives include the following:

- *Jingle Dancer* by Cynthia Leitich Smith
- *Fry Bread* by Kevin Noble Maillard
- *We Are Still Here* by Traci Sorrell
- *When We Were Alone* by David Robertson
- *We Are Water Protectors* by Carole Lindstrom
- *Indian No More* by Charlene Willing McManis with Traci Sorrell

Picture Books

Picture books can be used to expand on the limited information in textbooks. Using picture books as the source of information to provide students with both text and illustrative depictions increases engagement and meaning. Picture books offer a safe medium to facilitate difficult conversations, including the oppression of certain groups that have been marginalized or whitewashed. However, educators should be cautious when selecting books for inclusion in the classroom because many books perpetuate stereotypes and historical inaccuracies (Mendoza & Reese, 2001) (see Chapter 4: "Examining Stereotypes"). Chapters 3 and 5 of this book offer some guidelines for selecting books and evaluating a classroom library. This is another good reference: bit.ly/3VnWobu

Critical Comprehension
Lesson Series

Interrogating the Past and the Present

The lessons in this series examine people and events across time and how they have impacted the past and present. Specifically, they include the perspectives of historically marginalized groups to help students broaden perspectives, challenge stereotypes, and expand their understanding of the past and the present. They also provide opportunities to consider the ways in which learning about the past can help young people make informed decisions and take action for a better future.

The lessons and texts included in this chapter are intended to be a starting point and do not offer an in-depth history of any particular time period or group of people. Each lesson features one book but also includes a list of alternatives for additional work to extend thought and insight. We encourage you to adapt the lessons based on the interests and inquiries of your students.

Table of Lessons for Interrogating the Past and the Present	
LESSON FOCUS	**ANCHOR TEXT**
1. Challenging misconceptions about Native Americans	*Fry Bread* by Kevin Noble Maillard (enrolled member of the Seminole Nation of Oklahoma)
2. The transcontinental railroad	*Locomotive* by Brian Floca
3. The Tulsa Race Massacre	*Unspeakable: The Tulsa Race Massacre* by Carole Boston Weatherford
4. The Holocaust	*Rose Blanche* by Ian McEwan
5. Desegregation	*Separate Is Never Equal* by Duncan Tonatiuh
6. The fight for democracy	*The Hill We Climb* by Amanda Gorman
7. The Statue of Liberty	*Her Right Foot* by Dave Eggers

Note: The blank spaces are an invitation for you to add your own related topics and texts.

Lesson 1: Challenging Misconceptions About Native Americans

Fry Bread • by Kevin Noble Maillard
(enrolled member of the Seminole Nation of Oklahoma)

 First Read: Movie Read

This first visit, the "movie read," focuses on taking in the story without interruption (see Chapter 1, p. 21). In *Fry Bread* author Kevin Noble Maillard (enrolled member of the Seminole Nation of Oklahoma) focuses on a staple food that he describes as a community anchor for many Native American nations and uses it to depict the complex history of a modern family. The book includes representations of the diversity within the Native community in a way that affirms Native lives today. This book also highlights the harm to Native peoples caused by the US government.

 Second Read: Reading With the Text

For the second read, invite students to share their observations, reactions, and questions.

Ask students:

- *What is the book about?*
- *What do you notice?*
- *What surprised you?*
- *What are you thinking?*
- *What are you wondering?*

Studying Similes and Metaphors

Notice how the author uses the repeating phrase "Fry bread is . . ." as the main idea followed by details to describe the food's shape, sound, color, flavor, and so on. Discuss how the author used similes and metaphors to share about fry bread. Provide students with sticky notes to record a simile or metaphor they notice as you reread the book. Then invite students to place the sticky note under the appropriate section of a two-column anchor chart, one column labeled "Simile," and the other "Metaphor."

FIGURE 6.2

Interrogating the
Past and the Present

Discuss students' observations and return to the text and locate the metaphors and similes. Use this time to compare and contrast the two.

Class Recipe Book

Ask students:

- *What does it mean when the author says, "Fry bread is time"?*

- *What meal do you like to share with the people you care about?*

Read the recipe at the end of the book and discuss the ingredients and steps involved. Then, using this recipe as a mentor text, invite the students to choose a dish that is meaningful to them and write a recipe. They might seek insight from an elder in their family to develop the recipe. They could write a story describing the origin of the recipe and the tradition of the food in their family. For example, is the recipe prepared and shared on special occasions or at any time? Has the recipe been passed down from previous generations?

Encourage students to include a simile or metaphor in the title of this recipe. Model with your own example first. Create a class recipe book of their recipes to be copied or digitalized and shared with their families and the class.

For Younger Students

For younger students, creating the recipe book could be a shared or interactive writing experience. For example, you may bring teacakes that you learned to bake with your grandmother. Share the recipe and tell the story of making them when you were the age of your students. The metaphor may be "teacakes are love" or "teacakes are memory."

 Return Read: Reading Critically

Before beginning the return read, focus on the cover and revisit students' comments from the first read.

Ask students:

- *Is this the cover you would have imagined for the story? Why or why not?*

- *What surprised you about the cover? What didn't surprise you about the cover?*

Have a close look at the endpapers and the insides of the book cover. The endpapers at the front and back of the book are full of the names of tribal nations.

Ask students:

- *What do you notice about the endpapers?*

- *Do you recognize any of the names on the papers?*

- *Why do you think the author included these names on the endpapers?*

Endpapers

Debbie Reese (tribally enrolled at Nambé Owingeh, a sovereign Native nation) in her review of *Fry Bread* shared that the author Kevin Noble Maillard (Seminole Nation, Mekusukey Band) told her that to create the endpapers for the book, hundreds of phone calls were made to tribal offices to confirm the way they should be listed. The endpapers include more than 500 tribal nation names with a nation-to-nation relationship with the United States. These relationships are treaties, which are solemn agreements between the United States and American Indian nations. Enrollment in tribal nations is an important status that means one is counted in that nation's census. If a tribe cannot state who its citizens are, then it loses its identity as a sovereign nation (Reese, 2019b). Sovereignty means that Native American nations preexist the United States and tribal sovereignty is recognized and protected by the US Constitution, legal precedent, and treaties.

While reviewing the endpapers, Reese (2019b) discovered there are several groups included who are recognized by a state but are not necessarily true tribal nations. "Tribal recognition in the United States is a relationship between the sovereignty of the United States and the sovereignty of a tribal entity, and these organizations have no sovereignty. They only have whatever rights the state may grant to them" (Crawford, 2019). Non-true tribal nations can range from loose affiliations of people who believe they have American Indian ancestry, to well-organized groups that obtain 501(c)3 nonprofit status, to others that go on to become recognized by individual states (Crawford, 2019).

Pause after each page to read the corresponding text from the author's note and discuss the information. Continue in this pattern through the end of the book. For example, after reading the page, "Fry bread is food . . ." stop to read the corresponding sections in the author's note. Here, the author describes how there are many different ways to make fry bread.

Ask students:

- *Have you ever tried food from cultures other than your own?*

- *What foods have you tried?*

- *Have you ever heard of fry bread?*

- *Have you ever tried Native American or Indigenous food?*

After reading, "Fry bread is shape . . ." read the corresponding section in the author's note: "Just like people, there is no one shape, body type, or shoe size that makes anyone better than anyone else." Discuss the notion that people, just like fry bread, have different shapes. This can lead to important discussions and reminders about positive body image.

Ask students:

- *How does this connect with the book Beautifully Me (see Chapter 4)?*

- *Why is it important to honor all body shapes and sizes?*

Return Read Extension

Encourage students to notice the diversity of the characters throughout the book as well as in other books, posters around the school, advertisements, and so on. Are different body types represented accurately? (Note: This could connect with the lesson on beauty in Chapter 4.)

Continue reading the pages of the book and the corresponding section in the author's note. For the page, "Fry bread is color . . ." notice the diversity in skin tones and hair textures on the page and throughout the book. The author's note discusses how most people inaccurately think Native Americans have only black or brown hair.

Ask students:

- *Based on the images of Native people you've seen in TV, movies, books, or online, how are Native people represented? (Do an online image search and analyze the results.)*

- *How similar or different are they from the representation featured in Fry Bread? What does this suggest?*

Interrogating the
Past and the Present

The page "Fry bread is art . . ." discusses the history and cultural tradition of doll making and basket weaving. The author's note mentions the craft of basket weaving in the Black community. This could be an opportunity to learn more about the Gullah Geechee people and their connections with the Seminoles. Additionally, students can share the art and craft traditions passed down in their own families and cultures.

The section detailing "Fry bread is history . . ." explores the troubled past during colonization including war, conflict, and violence. It disrupts the notion of the friendly cooperative relationships often taught during Thanksgiving.

Ask students: *Do you notice the shift in the mood evoked as the illustrations move from colorful and whimsical to dark colors with shadows of people on the long walk and the serious facial expressions of the elders teaching the young people who listen inquisitively?*

Read the corresponding section of the author's note to explain "the long walk," "the stolen land," and "genocide." Discuss the injustices Native Americans faced, including President Andrew Jackson's Indian Removal Act of 1830, also known as the Trail of Tears. This can be an entry point for further research. Compare with movements today, such as those surrounding the Dakota Access Pipeline. Read *We Are Water Protectors* by Carole Lindstrom.

Read the pages "Fry bread is place . . . ," "Fry bread is nation . . . ," and "Fry bread is us . . ." Explain that Indigenous people lived here long before and are still here.

Ask students:

- *What is the message behind "we are still here"?*
- *Why is the notion "we are still here" so important?*

Layering Texts

Read *We Are Still Here* by Traci Sorrell. Invite students to research the Indigenous people of the land where their school resides and create a land acknowledgment statement to share with the school and the community.

Discuss how fry bread was food for survival when the US government displaced Natives from their homelands and limited their access to healthy food from the land. Natives no longer had access to familiar meats, fruits, and vegetables, such as corn. The government provided rations, including powdered, canned, and dry goods, which led to the creation of fry bread. (See the introduction to the author's note.)

Research food deserts, access to quality healthcare, and long-standing health problems in Native communities. (See the section "Fry Bread Is Sound" in the author's note.)

View and discuss the TED talk "What's Wrong with Our Food System."

Access the TED talk on our food system here.

Additional Texts and Resources

- *Birdsong* by Julie Flett (Swampy Cree-Red River Métis)

- *Indian Shoes* by Cynthia Leitich Smith (citizen of the Muscogee Nation)

- *Josie Dances* by Denise Lajimodiere (citizen, Turtle Mountain Band of Chippewa)

- *On the Trapline* by David A. Robertson (member of the Norway House Cree Nation)

- *The Forever Sky* by Thomas Peacock (member of the Fond du Lac Band of Lake Superior Chippewa)

- *When We Were Alone* by David Robertson (enrolled member of the Norway House Cree Nation)

- Book review from Debbie Reese
  bit.ly/3ONgSYR

Lesson 2: The Transcontinental Railroad
Locomotive • by Brian Floca

 First Read: Movie Read

This first visit, the "movie read," focuses on taking in the story without interruption (see Chapter 1, p. 21). *Locomotive* tells the story of a family's journey on a cross-country train traveling from Omaha to Sacramento in the summer of 1869 after the completion of the transcontinental railroad.

 Second Read: Reading With the Text

Before rereading the book, ask students what they recall from the first read about passengers riding the first transcontinental railroad in 1869. Record their comments under the "K" for "know" in a KWL chart. Then ask students to share what they are wondering or want to know and record that under the "W" column of the KWL. Reread the book with the lens of their inquiries and questions from the "W" column. After reading, invite students to share what they learned and record it in the "L" column of the KWL. Alternatively, students can record their thinking on sticky notes to share (see Figure 6.4).

We have adapted the KWL to represent a more fluid notion of reading and learning as inquiry.

K: What we know based on our current thinking and beliefs.

W: What we are now wondering about.

L: What we learned as a result of new understandings and what new questions we have.

FIGURE 6.3

LOCOMOTIVE · BRIAN FLOCA

Interrogating the
Past and the Present

K	W	L
• It connected the east and west. • There were two and they connected in the middle. • It made the transportation of goods and people easier and faster. • People slept on the train. • It went through tunnels in the mountains.	• Who built the railroad? • How fast does the train go? • How much did it cost to ride the train? • Did anybody get hurt? • Did people choose to work on the railroad? • Were the workers paid fairly?	

FIGURE 6.4   I Know I Wonder Chart

© Lester Laminack

Return Read: Reading Critically

For the return read, begin by reviewing what students learned (KWL chart). Display and read the endpapers, then ask students what else they know about what was happening in the United States at that time. For example, the Civil War ended, and President Abraham Lincoln signed the Emancipation Proclamation. Also, many Irish immigrants came to the United States because of the potato famine in Ireland.

Ask students:

- *What do you notice about the map and illustrations?*
- *Who is included/excluded (e.g., Native American territories are not included in the map, nor are they illustrated)?*

Read page 1: "A new road of rails made for people to ride."

Ask students:

- *Who was the road of rails made for and by whom?*
- *Do you think there was any impact on people or wildlife as a result?*

Read page 2: "Men came from far away to build from the East, to build from the West . . ."

Ask students: *Did only men work on the railroad? Only adults?*

Continue reading: "men came from far away."

Ask students:

- *Where did they come from specifically?*
- *What are their stories?*
- *Did they have to leave their families behind?*
- *What do you notice about the illustrations?*

Read page 3 (Omaha, Nebraska) where people are waiting for the train to arrive.

Ask students:

- *Who's riding the train?*
- *What do the passengers have in common?*

- *[Note: Scaffold students' understanding of the group who was privileged to be passengers and prompt questioning why others were not on board.]*
- *Who isn't riding the train?*

Turn to the middle of the book to the page labeled "The Great Plains." Notice how the perspective changes to more of a bird's-eye (or drone) view of the train within the broader landscape. This is a little different than the previous illustrations from within the train focused on the passengers and inner workings of the train. Reread: "Here the bison used to roam."

Ask students:

- *Where did the bison go?*
- *What happened to them?*

Pause here to remove the book jacket to display the alternate illustration of the bison. You may prefer to do so after reading.

Continue reading: "Here the Cheyenne lived, and Pawnee and Arapaho."

Ask students: *How might this language be problematic?*

Pause and reference the book *We Are Still Here* by Traci Sorell (see Lesson 1). You may also discuss the genocide of Indigenous people and how the building of the railroad affected their land, resources, and homes (connect to Lesson 1).

Turn to the page labeled "Sherman, Wyoming." Read the first two sentences.

Ask students: *What do you know about the porters?*

Explain that many people who had been enslaved during that time found work as porters when they were freed. The availability of employment as porters for formerly enslaved men was instrumental in the Great Migration. Go back four pages to the illustration of the boy selling newspapers. Pullman porters had greater access to information, different people, and different places. You can explore this further with the book *I, Too, Am America* by Langston Hughes, illustrated by Bryan Collier.

Turn to the page with the Summit Tunnel and the previous page.

Ask students:

- *Do you think it was dangerous work to build these tunnels?*
- *Who did that work? Who didn't do the work?*

Turn to the page labeled "Sacramento, California." On this page, the train finally arrives, and the family is reunited.

Ask students:

- *Who's riding the train?*
- *Who isn't riding the train?*
- *Who isn't reunited?*

So many voices are not included in the book, yet the train itself is personified and referred to as "she" and "her."

Ask students: *What do you think this suggests?*

Read the author's note for additional information. Note, however, that there is limited mention of the Chinese laborers who made up 90 percent of the workforce and who were not invited to the celebration at the completion of the railroad. They were not employed to work on the trains, and they were not among the passengers on board the trains.

Ask students: *What other perspectives are limited or missing?*

Layering Texts

To deepen students' understanding of the transcontinental railroad and provide additional perspectives, we offer the following additional texts:

"The Railroad That Changed America" video.

- View together the Scholastic article and video "The Railroad That Changed America" (see QR code in margin). Ask the guiding question "What impact do trains have on the United States?" during reading. After reading, ask students to describe the five ways the transcontinental railroad changed America. Discuss how the railroad transformed the nation but may not have benefited all people equally.

- Read *Coolies* by Yin to learn more about the transcontinental railroad from the perspective of the Chinese immigrant workers who built the railroad. In this story, the reader meets two young boys who leave their family in China to travel to California in search of work. While working on the transcontinental railroad, Shen and his brother Little Wong face difficult working conditions, discrimination, and even avalanches. Based on real events, this story tells the harsh realities of many Chinese immigrants working on the railroad system in 1865. Pairing this book with *Locomotive* and other resources enables readers to further their understanding

Interrogating the Past and the Present

of westward expansion to include the inequities and discrimination faced by the Chinese American laborers.

Ask students:

- *Consider whose perspective is centered in this book. How does it compare with the perspective presented in Locomotive?*

- *How were the workers treated in comparison with the treatment of other workers during time periods both past and present?*

Read *I, Too, Am America* by Langston Hughes to learn more about the Pullman porters who worked on the trains. Consider reading *This Is the Rope: A Story from the Great Migration* by Jacqueline Woodson as a follow-up read to this text set.

Ask students:

- *Consider whose perspective is centered in the book. How does it compare with the perspective presented in Locomotive and Coolies?*

- *How does the story of the transcontinental railroad in these texts compare with the story told in our textbook?*

- *What new information do you have now?*

- *What questions can you ask that you could not have asked before reading these books?*

Read *Black Heroes of the Wild West* by James Otis Smith to learn about the role of cattle drives and railroads during the mid- to late 1800s as well as the railroad companies' role along with the US government in exterminating millions of buffalo. Return to the cover of the book *Locomotive* and remove the book jacket to compare the illustrated cover without the buffalo.

Ask students:

- *Why do you think the author/illustrator created two different illustrations (the book cover and the book jacket)?*

- *What is the author's/illustrator's message?*

Interrogating the
Past and the Present

Lesson 3: The Tulsa Race Massacre

Unspeakable: The Tulsa Race Massacre •
Carole Boston Weatherford

 First Read: Movie Read

FIGURE 6.5

This first visit, the "movie read," focuses on taking in the story without interruption (see Chapter 1, p. 21). Weatherford shares the often-untold story of Greenwood, a thriving Black community in Oklahoma that experienced a devastating attack resulting in the loss of businesses, homes, and lives in 1921.

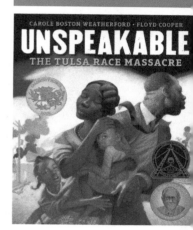

Begin by reading the first part of the title (Unspeakable). **Ask students** to share what comes to mind when they hear the word "unspeakable," and record their responses on chart paper.

They may respond with comments such as "something really awful or bad that cannot be expressed in words" or "someone or something horrific that nobody wants to mention like Voldemort" or "being at a loss of words that makes your jaw drop" or "speechless."

 Second Read: Reading With the Text

Open the book to display the illustration on the front and back covers.

Ask students: *What are you thinking as you study the cover of the book?*

Show students the endpapers at the beginning and end of the book.

Ask students:

- *Compare the endpapers at the beginning and end of the book. What do you notice?*

- *Why do you think Floyd Cooper, the illustrator, chose to use different mediums?*

As you reread the book, point out the use of the repeated phrase "once upon a time" across several pages.

Ask students: *What do you think the author's intention is for the use of the repeated phrase "once upon a time"?*

Pause throughout the reading to discuss the historical context, including segregation.

Interrogating the
Past and the Present

Ask students: Why did Black people flee the South in the late 1800s?

Point out the success of the community with many thriving Black-owned businesses, newspapers, churches, doctors, lawyers, hair salons, movie theaters, and so on. Mention how the people had access to quality health-care and education.

Ask students: *What are some examples of the ways Black people thrived in this community despite racism and segregation?*

Continue reading and pause at the page where the mood shifts to a dark background with white font and the white girl in light with the Black boy in the shadows. "But in 1921 . . ."

Ask students: *Why do you think the author shifts from the repeated phrase "once upon a time" and begins with "But in 1921 . . ."? What does this indicate?*

 ## Return Read: Reading Critically

Return to the discussion from the first reading where students discussed the title's first word, "Unspeakable."

Ask students: *Why do you think the author chose the title "Unspeakable"?*

Encourage students to think about why many people are unfamiliar with the Tulsa Race Massacre. Explain that this event was mostly suppressed and was not investigated for seventy-five years. Tulsa's power structures avoided publicizing for fear of "bad press." It took approximately one hundred years before Oklahoma's education system made strides to teach about the event. Discuss how shame and silencing of traumatic events may result in more harm.

Ask students:

- *Can you think of examples of how silence is used to avoid difficult conversations?*

- *And how does that cause harm or create more problems?*

For example, you may highlight why this story is often silenced.

Ask students:

- *Why do you think this violent incident was not investigated for more than seventy-five years?*

- *Why is it important to learn about the past (including hard history) to move toward a better tomorrow?*

Return to the end of the book where the author writes, "Tulsa's Reconciliation Park . . . is a place to realize the responsibility we all have to reject hatred and violence and instead choose hope."

Ask students:

- *What does the word "reconciliation" or "reconcile" mean?*

- *How can we all work together to reconcile racism in the past as well as the present?*

Let's Talk! Facilitating Critical Conversations with Students

Use this guide to support your work as you engage students in critical conversations:

bit.ly/3EQOTD1

Consider using this discussion guide by Dr. Sonja Cherry-Paul too.

Additional Texts to Explore Black History and Genius

- *Before She Was Harriet* by Lesa Cline-Ransome
- *Born on the Water* by Nikole Hannah-Jones and Renee Watson
  - Educator guide: bit.ly/3ualf6V
- *Counting on Katherine* by Helaine Becker
- *Heart and Soul: The Story of America and African Americans* by Kadir Nelson
- *Hidden Figures* by Margot Lee Shetterly
- *Mae Among the Stars* by Roda Ahmed
- *The Other Side* by Jacqueline Woodson
- *Stamped for Kids* by Sonja Cherry-Paul
  - Educator guide by Dr. Sonja Cherry-Paul: bit.ly/3FfhfYT
- *The Talk: Conversations About Race, Love & Truth* by Wade Hudson and Cheryl Willis Hudson
- *The Undefeated* by Kwame Alexander
- *Woosh! Lonnie Johnson's Super-Soaking Stream of Inventions* by Chris Barton

Interrogating the
Past and the Present

Lesson 4: The Holocaust
Rose Blanche • By Ian McEwan

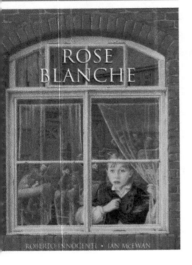

 ### First Read: Movie Read

This first visit, the "movie read," focuses on taking in the story without interruption (see Chapter 1, p. 21). This fictional story of the Holocaust is told from the perspective of Rose Blanche, a German girl, and is a tribute to the German resistance group to Adolf Hitler's regime called the White Rose Movement.

Before reading, explain that the story is set in Germany during World War II when Hitler ruled the country. Display Germany on a map.

Define Holocaust: The Holocaust was the systematic, state-sponsored persecution and murder of six million Jews by the Nazis. In 1933, the Nazis rose to power in Germany and believed that Germans were "racially superior" and deemed the Jews "inferior."

 ### Second Read: Reading With the Text

Begin reading the first page and point out how the book is told from the perspective of Rose, a young German girl with blond hair and blue eyes.

One day the first truck arrived, and many men left.

Ask students: *Where do you think they are going?*

Notice the way the people seem happy waving to the soldiers. Notice the flags and that Rose seems to be holding the flag with the swastika.

Ask students: *Have you seen those symbols before? What do they mean?*

Explain to students that the swastika is a symbol of the Nazi party.

Continue reading. It seems like little has changed from Rose's perspective other than lots of trucks.

Ask students:

- *What are the trucks doing there?*
- *What else is happening that Rose may be unaware of?*

Notice the reflection on the page where Rose is walking along the river.

Ask students:

- *What is the intended message?*
- *Why does the reflection show her walking along a barbed fence?*
- *How is this an example of foreshadowing?*

When one truck stops to repair the engine, a boy jumps out of the back and tries to run away.

Ask students:

- *Why is the boy in the truck?*
- *Where is he going?*
- *Why does he want to run away?*
- *Why does the mayor stop him?*
- *Why doesn't the mayor stop Rose?*
- *What do you think Rose is thinking?*

On the next page when the mayor returns the boy to the soldiers the author states the sky was gray.

Ask students:

- *Why is this an important detail?*
- *What do you notice about the tone of the story based on the illustrations thus far?*

Notice that the only color we see is the red in Rose's clothing and in the flag and arm patches.

Rose curiously follows the truck with the little boy. Nobody notices her.

Ask students: *Why didn't they notice her, but they noticed the boy?*

She walks to the edge of town where she has never been before.

Ask students:

- *How would you describe Rose based on her actions thus far?*
- *Why do you think the author states again that the clouds are gray?*

Pause at the page when Rose discovers the hungry children behind the barbed wire.

Ask students:

- *Who are these children?*

- *Why are they there?*

- *How did they get there?*

- *Why are they hungry?*

- *What role does the setting play here (e.g., The sun was setting, and it was windy. Rose was cold.)?*

Continue reading. Weeks passed by.

Ask students:

- *Why do you suppose Rose took lots of bread and other food to school but got thinner?*

- *Why was the mayor getting bigger?*

Explain that the yellow star on the children's clothing indicates that they were Jewish. Note the contrast of bright yellow with the gray tones in the illustrations.

The snow melting suggests a change of season. This may indicate a change in the story as well because now the soldiers are returning from the far side of the river. They look tired and worn down.

Ask students:

- *Why do you suppose this is so?*

- *What have they been doing?*

- *Why did they come at night with no lights on?*

- *Why didn't they stop?*

People in the town fled. Soldiers were among them.

Ask students: *Where are they going? Why are they fleeing?*

Continue reading. Fog erased the road, making it difficult to see. Rose hopped around to avoid the mud puddles. When Rose returns with food for the children, they were gone.

Ask students: *Where did they go? What happened?*

Continue reading. Shadows moved between the trees, and it was hard to see them.

Ask students: *What is meant by the line "Soldiers saw the enemy everywhere"?*

Keep reading. Then there was a shot.

Ask students: *What happened?*

Other soldiers with different uniforms and different languages arrive in town. Rose's mom waited a long time for her girl. Meanwhile, the season has changed to spring.

Ask students: *What can we infer happened?*

Finish reading.

Ask students:

- *What does the image on the last page, the image of the withered blue flower once held by Rose on the barbed wire, suggest?*

- *How did Rose's thinking change throughout the story? What changed about her thinking?*

- *What danger was Rose in because of what she did? Why did she continue to help anyway?*

- *What would you have done if you were Rose?*

Note: The last question sets up students for the Return Read: Reading Critically.

 ## Return Read: Reading Critically

Display a variety of images of modern people experiencing hardship (e.g., refugees, protesters, flood victims). Using a gallery walk, invite students to move around the room to examine the illustrations. Students will work together with their peers to answer the following questions that can be listed in a handout and placed on a clipboard.

Ask students:

- *Why is/are the person/people in trouble?*
- *What could be done to help?*
- *Where might help come from?*
- *What/who could prevent help?*

Return Read Extension

Other groups targeted by Nazis included people with disabilities, Black people, gay men, and Jehovah's Witnesses, to name a few. Like the way

Jews were forced to wear the yellow star of David, pink triangles were sewn onto the shirts of gay men in the concentration camps as a badge of shame and dehumanization. It was later reclaimed as a symbol of liberation and empowerment in the 1970s. In 1978, Gilbert Baker designed the rainbow flag as a symbol of hope and pride for the LGBTQ+ community. To learn more about the history of the rainbow flag, read the following:

- *Sewing the Rainbow: A Story About Gilbert Baker* by Gayle E. Pitman

- *Pride: The Story of Harvey Milk and the Rainbow Flag* by Rob Sanders

Additional Resources for Studying About the Holocaust

- *Anne Frank: The Diary of a Young Girl* by Anne Frank (chapter book)

- *The Boy in the Striped Pajamas* by John Boyne (chapter book)

- *Nicky & Vera: A Quiet Hero of the Holocaust and the Children He Rescued* by Peter Sis

- *Number the Stars* by Lois Lowry (chapter book)

- *The Butterfly* by Patricia Polacco

- *The Harmonica* by Tony Johnston

- *Erika's Story* by Ruth Zee

- *The Yellow Star: The Legend of King Christian X of Denmark* by Carmen Agra Deedy

- *The Cats of Krasinski Square* by Karen Hesse

- *The Number on My Grandfather's Arm* by David Adler

- *Six Million Paper Clips: The Making of a Children's Holocaust Memorial* by Peter W. Schroeder

- United States Holocaust Memorial Museum's Teaching Materials by Topic: bit.ly/3uc7iW7

- Historical Association's Rose Blanche resources: bbit.ly/3OR8ibA (Note: We do not recommend doing the role-playing suggested in these lessons.)

For Older Students

Discuss genocide (the deliberate, systematic, and widespread destruction of a racial or cultural group).

Display the pyramid of hate from the Anti-Defamation League, which can be found at bit.ly/3AYbvAg

Connect to lessons about bias in Chapter 5 and show how these behaviors can lead to discrimination and ultimately genocide.
Resource: bit.ly/3UmioSl

Lesson 5: Desegregation

Separate Is Never Equal: Sylvia Mendez and Her Family's Fight for Desegregation • by Duncan Tonatiuh

FIGURE 6.7

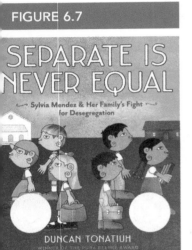

First Read: Movie Read

This first visit, the "movie read," focuses on taking in the story without interruption (see Chapter 1, p. 21). *Separate Is Never Equal: Sylvia Mendez and Her Family's Fight for Desegregation* takes place seven years before the *Brown v. Board of Education* (1954) ruling. It is the story of Mexican-born Gonzalo Mendez and Puerto Rican Felicitas Mendez who challenged the segregated school system in California when their children were turned away from the local school and sent to a run-down school for Mexican American children in the 1940s. The legal case, *Mendez v. Westminster* (1947), paved the way for the desegregation of schools in the United States.

Second Read: Reading With the Text

After reading the book a second time, focus on the students' overall responses and reactions to the story.

Ask students:

- *What is the book about?*

- *What message do you take away from the story?*

- *What comments do you have about the book?*

- *What do you think about what happened to the Mendez children?*

- *What connections can you make to Sylvia's experience?*

- *What questions come to mind after reading the story?*

- *What surprised you about the story?*

Record the responses on a chart paper or invite students to record their thinking on sticky notes (see Figures 6.8 and 6.9).

FIGURE 6.8   Students Respond Using Sticky Notes

FIGURE 6.9   Students Share Sticky Notes on a Chart

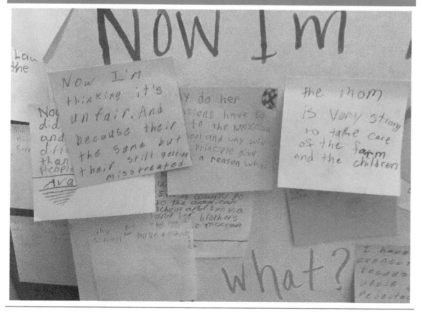

Return Read: Reading Critically

Begin the return read by focusing on the book cover.

Ask students:

- *What do you notice about how the illustrator positioned the characters on the cover?*

- *What connections can you make between the title of the book and the way the characters are positioned in the illustration?*

- *Why do you think the illustrator chose the colors they did for the two school buildings?*

- *How is the illustrator using color to visually represent segregation?*

Continue reading the book and stop on the page where the young white boy points at Sylvia and yells "Go back to the Mexican school! You don't belong here!"

Ask students:

- *Why do you think Duncan Tonatiuh chose to begin the book with this scene?*

- *How did this scene make you feel?*

- *Focus on the illustrations. Who would you identify as a perpetrator? A victim? A bystander?*

- *What effect did positioning the characters, as they are in the spread, have on you as a reader?*

Read on and stop on the page after the spread where Aunt Soledad is enrolling the children.

Ask students:

- *What went through your mind as you read about how Sylvia looked at her cousins' light skin and auburn hair and then looked at her brothers and her own hands and bare arms and wondered, "Is it because we have brown skin and thick black hair?"*

- *Why do you think the author included this scene in the book?*

- *What questions came to mind?*

- *Have you ever seen anyone who was treated in this way?*

- *Have you ever experienced being treated in this way?*

Share with students the meaning of colorism and the graph in the information box.

Ask students:

- *What effect does colorism have on the lives and livelihood of people and groups of people?*
- *What effect did colorism have on the Mendez children?*
- *Who benefits from colorism?*
- *Who is put at a disadvantage because of colorism?*
- *Have you ever experienced colorism?*
- *What can you do to contribute to disrupting or stopping colorism?*

Avoiding Harm

Some students may see this as an opportunity to share their experiences as a way to teach others to be better. Other students may be made vulnerable by being asked these questions. As such you will need to decide which questions to ask, based on your own students.

Colorism

Colorism is a type of discrimination that is based on skin color where lighter skin color is sometimes favored over darker skin color within a racialized or ethnic group. For example, Latinx people in the United States may face discrimination because they are Latinx (a form of racism), but the extent of the discrimination may vary based on their skin color. Those with darker skin experience more incidents of colorism. Unfortunately, discrimination based on skin color also occurs *within groups* of Latinx people just as much as it can be directed at Latinx people by non-Latinx groups (see Figure 6.10).

In extreme cases colorism has resulted in those affected by it bleaching their skin, thus contributing to a multibillion-dollar skin-bleaching industry around the world.

(Continued)

(Continued)

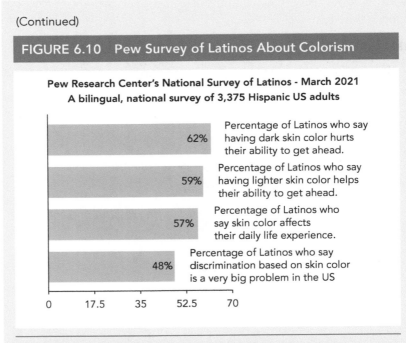

FIGURE 6.10   Pew Survey of Latinos About Colorism

Pew Research Center's National Survey of Latinos - March 2021
A bilingual, national survey of 3,375 Hispanic US adults

62% — Percentage of Latinos who say having dark skin color hurts their ability to get ahead.

59% — Percentage of Latinos who say having lighter skin color helps their ability to get ahead.

57% — Percentage of Latinos who say skin color affects their daily life experience.

48% — Percentage of Latinos who say discrimination based on skin color is a very big problem in the US

Source: Adapted from Noe-Bustamante et al., 2021.

To continue to learn about colorism, read the book *Sulwe* by Lupita Nyong'o or view the author's read aloud on Netflix Jr's Bookmarks series. bit.ly/3AVSlv6

Focus on the spread where the children are having lunch in the yard at the Mexican school.

Ask students:

- *How would you describe the conditions at the Mexican school?*
- *Why do you think the author chose to include the electric wire fence to keep the cows in?*

Turn to the swimming pool spread.

Ask students:

- *Why do you think the author chose to include the sign at the pool?*
- *How did seeing that sign influence your reaction to the image?*
- *Why do you think the illustrator chose to include the bars in front of the Mexican children? What do the bars stand for?*
- *How did seeing the bars influence your reaction to the image?*

Recap instances in the book where Aunt Soledad and Mr. Mendez had experiences with people, such as the secretary at the school, who gave them firm answers like "rules are rules" or "That is how it is done," without offering any explanation for their answers.

Ask students:

- *What do responses like this tell you about people?*

- *Why do you think they would respond in this way?*

- *What are better ways for them to respond?*

Revisit the courtroom scenes.

Ask students:

- *What were some of the claims about Mexican children being made by members of the school board and why were they making such claims?*

- *What were lies that were told in the courtroom and by whom?*

- *What could be the reasoning behind such lies?*

- *What were the truths that were told? How were these truths revealed?*

Return to the cover of the book.

Ask students: *Now that you have spent more time with the story, what can you say about the phrase "separate is never equal"?* (Alternatively, students could be given the option to draw or sketch their response or choose an art card to represent their thinking.)

Share Sylvia Mendez's bio-note with the students.

Ask students: *What are some things you might do if you encounter a situation where someone or some group is being treated in the way Sylvia and her family were treated?*

Sylvia Mendez Bio-Note

FIGURE 6.11

Sylvia (second from right) discusses *Separate Is Never Equal* with a group of families in the Washington, DC, area. (Printed with the permission of Sylvia Mendez.)

In 1943, when Sylvia was in third grade, she and her siblings were denied admission to the "white school" near their home. They were told they had to attend the school for Mexican American children.

Sylvia's family fought back and launched a lawsuit, which resulted in a landmark court case known as *Mendez v. Westminster*. The civil rights attorney David Marcus filed the lawsuit based on the argument that segregating children by ethnicity was a violation of the equal protection clause of the Fourteenth Amendment.

The court case, which ended in 1947, became the first successful federal school desegregation decision in the nation. The case became an example for future court rulings and paved the way for later actions, such as California Governor Earl Warren pushing the state legislature into repealing laws that segregated Asians and Native American school children. It also paved the way for the historic *Brown v. Board of Education* case decided by the US Supreme Court in 1954.

Through the years, Sylvia has worked tirelessly to bring awareness to this historical injustice against Mexican American children. For years she made herself available to speak at schools, community groups, and various educational forums to educate others regarding her parents' fight for the desegregation of schools in California.

Resources and Books

Sylvia and Aki by Winifred Conkling

Mendez v. Westminster: School Desegregation and Mexican-American Rights by Philippa Strum

Sylvia Mendez's web page
bit.ly/3uj9ue8

Voices of History—Sylvia Mendez
bit.ly/3B0h01z

Mendez v. Westminster: Paving the Way to School Desegregation
bit.ly/3VDOniC

In the endnotes, Duncan Tonatiuh writes, "I also hope that [young people] will see themselves reflected in Sylvia's story and realize that their voices are valuable and that they too can make meaningful contributions to this country."

Ask students: *What meaningful contributions can you make to this country?*

Additional Books About School Desegregation

- *Let the Children March* by Monica Clark-Robinson

- *Little Rock Nine* by Marshall Poe

- *The Lions of Little Rock* by Kristin Levine

- *The Story of Ruby Bridges* by Robert Coles

- *Through My Eyes* by Ruby Bridges

Interrogating the
Past and the Present

Lesson 6: The Fight for Democracy
The Hill We Climb • by Amanda Gorman

FIGURE 6.12

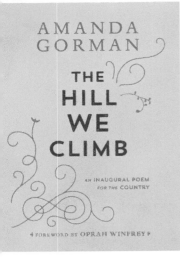

AMANDA
GORMAN

THE
HILL
WE
CLIMB

AN INAUGURAL POEM
FOR THE COUNTRY

FOREWORD BY OPRAH WINFREY

Amanda Gorman's
poem "The Hill
We Climb."

Interrogating the
Past and the Present

First Read: Movie Read

This first visit, the "movie read," focuses on taking in the story without interruption (see Chapter 1, p. 21). View the video of Amanda Gorman reciting her poem for the 2021 presidential inauguration. (Scan the QR code in the margin to access the video and full text of the poem.)

Second Read: Reading With the Text

Provide students with copies of the poem. Scan the QR code in the margin for both the video of Gorman reading her poem and the full text.

Begin by reading and discussing the significance of the poem's title.

Ask students: *Who might "we" refer to?*

Read the poem, pausing to annotate and discuss along the way.

Ask students:

- *What do you notice?*
- *What are you thinking?*
- *Can you make any connections to other texts, historical events, or current events?*

Ask students:

- *What do you notice? What stands out to you?*
  - *Repetition?*
  - *Stanzas with purpose?*
  - *Rhyme?*
  - *Mood? (created for reader)*
  - *Tone? (poet's attitude)*
  - *Metaphors/similes?*
  - *Word choice?*
  - *Imagery?*
  - *Purpose/message?*
  - *Emotional response/impact on reader?*
- *What do you wonder?*

After reading, invite students to return to the poem, select a line that stood out to them, and share it with the class along with why that particular line resonated.

Summarize the poem and discuss the author's message.

To connect with the lessons in Chapter 2 on identity, invite discussion about the way Gorman describes herself in the poem.

Ask students:

- *Which of her own identities does she name?*

- *Why do you think she chooses to name these identities in this poem about American democracy?*

 ## Return Read: Reading Critically

In the previous read, you discussed the significance of the title "The Hill We Climb."

Ask students: *The hill is a metaphor that suggests effort or struggle. What does the use of this metaphor suggest about our democracy?*

As you return to the poem for this read, pause and discuss some of the lines in the questions that follow.

Ask students:

- *What is the "never-ending shade" or the "loss we carry" Gorman references at the beginning of the poem?*

- *What do you think is meant by the phrase "quiet isn't always peace"?*

- *What do you think the line "the norms and notions of what just is, isn't always justice" means? Do you agree? Why or why not?*

- *What is Gorman's message about closing the divide and putting our differences aside?*

Invite students to reflect and connect with the following lines:

> That even as we grieved, we grew
>
> That even as we hurt, we hoped
>
> That even as we tired, we tried

Ask students:

- *What does it mean to you to be American?*

- *How does your definition compare with what Gorman describes as "being American"?*

- *Now that we have read several books, how are your ideas changing? What is causing that change?*

Reread the end of the poem:

> For there is always light,

> If only we're brave enough to see it,

> If only we're brave enough to be it.

Ask students:

- *What is the light we need to see?*

- *How can we be the light?*

- *Why is it necessary to be brave to do so?*

- *How does this connect with the Statue of Liberty's torch as a symbol of enlightenment—lighting the path to liberty and freedom? (Connect to the lesson using* Her Right Foot, *by Dave Eggers, the centerpiece of the next lesson in this chapter.)*

Return Read Extension

In an interview with the *New York Times*, Gorman said, "Now more than ever, the United States needs an inaugural poem. Poetry is typically the touchstone that we go back to when we have to remind ourselves of the history that we stand on, and the future that we stand for."

Ask students:

- *What do you think she means?*

- *How does poetry capture our feelings or attitudes in a way that traditional speeches or prose do not?*

- *How did "The Hill We Climb" seek to accomplish these goals?*

Return to the following lines:

> We the successors of a country and a time
>
> Where a skinny Black girl
>
> descended from slaves and raised by a single mother
>
> can dream of becoming president
>
> only to find herself reciting for one

Explain that Gorman is a descendant of enslaved people. Provide some context and then read Chapter 3 in *Stamped for Kids* by Sonja Cherry-Paul. Introduce Phyllis Wheatley as another Black poet and discuss how her poetry was a way to disrupt slavery because it demonstrated her brilliance. That challenged the myth held by many whites that Black people were born as savages.

Watch Amanda Gorman's TED-Ed student talk.

Additional Texts to Highlight the Struggle for Democracy

- *Bright Star* by Yuyi Morales

- *Change Sings* by Amanda Gorman

- "Still I Rise" by Maya Angelou

Resource:

Read the *New York Times* article titled "Why I Almost Didn't Read My Poem" by Amanda Gorman and discuss why she almost didn't read her poem bit.ly/3iqP68t

---

Interrogating the
Past and the Present

Lesson 7: The Statue of Liberty
Her Right Foot • by Dave Eggers

FIGURE 6.13

 First Read: Movie Read

As we learn about important symbols in our country, most of us think of the Statue of Liberty as a symbol of freedom and a welcome to immigrants. Before reading, begin by asking students what they already know about the Statue of Liberty and record on the chart under "I think . . ." Record students' wondering in the column "I wonder . . ." Then display a photo and/or replicas of the statue and ask students to share their observations and update the chart.

This first visit, the "movie read," focuses on taking in the story without interruption (see Chapter 1, p. 21). In this nonfiction book, the author provides background about the Statue of Liberty, including that it was a gift from France, was shipped in crates, and was reassembled in New York, and little-known details about the statue, including her right foot in mid-stride.

Second Read: Reading With the Text

Explain how reading nonfiction helps us learn new information. After the second read, invite students to share what they learned about the Statue of Liberty and update the chart from the first read (see Figure 6.14).

Ask students:

- *What new information did you learn about the Statue of Liberty?*

- *What are you thinking or wondering now?*

Interrogating the Past and the Present

218

FIGURE 6.14   Statue of Liberty Chart

BEFORE READING		AFTER READING	
I THINK . . .	I WONDER . . .	NOW I'M THINKING . . .	NOW I'M WONDERING . . .
• It's tall • In New York • Welcomes immigrants • Means freedom		• Gift from France • Made of copper • Assembled first in Paris • Shipped in more than 200 crates and reassembled in New York	

Return Read: Reading Critically

For the return read, focus on the statue as a symbol of liberty. Explain that just like authors have an intention for their writing, so do artists/sculptors. They want us to interpret their art and consider the message being conveyed. Throughout the book, the author describes intentional details the sculptor included in the Statue of Liberty. (Connect to the discussion on similes and metaphors in Lesson 1 with the book *Fry Bread*.)

For example, as you reread the book, pause on the page where the author describes the torch as a symbol of enlightenment and lighting a path to liberation and freedom and discuss.

Ask students:

- *What is enlightenment?*

- *How does Lady Liberty's torch light a path to liberation and freedom?*

  o *Compare the words "light a path" with "enlightenment" as a way to shine a light in darkness and make things visible to provide new information that brings a different understanding.*

- *Why do you think Bartholdi included the torch in her hand?*

Return to the spread in the middle of the book without any illustrations: "But there is one thing you might not know . . . you probably have not seen pictures of her feet." Continue reading and discuss how the statue is walking mid-stride.

Ask students:

- *Where is she going?*
- *Why do you think Bartholdi sculpted her right foot in mid-stride?*
- *What does this suggest?*

Continue reading. Pause and discuss the page that describes her feet in broken chains.

Ask students:

- *Why do you think Bartholdi included broken chains around Lady Liberty's feet?*
- *Why did he want us to think about her being freed from bondage?*

Continue reading. Near the end of the book the author writes, "If the Statue of Liberty is a symbol of freedom, if the Statue of Liberty has welcomed millions of immigrants to the United States, then how can she stand still?"

Ask students: *What is Bartholdi suggesting about the Statue of Liberty and immigrants?*

Continue reading the next page: "Liberty and freedom from oppression are not things you get or grant by standing around like some kind of statue. No! These are things that require action. Courage. An unwillingness to rest."

Ask students:

- *What is oppression?*
- *What does the author mean by "things you get or grant"?*
- *What are some examples of people over time who have demonstrated courage to take action for liberty and freedom?*

Record their responses on a chart and invite students to conduct research to explore various movements and change makers.

At the end of the book, the author discusses how the Statue of Liberty is an immigrant, too, and offers an explanation for why she's moving.

Ask students:

- *Are all immigrants treated the same when they arrive in the United States?*

- *How can we take steps to move forward to accept and welcome others?*

Additional Texts to Explore

- At the end of the book, the author includes a photograph of the New Colossus poem on the pedestal of the statue. To learn more about this poem's origin, read the book *Emma's Poem: The Voice of the Statue of Liberty* by Linda Glaser.

- *Dreamers* by Yuyi Morales

- *Front Desk* by Kelly Yang (chapter book)

- *Grandfather's Journey* by Allen Say

- *I, Too, Am America* by Langston Hughes

- *Refugee* by Alan Gratz (chapter book)

For Younger Students

Read *Bright Star* by Yuyi Morales. Make connections to the book *Dreamers* by the same author.

Ask students: *How will you shine your light?*

READING FOR ACTION

After reading with and reading critically a collection of texts focused on interrogating history, invite students to reflect on what they learned and how their thinking has changed.

Ask students: *What will we do with this new insight? How can we take action?*

SOME IDEAS/SUGGESTIONS

- Work to disrupt the commonplace by seeking counternarratives.

- "Tulsa's Reconciliation Park . . . is a place to realize the responsibility we all have to reject hatred and violence and instead choose hope" (from *Unspeakable: The Tulsa Race Massacre*). How can we take action to reject hate and violence and choose hope? What are some examples from your own life and/or examples of ways you've seen or heard about others doing so?

- Amanda Gorman invites us to see the light and be the light in her poem "The Hill We Climb." In what ways will you be brave enough to see and be the light?

- In the book *Her Right Foot*, the author explains how liberty and freedom require courage, action, and unwillingness to rest. How can you take action to fight for liberty and freedom?

- How can we move forward to welcome immigrants and refugees?

Consuming Critically

7

Following a study of needs and wants and how these are met in different environments for plants and animals, Chris Hass read *Those Shoes* by Maribeth Boelts to the third graders in his class. On a return visit with the book, he asked students to think about whether the story reflects a need, a want, or both.

Hadley: I think the shoes are both because he needs new shoes, but he wanted that brand.

Dr. Hass: Oh, you think the specific brand was a want?

Hadley: Yeah, because he could have used a lot of different shoes, but he wanted that expensive shoe.

Other students chimed in and added that the boy wanted those specific shoes because so many other kids had them. Dr. Hass nudged their thinking by asking, "What else makes us want something we may not actually need, other than seeing other kids with these things?" Several students replied with "seeing it on display in the store," "seeing ads on the internet or in a magazine," "hearing other people talk about how cool it is," and "knowing that it is expensive." A reading of this book and the follow-up conversation could go in many directions, but Dr. Hass opens the conversation by inviting students to reflect on the relationship between needs and wants. That naturally moved to an exploration of how the media and advertising attempt to sell products and ideas, which lays the foundation for developing critical media literacy with young readers.

From the time we are born we are immersed in advertisements and messages from family, friends, and the media that result in brand loyalty to the products in our cupboards, refrigerators, bathrooms, closets, toy boxes, and driveways. Throughout our lives we are exposed to advertising through TV, radio, billboards, social media, internet searches, and print.

We are surrounded by franchised grocery markets, fast food restaurants, gas stations, and more. Brand names stand boldly along our highways and quietly infiltrate our notions of what we should buy. For many families, the result is unquestioned loyalty to particular products and specific brands. Imagine a parent shopping for groceries with a young child. The parent says to the child, "Walk to the end of the aisle and get a jar of peanut butter." The child walks to the section where several brands and varieties are presented but reaches for the brand that is used at home and brings it back to the parent. Think about that. The parent asked the child to get a jar of peanut butter without specifying which brand. The child knew where to look and was met with several brand options yet ignored the other brands to reach for the one that is the choice of their family. For the child, that brand IS peanut butter. Throughout our lives advertising influences us in ways we aren't even conscious of.

Focused marketing campaigns influence our notions of product quality, brand selection, and even our language when referring to the products we use daily. Consider items we use almost every day where the brand has become the generic name for all products of the type. How often do you hear someone refer to a tissue as a Kleenex without regard to the brand, or refer to window cleaner as Windex? In some parts of the country, all soft drinks are referred to as Coke. That is the power of advertising in our lives.

Reflection prompts us to examine other ways that our thinking, behaviors, attitudes, and language have been unconsciously shaped by logos, signage, jingles, billboards, newspapers, social media outlets, television, music, movies, and more. Consider the influence of the media on our notions of beauty, body image, relationships, health, success, politics, product quality, and safety. These notions are, in many ways, shaped by focused marketing tactics that pepper children daily. According to Guttman (2020), "In 2018, kids advertising spending amounted to 4.2 billion U.S. dollars worldwide," with an expenditure forecasted to reach "4.6 billion U.S. dollars by 2021, out of which an estimated 1.7 billion is projected to stem from digital advertising formats."

An American Academy of Pediatrics (AAP) policy statement further notes "newer forms of advertising found in mobile and interactive media and smart technologies, often powered by personal data, are more difficult to identify. They do not necessarily occur in a predictable manner and are often integrated into the content" (Radesky et al., 2020). Newer forms of advertising discussed in the policy statement include user-created content (e.g., unboxing videos, toy-play videos, influencers reviewing or using products with sponsorship from companies) on social media platforms, such as TikTok or Instagram, and video-streaming services, such as YouTube. Such content involves commercial content and marketing messages. Commercial content is often inserted as hidden ads, pop-up ads, and ads with incentives, such as free game tokens. Characters in the apps can also encourage in-app purchases in some games.

Streaming-Only Homes
See Fewer/No Commercials

Take a look at this article from GeekWire: "Analysis: Kids in 'Netflix Only' Homes Avoid 230 Hours of Ads a Year" (https://bit.ly/3uG13Ky).

According to this report:

- the average child watches 2.68 hours of TV a day, or almost 980 hours per year;

- one hour of TV contains 14.25 minutes of ads, or 24 percent of airtime; and

- "Netflix only" homes spare kids 230 hours of ads a year, or 9.6 days of ads.

Families who can afford to pay the Netflix subscription fees are put at an advantage in terms of being able to have a seamless viewing experience and avoiding all the TV ads.

Take a mental walk through the grocery store with attention to the placement of milk in the back of the store and sugary cereals at the eye level of children riding in a shopping cart, while the bulk discount brand of cereal is found on the bottom shelf. Notice the placement of candy, gum, and snacks in the checkout line. Note where brand name products are placed and which items are given prime shelf space or stand-alone displays. How much of this intentionally markets products to children?

Consider how advertisements and product placement position consumers of every age. What products, goods, services, or ideas are they attempting to sell, and to whom? The AAP report cited previously contends that children "must be able to discriminate between commercial and noncommercial content and identify advertising's persuasive intent" if we expect them to critically process ads. When students become aware of the intent of product manufacturers, they can become more critical consumers who question and make conscious and informed decisions about their needs and wants.

As technology has become more readily available and children have gained greater and more independent access, the amount of time they spend with tablets, streaming, and television increases. Perhaps of greater concern is that this independent use may be unsupervised by busy adults, leaving even young children to receive these powerful messages with no adult to filter or help interpret what is perceived. Without adult interaction, children are not likely to recognize the attempts to manipulate their desire for the products being shown.

So, how do we equip children to become critical consumers who are able to lift the veil and see the intent behind commercials and advertising campaigns? We begin this series of lessons with a study of texts related to marketing and advertisements.

A few days after reading *Those Shoes* with his class, Dr. Hass introduced the notion of commercials. He asked the students to share a few of their favorite commercials, then they watched a selection together. While watching he made note of their reactions and questions. The general observation was their favorite commercials are the ones that make them laugh. The students pointed out that a commercial for spicy Doritos seems to be made for kids because it includes funny animals.

When he asked the class what the purpose of commercials is, students were quick to note commercials are made to make you want to buy things. Dr. Hass nudged, "How do they do this? What do commercials do to make you want to buy something?"

Thomas: They show you what the thing can do in the commercial. Like, they show how it works and how it's a good thing to have.

Blaize: And they tell lots of stuff about it.

Dr. Hass: What do you mean?

Blaize: They, like, let you know what it is and why it's good.

Dr. Hass: Hmm, do they always do this? I ask because we watched a number of commercials last time and most of them just made us laugh, like the spicy chip commercials where the animals dance.

Blaize: Yeah, but it showed you the chips were spicy because the sloth ate a chip and was like, "AH!"

For Older Students

Cost of Advertising Discussion

The cost of a 30-second commercial for the 2022 Super Bowl was $6.5 million, which equals $217,000 per second. Every second counts.

This opens an opportunity to examine commercials with a focus on editing and mathematics.

Ask students:

- *When developing a commercial, what would you include? Why?*

- *What would make a good commercial?*

- *What would make a bad commercial?*

- *If your commercial were limited to 15 or 30 seconds, how would you determine what to include?*

- *How much time would you devote to each of the things you include?*

- *What research would you have to do to make sure that you are getting the most information out to your audience in a limited amount of time?*

- *What are things you would need to consider to get your message out to the most diverse audience possible?*

Resource: "Super Bowl LVI Commercials Cost $6.5 Million Per Ad," https://bit.ly/3SvjprZ.

For Younger Students

Examining Commercials and Advertising

Young children can learn to look closely to examine the purpose of commercials and advertising and learn to critically examine specific advertisements to become critical consumers (Wright & Laminack, 1982). Through a close examination of advertising with exploration of the language used, the explicit and implicit claims made, and the techniques employed by the campaign, children can recognize how advertising attempts to manipulate their thinking and desires.

Ask students:

- *What language is used in the commercial to convince you to want the product?*

- *Is the commercial promising something to you?*

- *What images in the commercial lead you to want the product?*

- *What is the commercial trying to convince you about?*

Critical Comprehension
Lesson Series

Consuming Critically

These lessons are designed to launch the exploration of both consuming critically (critical thinking about what you buy) and media literacy (critical thinking about the advertising itself). The lesson series begins with the exploration of wants and needs using a picture book to show how advertising campaigns attempt to manipulate buyers to give in to their desires without regard for their needs. The lessons then move to more specific concepts around marketing through an exploration of print advertisements and television commercials. A picture book is used as a springboard to launch inquiry into marketing gender norms of clothing, and the collection closes out with a close look at the principles that drive product placement in grocery stores.

Table of Lessons for Consuming Critically	
LESSON FOCUS	**ANCHOR TEXT**
1. Exploring wants and needs	*Those Shoes* by Maribeth Boelts
2. Print marketing	Print ads
3. Messages in commercials	Vroom commercial
4. Gender bias in clothing	*Sparkle Boy* by Lesléa Newman
5. Product placement/marketing	Grocery Stores and Supermarkets Product Placement Guide from Kuusoft

Note: The blank spaces are an invitation for you to add your own related topics and texts.

Lesson 1: Exploring Wants and Needs
Those Shoes • by Maribeth Boelts

 First Read: Movie Read

This first visit, the "movie read," focuses on taking in the story without interruption (see Chapter 1, p. 21). When a specific shoe becomes the most desired shoe in school, Jeremy longs to have "those shoes." Page by page more and more students come to school sporting a pair, until Jeremy and his classmate, Antonio, appear to be the only two without them. Though Jeremy really wants "those shoes," his grandma reminds him that he needs new winter boots. Jeremy finds a pair at a thrift store and though they are too small, he buys them with his own money hoping they will stretch. When Antonio's shoe comes apart on the playground, Jeremy makes a big decision.

 Second Read: Reading With the Text

Before you begin the second read, offer a summary of the story. Then show the cover.

Ask students: *What makes everyone want these particular shoes so badly?*

Continue reading and pause after Grandma says, "There's no room for 'want' around here—just 'need' . . . And what you *need* are new boots for winter."

Ask students:

* *What is the difference between a "want" and a "need"?*

* *Can you give examples from this story?*

Make a chart of wants and needs and list the examples students generate. Examine their examples for common threads and develop a definition for each term.

Read to the scene where Jeremy's shoe comes apart and Mr. Alfrey offers him a pair of shoes to replace them. Point out the large billboard looming above the buildings beyond the playground.

Consuming Critically

Ask students:

- *Where else have we seen this image? (Show them that the shoe has now been presented on a billboard three times.)*
- *How do these billboards help make that shoe so desirable?*
- *What happens in the story to make everyone want the same shoes?*
- *How does desire grow to the point that everyone wants those shoes?*

Read the next spread.

Ask students:

- *Why are the kids laughing?*
- *What does that laughter reveal about them?*
- *Why is Antonio the only one not laughing?*

Read the next two pages, stopping where "Grandma shakes her head."

Ask students:

- *Does Grandma want Jeremy to have those shoes?*
- *How do we know?*
- *What makes her decide not to buy them for him?*

Read the next three spreads, stopping where Jeremy says, "Sometimes shoes stretch."

Ask students:

- *When Jeremy finds a pair of "those shoes" at a thrift shop, why does he spend his own money to get them even though they are too small?*
- *Why does Grandma permit him to make the purchase even though she knows they do not fit?*

Read to the end of the book.

Ask students:

- *How does Jeremy reach the decision to give up "those shoes"?*
- *What does that show us about the difference between want and need?*

Return Read: Reading Critically

For the return read highlight comments from the second read regarding wants and needs and how our desire for something can be influenced by others.

Ask students:

- *How do companies try to make us want the things they make?*

- *How do these companies send us messages about what it means to "fit in" with a certain crowd or group?*

- *Can you imagine the TV commercial about "those shoes" that Jeremy and his classmates may have seen? What words and images would be used to market them to kids? What about to their parents/caregivers? Who might they have wearing those shoes in the commercial? Why would they have that person wearing those shoes? What sort of things might they tell you about those shoes?*

Design a product, such as a shoe, and a commercial to market it.

Lesson 2: Print Marketing
A collection of print advertisements

FIGURE 7.2

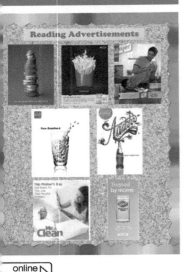

online resources

When selecting print advertisements for this lesson on critical reading, consider the following:

- Is the product clearly featured?
- Does the product or service fall within the realm of experience for your students?
- Is the ad visually appealing?
- Does the language, image, or both present a clear suggestion, message, or promise?
- Are there elements intended to draw the consumer in for a closer look?

First Read: Movie Read

This first visit, the "movie read," focuses on taking in the text without interruption (see Chapter 1, p. 21). Show several print ads marketing items such as toys, clothing, food, cleaning products, and other things that may be of interest to students. For this first read simply have students spend time looking through the ads.

Second Read: Reading With the Text

Before beginning the second read, remind students of the billboards in *Those Shoes*, from Lesson 1, and recap their thoughts on what caused everyone to want "those shoes" so badly.

Have students take a close look at the ads from the first read.

Ask students:

- *What products are being advertised?*
- *What is featured for each product in the ads?*

Now, guide the students to read each ad with attention to the images and the language, noticing messages, suggestions, or promises.

Ask students:

- *What are the advertisers trying to sell?*
- *What messages, suggestions, or promises are presented in the words or the images in these ads?*

- *What do the advertisers want us to think, believe, or feel about the product?*
- *Who are they marketing the product for? How do you know?*

Make a chart listing the products across the top (see Figure 7.3). Under each product list the message, suggestion, or promise for that product.

FIGURE 7.3 Products Chart			
	PRODUCT: HEINZ KETCHUP	**PRODUCT: MR. CLEAN**	**PRODUCT: COCA-COLA**
Message, Suggestion, or Promise	It tastes like fresh tomatoes. They use only fresh tomatoes to make it. No other company does it this way.	Mr. Clean makes cleaning quicker so you can be with your family.	It is refreshing. It makes you happy.

 ## Return Read: Reading Critically

Guide students to examine the message, suggestion, or promise and consider how the advertisers are attempting to position the consumer to think about their product. For example, X brand glass cleaner cuts grime and leaves no streaks. They show a well-dressed person smiling holding a paper towel and a bottle of the product. They want us to think brand X makes it easy.

Ask students:

- *How do these ads position us to think about the product?*
- *How do these advertisers use the images and language to position us to want their product?*
- *What lifestyle is the company promoting? Does the company want us to think about fun, good health, our energy, or something else?*

Place each print ad in the center of a sheet of chart paper. Use the upper left area to name the product. Use the upper right area to list the messages, suggestions, or promises conveyed in the ad. Use the bottom left of the chart to list what the advertisers want us to think, feel, or do. Leave the bottom right area blank for now; it will be filled in later in the lesson (see Figure 7.4).

Consuming Critically

FIGURE 7.4 Critical Read Product Chart	
Product LEGO bricks	**Message/Suggestions/Promise** They are brain food like milk. They are good for your brain.
What the advertiser wants us to think, feel, or do Playing with LEGO bricks makes you smarter.	

Highlight comments from the second read regarding the messages, suggestions, or promises of the advertisers. Recap comments about how the ads are attempting to position us toward the product. Remind students that ads can include an implicit or hidden message that may suggest a product or task is for a particular type of person or group. Return to the print ads and search for hidden messages or suggestions.

Ask students questions, such as the following, related to each ad you show:

- *Does the language or the image in the ad suggest that the product is for girls?*
- *Does the product imply that it takes a man to use it?*
- *Does the product suggest that only men can mow the grass or wash cars?*
- *Does the product imply that only mothers cook, clean the house, or do laundry?*
- *Does the product imply that milk is the best brain food? What does this mean for those who are lactose intolerant?*

This time as you revisit the ads, search for those hidden messages and use the lower right corner of the chart in Figure 7.4 to list them.

Ask students: *Are there any hidden messages in these ads?*

You may find it helpful to view this brief video showing a young Meghan Markle using her voice to prompt Procter & Gamble to change the wording of one of their commercials:

bit.ly/3VIz602

Lesson 3: Messages in Commercials
Vroom commercial
bit.ly/3OTHp6L

 First Read: Movie Read

This first visit, the "movie read," focuses on taking in the text without interruption (see Chapter 1, p. 21). The Vroom commercial in this lesson suggests that car dealerships cater to men and ignore women who are interested in buying a car. The commercial attempts to convince the viewer that if you buy your car through Vroom, women and men are treated equally.

 Second Read: Reading With the Text

Before you begin the second viewing, recap the commercial.

Begin the second read by viewing the commercial and pausing when the woman asks about an SUV with a V8 engine and is ignored by all the salespeople.

Ask students:

- *What is happening here?*

- *Why do you think that is happening?*

Continue viewing and pause at the point when the salesperson says, "Bro, I've got a sick SUV back here that has your name all over it."

Ask students:

- *Now what is happening?*

- *What is the commercial suggesting about buying a car at a dealership?*

- *What is the company's intention?*

Continue the commercial to the end.

Ask students: *What message is the commercial sending to people who want to buy a car through Vroom?*

Summarize students' thinking on a chart for future reference.

Consuming Critically

For Younger Children

Ask students:

- *What is the commercial about?*
- *What are some things you notice about the commercial?*
- *What do you wonder about it?*
- *What is one of your favorite commercials? Why?*

View some of the commercials mentioned by the students and ask similar questions.

 ## Return Read: Reading Critically

Recap the insights recorded on the chart at the conclusion of the previous read. Highlight comments regarding gender bias when buying a car. Watch the commercial and pause at the point when the salesperson says, "Bro, I've got a sick SUV . . ."

Ask students:

- *What does the commercial suggest about the way women and men are treated differently when buying a car at the dealership?*
- *How was the male puppet treated differently than the woman?*
- *Are there any female salespeople at the car dealership in this commercial?*
- *Why would the advertiser show only male salespeople in this commercial?*
- *Did the woman expect the salespeople to be men?*
- *Do you think she expected they would ignore her? Why?*
- *What detail is included in the commercial that reveals she expected their behavior?*

Watch the rest of the commercial.

Ask students:

- *When the scene shifts to the woman standing in front of her house and her SUV is delivered on a truck, why do you think the advertiser has a Black woman salesperson at the delivery?*
- *What message is the commercial sending?*
- *Who is the target market for this commercial?*

For Younger Children

Ask students:

- *Why is there a puppet in the commercial?*

- *What role does the puppet play in the conversation?*

- *How did the salespeople treat the puppet? How is the way they treated the puppet different from the way the woman was treated?*

Guide students to create a new commercial where men and women are treated the same when they make a purchase. They could make stick puppets to perform the commercial.

Return Read Extensions

Examine other commercials.

Ask students:

- *Who is included in the commercial? Who isn't?*

- *Who has power in the commercial?*

- *Who benefits?*

- *What changes could be made to make the commercial more inclusive and equitable?*

Additional Commercials to Explore

- Doritos Super Bowl commercial
  bit.ly/3VDjAlZ

- NFL commercial
  bit.ly/3VH1Whi

- Robo Alive commercial
  bit.ly/3EUhWFR

- Amazon ("Kindness, the Greatest Gift")
  bit.ly/3FdxYfc

Lesson 4: Gender Bias in Clothing
Sparkle Boy • by Leslèa Newman

Teaching guide for *Sparkle Boy* prepared by Lee and Low Publishers:

bit.ly/3ioNqfC

🎥 First Read: Movie Read

This first visit, the "movie read," focuses on taking in the story without interruption (see Chapter 1, p. 21). *Sparkle Boy* celebrates the delight that many children take in things that shimmer, glitter, and sparkle. Although he loves to play with his alphabet blocks, puzzles, and trucks, Casey also wants things that sparkle and shine, such as his sister Jessie's shimmery skirt and her glittery nail polish, and the sparkly bracelets his grandmother wears.

📖 Second Read: Reading With the Text

Before you begin the second read, show the cover and read the title.

Ask students:

- *Do you like to choose the clothes you wear? Why?*

- *Does anyone ever tell you that your choices are inappropriate?*

- *Have you ever been told that something you like is not right for you because it is only for boys? Or only for girls? What did you think? How did you feel? What did you do?*

Point out the shimmer and sparkle embedded in the cover art. Before you read, invite the students to give particular attention to things that attract Casey's attention, Jessie's reaction to his interest, and the response of the adults. As you read, pause in a few places and ask students to share their observations. Create a chart to record what they notice (see Figure 7.6).

FIGURE 7.6 Sparkle Boy Observation Chart		
WHAT ATTRACTS CASEY'S ATTENTION	**WHAT JESSIE SAYS/DOES**	**WHAT THE ADULTS SAY/DO**
The shimmer in Jessie's skirt.	Thinks boys can't have skirts that shimmer.	Mom gets a shimmery skirt Jessie has outgrown and lets Casey wear it.
The sparkle in Jessie's nail polish.	Says boys don't have nail polish and wants it on his toes so his socks will cover it.	Dad says it is not a problem and puts the sparkly nail polish on his fingernails.

Ask students:

- *What attracts Casey's attention?*

- *What do Jessie's comments suggest about her beliefs?*

- *What do the responses and actions of the adults reveal?*

 Return Read: Reading Critically

Begin with a close look at the illustrations. Start with the title page and point out what Casey is wearing in different scenes and the toys he plays with (blocks, puzzles, trucks). Engage students in a discussion about the ideas some people have about toys and clothes as "boy things" or "girl things." Point out that Casey has many "boy things" even though he is attracted to some things that others think of as "girl things."

Ask students:

- *Why do you think that the author and the illustrator feature both "boy things" and "girl things" for Casey?*

- *Who decides which things are for boys or girls?*

- *Are there things that are for girls only? For boys only?*

Guide students to notice that Casey is drawn to the sparkle, glitter, shimmer, and shine of objects. The objects with those qualities in this story happen to be a skirt, nail polish, and a bracelet.

Ask students:

- *How do you think Casey would have reacted if Jessie had worn a t-shirt that shimmered, or played with a toy car that had sparkly headlights?*

- *Would Jessie's reaction have been the same?*

Consuming Critically

Return to the chart and review the items Casey wanted and what attribute he was drawn to. Review Jessie's reaction to his interest and contrast that with the reaction of the adults.

Ask students:

- *Why does Jessie respond the way she does?*

- *Why does Jessie believe that some things are for girls only?*

- *How do you think Jessie feels when Mama says it is OK for Casey to wear a skirt and then brings one of her old ones for him to try on?*

- *Do Jessie's reactions change when Daddy says Casey can have glittery nail polish or when Abuelita gives him a sparkly bracelet? How do you know?*

- *Why do the adults have a reaction that is different from Jessie's?*

- *What causes Jessie's change of attitude at the library?*

Shift from the book to explore the presentation of clothing in department stores. You can do this by either going to a local department store and taking photos to share with students, looking through department store catalogs, or you could go to a local department store's website. Examine what is presented, including the use of color, design, accessories, texture, and materials. Make a chart of the observations (see Figure 7.7).

FIGURE 7.7   Department Store Observation Chart

	GIRLS	BOYS	BOTH/ NEUTRAL
Design	fancy, ruffles, sparkles, glittery, polka dots, floral, short/cropped	less ornate, plain, camouflage	plaid, stripes
Color	pinks, purples	green, blue, brown, orange	red, beige, white, black
Texture	silky, smooth, thin	thick, tough, durable	
Material	silk, satin, chiffon, polyester	denim, corduroy	cotton

Consuming
Critically

Ask students:

- *What colors are used more frequently in clothing for girls? For boys?*

- *Which colors are used most frequently for both boys and girls?*

- *What do these colors suggest about boys? Girls?*

- *What ideas are associated with those colors?*

- *What design features appear on girl clothes that are missing from clothes designed for boys? And on boy clothes that are missing from girl clothes? What does that suggest?*

- *Which materials are used more often in clothing for girls? For boys? For both?*

- *What does the choice of particular fabrics or materials suggest about boys? Girls?*

- *What do these suggest about how some people define boys and girls?*

- *How can clothing sections in stores be reimagined to be more inclusive?*

Lesson 5: Product Placement/Marketing

For this lesson, rely on a collection of images of various aisles and shelves at a local grocery store or a virtual visit to a local grocery store. These might include photos showing the placement of cereal, cookies, soft drinks, juice, dairy products, bread, chips and snacks, the bakery, or the shelves at the checkout station.

 ## First Read: Movie Read

This first visit, the "movie read," focuses on taking in the images without interruption (see Chapter 1, p. 21).

Second Read: Reading With the Text

For this read, review all the images from the grocery store looking closely to observe content, organization, design, and displays.

Ask students:

- *What do you notice?*
- *What items are presented?*
- *What are you wondering?*

Make note of their wonderings and observations.

Return Read: Reading Critically

Before you begin the critical read, engage the students in a brief conversation about their knowledge of where products are located in the grocery stores they are most familiar with.

Ask students:

- *What do you notice on the shelves when you are waiting in the checkout area at the grocery store?*
- *Where do you usually find milk and eggs and cheese?*
- *When you are looking for cereal, which shelf would you find sugary cereal on?*
- *Which shelf would you find all-natural and organic cereal on?*

Consuming Critically

- *Are products placed in the same areas in most of the grocery stores you have been in?*

- *Where would you find items from your own culture? Can you find these items in all the grocery stores you have been in?*

Read the two introductory paragraphs of the article "Grocery Stores and Supermarkets Product Placement Guide" by Kuusoft (https://bit .ly/3yTxCY6) for a close examination of the rationale and psychology behind the decisions regarding product placement and sales strategies for grocery stores.

Ask students:

- *Who is the author writing this for?*

- *What audience does she have in mind?*

- *Do you think she expected shoppers to read this article?*

Read the section under the first heading: *What is in-store product placement?*

Ask students:

- *How is product placement different from just putting things on the shelves?*

- *How does that make a difference for the store? The company? The customer?*

Read the section under the second heading: *Factors to take into consideration.*

Ask students: *What factors should a store manager consider when planning for product placement?*

List the factors as students name them. Take time to talk about what each one means and how it may impact sales. For instance, students may need guidance with considering the customer base's demographics, or the use of mirrors and lighting.

Read the section under the third heading: *Tips for smart supermarket product placement.*

Make a chart to record suggestions and add the reason for each (see Figure 7.9). As you read through this segment, pause after each of the six tips to record new insights.

Consuming
Critically

FIGURE 7.9 Suggestions Chart	
SUGGESTIONS FOR MANAGERS	**REASON FOR THE SUGGESTION**
Example: Place staple items at the back of the store.	Example: People want them and will have to go through the store passing all the other products to get them.
"Eye level is the buy level"	Put things kids like on the shelf they will see when walking with their parents or riding in the shopping cart. Put things adults like up high where they see them as they walk down the aisles.
Sales and marketing to put the product in your customers' minds before they come to the store	Add pictures of things you know people like in the advertisements so they will come to your store looking for them.
Encourage impulse buying by placing things at the checkout	Put candy and chips and toys and magazines and gum on the shelves at the checkout so people will pick them up while they wait in line.
Cross-selling and up-selling	Put things on the shelf that go together so people will get them all at once, e.g., picnic supplies.
Endcap displays	Use the shelves on the end of the aisle to get people's attention and make them notice the items you want to sell.

Ask students:

- *What do you know now that you didn't know before we read this article?*

- *What surprised you most about how these decisions are made?*

- *What will you look for the next time you visit the grocery store?*

- *How will you think about grocery shopping differently?*

Bring in several print ads from different local grocery stores. Cut out images of the items being advertised (cereal, canned vegetables, milk, eggs, coffee, toothpaste, etc.). Be sure you have a good variety of things found throughout a typical grocery store.

Consuming Critically

Begin with a recap of insights from the previous readings. Engage students in a conversation as if you are planning to open a new grocery store. For this conversation, they are the managers for that store and will be responsible for product placement. Give each group a collection of items you have cut out of the print ads.

Ask students:

- *Where would you place each of these items in your grocery store?*

- *Why?*

Ask each group to share the plan they made and use the information from the article to support the decisions they made. Combine information from all groups to create a plan for a grocery store.

Use a chart sheet to lay out the floor plan of a grocery store. Using the decisions made by each group, place the products "in the store" on the floor plan. As a whole group, return to the insights from previous readings and "walk through" your store. Discuss the rationale for the placement of each product and negotiate any changes.

Ask students:

- *How will this affect what you notice when you visit the grocery store next?*

- *How can you use this knowledge to help your family be more conscious and critical shoppers?*

- *How can this information help you avoid impulse buying at the grocery store?*

Additional Resources

NAMLE (National Association for Media Literacy Education) and these core principles may be a resource:

- bit.ly/3Un98xZ

- bit.ly/3OMYwY0

- bit.ly/3AUnTBd

READING FOR ACTION

After reading the world critically, invite students to reflect on what they have learned and how their thinking has changed.

Ask students: *What will we do with our new insights? How can we take action?*

SOME IDEAS/SUGGESTIONS

- How can you be more critical when making decisions about the products you buy?
- How can you consider who is being targeted in advertising as you make decisions as a consumer?
- How might you reimagine advertisements to be more equitable?
- How can you avoid being manipulated by information in the world around you?
- Contact the store manager with suggestions for products to include.
- Offer the store manager ideas about where to locate certain items.
- Suggest the addition of a comment box to be placed in the store for shoppers to make suggestions or share ideas for products to add to the shelves.
- Offer the store manager suggestions for making products more accessible to customers in a wheelchair.

Conclusion

Your Turn

Our aim in writing this book was to help expand the notion of teaching children to read beyond literal levels of understanding to reading with a critical stance and questioning the word and the world (Freire & Macedo, 1987). We believe children have the right to be critical consumers of text and messages in the world around them; to be curious, informed, and accepting of other perspectives and experiences; and to actively seek justice, equity, and belonging.

Now we invite you to pause and consider how your thinking has changed. When you read a favorite book, do you notice things you have never considered before? Do you find yourself questioning the author's intent or message? Do you read with an eye for the missing perspective? Do you leave with new insights and meaning?

We mentioned early on that this work begins with each of us. Now that you have spent time engaged in critical self-reflection, it's time to begin thinking about next steps, your daily teaching, and the units and lessons that remain ahead of you. We hope you are inspired to implement these lessons for critical comprehension in your classroom. We acknowledge that we cannot include a lesson on every topic, perspective, and voice in the pages of this book. This is why we invite you to apply the instructional framework from this book to design a typical unit for your grade level.

Planning for Critical Comprehension

To begin, we walk you through our process in finding the focus and creating the lessons for one of the chapters in this book. For this example, think of each chapter as a unit of study consisting of a series of lessons. As we map out our process on the left side of the planning document that follows, use the right side to map out a unit for your own classroom.

As you plan, keep in mind the critical questions listed for thinking beyond a single text (Figure 8.1).

FIGURE 8.1   Critical Questions

CRITICAL QUESTIONS
For Thinking Beyond a Single Text

- How does the text position the reader?
- Who is included or featured in the text/image? How are they represented? Why? Who benefits? Who is harmed?
- What information is featured? Is it presented as "the" truth, or does it make clear there are other perspectives to consider? Who benefits from this portrayal of information? Who is harmed or made invisible?
- Who/what is excluded from the text? Why? How does this exclusion position who/what is included? Why? Who benefits? Who is harmed?
- What are the counter narratives?
- What could be a more accurate/complete representation of the story? Where might I find those alternate perspectives?
- What questions might an alternate perspective answer?

DEVELOPING CHAPTER 3	DEVELOPING MY UNIT OF STUDY
Focus: Examining perspective	**Focus:**
What are some possible texts that could be part of this chapter or unit of study? Why?	**What are some possible texts that could be part of this chapter or unit of study? Why?**
• *Zoom* by Istvan Banyai • *Duck! Rabbit!* by Amy Krouse Rosenthal • *The True Story of the Three Little Pigs!* by Jon Scieszka • *Hey, Little Ant* by Phillip and Hannah Hoose • *Jamaica's Find* by Juanita Havill • *Last Stop on Market Street* by Matt de la Peña • *The Other Side* by Jacqueline Woodson • *Two Bad Ants* by Chris VanAllsburg • *They All Saw a Cat* by Brendan Wenzel • *Rosie's Walk* by Pat Hutchins • *Apt. 3* by Ezra Jack Keats • *Mirror Mirror* by Marilyn Singer This collection includes books to introduce the concept of perspective and examining multiple perspectives, as well as more complex notions, such as the role of power and perspective and how other perspectives may influence us.	

DEVELOPING CHAPTER 3	DEVELOPING MY UNIT OF STUDY
What are possible questions to ask and lessons to develop? • What books might serve as mirrors or windows (Bishop, 1990) for students? • Whose perspectives tend to be included? Whose are often excluded? Why? • What counternarratives can I include to expand perspectives? • How can I build off previous learning and student inquiry? • What other ways can I center students in teaching and learning? • How does this align with the standards? • What are the intended learning outcomes? • How can I integrate ELA and content learning? • What vocabulary needs to be taught? • How might these lessons help develop future lessons to explore the perspectives of historically marginalized groups to help students broaden perspectives, challenge stereotypes, and expand their understanding of the past and the present? • How does the author's/illustrator's craft contribute to the construction of meaning?	**What are possible questions to ask and lessons to develop?**
What work do I need to do first to become more critically conscious about the topic? • Develop a clear understanding of the difference between perspective and point of view. Too often they are used interchangeably but are in fact quite different. • Consider how to lead students to recognize whose perspective is featured and how to reframe the story from another perspective. • Consider how to layer texts to shift from basic to more complex notions of perspective. • Revisit the books and materials typically used and consider whose perspective is included or excluded. Consider how to diversify the materials selected to ensure students have both mirrors and windows (Bishop, 1990). • Consider whose perspectives tend to be included or excluded. • Reflect on ways to include multiple perspectives. • Seek counternarratives.	**What work do I need to do first to become more critically conscious about the topic?**

(Continued)

(Continued)

DEVELOPING CHAPTER 3	DEVELOPING MY UNIT OF STUDY
• Think about ways to consider the perspectives students bring. • Explore how to lead students to recognize and appreciate other perspectives. • Reflect on how to create space for students to share their perspectives openly. • Seek additional reading and learning opportunities.	
What other resources might be useful for exploring this topic? • A collection of fairy tales to reconstruct from a new perspective after reading *The True Story of the Three Little Pigs!* by Scieszka. • A collection of art that may be interpreted differently when viewed from different perspectives. • A collection of ads that advertise a similar product in different ways. • A series of movie titles or movie posters that are about the same topic or story.	**What other resources might be useful for exploring this topic?**

Now let's start creating individual lessons for the unit.

CREATING A LESSON FOR PERSPECTIVE CHAPTER/UNIT	CREATING A LESSON FOR MY UNIT OF STUDY
Focus: Widening the lens to reveal more	**Focus:**
What are some possible texts that could be used for a lesson on widening the lens? • *Zoom* by Istvan Banyai • *ReZoom* by Istvan Banyai • *Across Town* by Sara • *Flotsam* by David Wiesner • *The Other Side* by Istvan Banyai • *The Red Book* by Barbara Lehman • *They All Saw a Cat* by Brendan Wenzel	**What are some possible texts that could be used for a lesson on . . . ?**
What are some possible activities and questions to consider while reading *Zoom* by Istvan Banyai? • Given that the text is a wordless picture book, provide opportunities for students to describe what they see in each illustration and what they infer is happening in the illustration.	**What are some possible activities and questions to consider while reading . . .**

CREATING A LESSON FOR PERSPECTIVE CHAPTER/UNIT	CREATING A LESSON FOR MY UNIT OF STUDY
• Engage in shared or interactive writing to create the text to align with the illustrations for the book. • Use hands or cardboard paper towel or toilet paper tubes to make a spyglass to look through and zoom in on an object. Encourage students to describe the object with and without the spyglass. • Invite students to make their own Zoom books to widen and narrow the focus on a particular object or scene.	
What are possible ideas for reading with the text (second read)? What are possible questions to ask students? • What do you see? • What do you not see? • What are you thinking? • What are you wondering?	**What are possible ideas for reading with the text (second read)? What are possible questions to ask students?**
What are possible ideas for reading critically (return read)? What are possible questions to ask students? • Why do you think different people had different ideas about what the images represent? • Where do you think those ideas came from? • What would lead different people to interpret the images differently? • Who do you think would have an advantage in interpreting the images as farm scenes? As a magazine cover? • Who do you think might find it hard to imagine the images as farm scenes or as a scene on a magazine cover? • How did the different perspectives in each image influence your interpretation of the images? • What difference does it make to read an image or a text from different perspectives?	**What are possible ideas for reading critically (return read)? What are possible questions to ask students?**

CREATING A LESSON FOR PERSPECTIVE CHAPTER/UNIT	CREATING A LESSON FOR MY UNIT OF STUDY
Focus: Exploring multiple perspectives	**Focus**:
What are some possible texts that could be used for a lesson on exploring multiple perspectives? • *The Other Side* by Jacqueline Woodson • *Mirror Mirror: A Book of Reverso Poems* by Marilyn Singer • *Follow Follow: A Book of Reverso Poems* by Marilyn Singer • *Look! Look! Look!* by Tana Hoban	**What are some possible texts that could be used for a lesson on . . . ?**
What are some possible activities and questions to consider while reading *The Other Side*? • Discuss boundaries, barriers, and restrictions in general and then more specifically. • Discuss the purpose of a fence. • Revisit the use of metaphor. • Build background knowledge about the segregation era and Jim Crow laws. • Discuss the characters' actions, motives, and feelings. • Compare and contrast the actions, motives, and feelings of the children and adults. • Notice how the characters change and what factors influenced this change. • Ask students to consider how they can take action to make a difference in someone's life. • Do an author study of Jacqueline Woodson.	**What are some possible activities and questions to consider while reading . . .**
What are possible ideas for reading with the text (second read)? What are possible questions to ask students? • What do you notice? Wonder? • Why does the girl initially tell Annie she can't jump rope with them? • Why don't the girls speak? Discuss notions of feeling silenced. • How do the characters' perspectives change at the end of the story? What causes this shift? • Examine the illustrations. Give particular attention to illustrations that spread across the center of the book and note the placement of images.	**What are possible ideas for reading with the text (second read)? What are possible questions to ask students?**

CREATING A LESSON FOR PERSPECTIVE CHAPTER/UNIT	CREATING A LESSON FOR MY UNIT OF STUDY
What are possible ideas for reading critically (return read)? What are possible questions to ask students? • How is the fence a metaphor for racism in the United States both past and present? • What are other examples of fences that create barriers for some? How do those fences empower some and harm others? • How can we mend or take down those fences? • Invite students to create an artist's representation of the fence as a symbol for barriers or inequities. • Discuss the famous Clark doll study. • Connect the notion of the fence as a barrier with other limitations and restrictions during Jim Crow. Discuss how systemic racism advantages some while oppressing others.	**What are possible ideas for reading critically (return read)? What are possible questions to ask students?**

Now that you have read an example of our process for developing one chapter and two lessons, we invite you to use a similar process to plan for a unit or topic you teach using the instructional framework from this book. Review the standards and the curriculum for your grade level and consider how you could reimagine the curriculum to include reading with the text (second read) and reading critically (return read).

For example, you may typically explore the water cycle in science and communities in social studies. What if you develop a unit that critically examines the two together? You might consider questions like the following:

• Why is water important for all communities?

• Why did communities historically develop near water?

• How does the water cycle impact a community?

• How did technology and innovation make it possible for communities to develop in areas without a river or lake nearby?

• Do all people have equal access to clean water? Why?

• What factors influence who gets access to water and who doesn't?

• What responsibility does a community upstream have for the quality of the water that flows into a community downstream?

• How do the actions of people affect the quality of water and access to water?

Now consider how to integrate the science and social studies standards with the ELA standards and curriculum. There will be opportunities for reading and research using stories and poems, fiction and nonfiction, reports, articles, and blogs. There will be opportunities for listening to podcasts and viewing videos. There will be opportunities for reading and conducting interviews, polls, and surveys. There will be opportunities for developing consciousness about water conversation and writing passionate pleas for protecting watersheds and access to clean drinking water. There will be opportunities for writing and creating poems, letters, blogs, posters, public service announcements, and music as students are moved by knowledge and insight. There will be opportunities for data collection and analysis of family water use, including record keeping and observation notes. There will be stories about swimming, fear of water, boating, losing an item in a stream, thunderstorms, hurricanes, puddles, and more.

In the chart that follows you will find that we have brainstormed a list of possible resources for this study. Additionally, we offer suggestions in each column for the first resource to spark your thinking. Now we invite you to select one or more of the additional resources and have a go at brainstorming ideas to complete the empty boxes.

TEXT	SCIENCE	SOCIAL STUDIES	ELA	TAKING ACTION
We Are Water Protectors by Carole Lindstrom Summary: An Ojibwe girl learns from her grandmother about protecting our planet, and the effort to protect the water supply of her people from the "black snake." This story reflects various Indigenous groups leading movements in North America to protect the right to clean water and demonstrates	Learn about how water is necessary for survival. Study watersheds and the harm of human impact. What are different examples of water pollution? Explore how oil or pollution gets into water sources. How is it harmful? Where are pipelines located? Who gets to decide where they go? Who benefits? Who is harmed?	Locate North Dakota and South Dakota on a map. Learn about the Dakota Access Pipeline and the NoDAPL protests to protect the water on Indigenous lands. Learn more about the Standing Rock Sioux Tribe. Make connections to current events and historical events. Explore access to clean water around the globe.	Explore theme and symbolism. What does the black snake represent? Explain the influence of cultural and historical context on characters, setting, and plot development. Create a text set with books related to water, such as *A Long Walk to Water* by Linda Sue Park, *Nya's Long Walk to Water* by Linda Sue Park, and *The Water Princess* by Susan Verde.	Research where the water you drink (at home or school) comes from. What actions can be taken to protect our water supplies? Why were the Standing Rock Sioux Tribe and other people protesting the Dakota Access Pipeline? Would you ever join a protest like the one on the Standing Rock Sioux Reservation? Why or why not?

TEXT	SCIENCE	SOCIAL STUDIES	ELA	TAKING ACTION
the social responsibility all people hold toward safeguarding our environment.	Research how we get gasoline we use for fuel.		Learn more about the author Carole Lindstrom.	If a pipeline was planned to go through your community, what would you do?
Young Water Protectors by Aslan Tudor, Kelly Tudor, and Jason Eaglespeaker				
View the video "One Year at Standing Rock" to learn about a teenage girl's experience as one of the original protesters. bit.ly/3OP8wQm				
View "Stand Up/ Stand N Rock," a protest song led by Native rapper Supaman. bit.ly/3XNuSGc				
Read the article "Signpost From Standing Rock Shows the Power of Solidarity." bit.ly/3ukrWDb				
Read the article "A Short History of the U.S. Government's Relationship with Native Americans." bit.ly/3ucvkjs				
Read the article "Army Corps of Engineers Rules Against Planned Dakota Access Pipeline Route." bit.ly/3inf3FU				

(Continued)

(Continued)

TEXT	SCIENCE	SOCIAL STUDIES	ELA	TAKING ACTION
Read the article "Final Leg of Dakota Access Project Halted, Yet Neither Side Calls It Quits." bit.ly/3OP6GPr				

Take a fresh look at your classroom library. Consider how critical examination of one book about the water cycle could lead to further reading about access to water in various communities. As a result, your classroom library becomes more vibrant and alive as you and your students begin to realize how reading critically broadens and deepens our insights and our questions. New questions prompt further reading and research. New information ignites the mind and the urge to create through writing, art, music, dance, drama, speech, and more.

A Call to Action

The time is now. If we seek a better world for the next generation, it is our responsibility to take action. "Without action, there can be no change" (Hass, 2020, p. 149). The decisions we make every day about what we include (and exclude), whose voices and stories are centered (and silenced or ignored), and the way we create space for critical awareness and curiosity can be transformative. By centering children as agentive learners who question texts, authors, and authority, who seek multiple perspectives to weave a more complete tapestry of truth, and who critique and respond to injustices, we empower them to be the change. Reading critically positions us with the power to make informed decisions to advocate for equity and justice. We can take action and be part of the change. Or we can choose inaction and be complicit in a system that advantages some and disadvantages others. People have risked their lives to learn to read and write and fight for more equitable education, freedom, and a better life. This work begins with you. Be brave to be vulnerable.

Consider working with a group of colleagues who are also interested in doing this work. Like the three of us, you can support and challenge each other to dig deeper and grow. We acknowledge that as humans we are flawed and thus, we won't get it all right. We are learning too. We hope that you will share your journey with other educators and with us.

References

Adichie, C. (2009). *The danger of a single story* [Video]. TED Conferences. https://www.ted.com/talks/chimamanda_ngozi_adichie_the_danger_of_a_single_story?language=en

Alexander, M. (2010). *The new Jim Crow: Mass incarceration in the age of colorblindness*. The New Press.

Amodio, D. M., & Devine, P. G. (2006). Stereotyping and evaluation in implicit race bias: Evidence for independent constructs and unique effects on behavior. *Journal of Personality and Social Psychology, 91*(4), 652–661.

Annie E. Casey Foundation. (n.d.). *Parental incarceration*. https://www.aecf.org/topics/parental-incarceration?gclid=CjwKCA-jw682TBhATEiwA9crl3wEBYFqNXK6qG-P8HyausdtJ7g5PVCXGWsBtoSs_V2GQnTJ-vFZEnCRoCRoIQAvD_BwE

Au, K. (1980). Participation structures in a reading lesson with Hawaiian children: Analysis of culturally appropriate instructional event. *Anthropology & Education Quarterly, 11*(2), 91–115.

Baker-Bell, A., Tamara, B., & Johnson, L. (2017). The pain and the wounds: A call for critical race English education in the wake of racial violence. *English Education, 49*(2), 116–129.

Bell, D. (2018). *Faces at the bottom of the well: The permanence of racism*. Basic Books.

Bell, D. A. (1976). Serving two masters: Integration ideals and client interests in school desegregation litigation. *Yale Law Journal, 85*(4), 470–516.

Bian, L., Leslie, S., & Cimpian, A. (2017). Gender stereotypes about intellectual ability emerge early and influence children's interests. *Science, 355*(6323), 389–391.

Bian, L., Leslie, S. J., & Cimpian, A. (2018). Evidence of bias against girls and women in contexts that emphasize intellectual ability. *American Psychologist, 73*(9), 1139–1153.

Bishop, R. S. (1990). Mirrors, windows, and sliding glass doors. *Perspectives: Choosing and Using Books for the Classroom, 6*(3), ix–xi.

Bomer, R., & Bomer, K. (2001). *For a better world: Reading and writing for social action*. Heinemann.

Boutte, G. S. (2008). Beyond the illusion of diversity: How early childhood teachers can promote social justice. *Social Studies, 99*(4), 165–173.

Boyd, F. B., Causey, L. L., & Galda, L. (2015). Culturally diverse literature: Enriching variety in an era of Common Core State Standards. *The Reading Teacher, 68*(5), 378–387.

Brophy, J., & Alleman, J. (2009). Meaningful social studies for elementary students. *Teachers and Teaching, 15*(3), 357–376.

Brown, B. (Host). (2021, November 24). The anatomy of trust [Audio podcast episode]. Brené Brown. https://brenebrown.com/podcast/the-anatomy-of-trust/

Bullock, R. T. (2021, August 10). Name discrimination is one of the first types of racism kids face. WRAL News. https://www.wral.com/name-discrimination-is-one-of-the-first-types-of-racism-kids-face/19819845/

Campano, G., Ghiso, M. P., & Welch, B. (2016) *Partnering with immigrant communities: Action through literacy.* Teachers College Press.

Casambre, N. J. (1982). The impact of American education in the Philippines. *Educational Perspectives, 21*(4), 7–14.

Christ, T., & Sharma, S. A. (2018). Searching for mirrors: Preservice teachers' journey towards more culturally relevant pedagogy. *Reading Horizons, 57*(1), 55–73.

Christensen, L. (n.d.). *Warriors don't cry: Acting for justice.* Rethinking Schools. Retrieved July 20, 2022, from https://rethinkingschools.org/articles/warriors-don-t-cry-acting-for-justice/

Comber, B., & Simpson, A. (2001). *Negotiating critical literacies in classrooms.* Lawrence Erlbaum Associates, Inc.

Comber, B., Thompson, P., & Wells, M. (2001). Critical literacy finds a "place": Writing and social action in a low-income Australian grade 2/3 classroom. *The Elementary School Journal, 101*(4), 451–464.

Conaway, W., & Bethune, S. (2015). Implicit bias and first name stereotypes: What are the implications for online instruction? *Online Learning, 19*(3), 162–178.

Corbett, C., & Hill, C. (2015). *Solving the equation: The variables for women's success in engineering and computing.* AAUW. Retrieved August 2, 2022, from https://www.aauw.org/app/uploads/2020/03/Solving-the-Equation-report-nsa.pdf

Craft, J. (2019). *New kid.* Quill Tree Books.

Crawford, G. D. (2019). "Fake tribes" can threaten federally recognized ones, genealogist says. *Tahlequah Daily Press.* https://www.tahlequahdailypress.com/news/fake-tribes-can-threaten-federally-recognized-ones-genealogist-says/article_79c715a4-f9ac-5bba-8871-f1599342d07d.html

Crenshaw, K. (1989). Demarginalizing the intersection of race and sex: A Black feminist critique of antidiscrimination doctrine, feminist theory and antiracist policies. *University of Chicago Legal Forum, 1989*(1), 139–167.

Cully, C. F. (Host). (2022, March 8). How kids can develop a healthy body image. [Audio podcast episode]. In *Dear Highlights.* Blubrry. https://blubrry.com/dear_highlights/84080232/how-can-kids-develop-a-healthy-body-image/

Davis, G. (2019). What 2.7M YouTube ads reveal about gender bias in marketing. *Think with Google.*

Davis, G. (2022). *Creator's checklist to disrupt gender bias in film and television.* Geena Davis Institute on Gender in Media.

Demoiny, S. B., & Ferraras-Stone, J. (2018). Critical literacy in elementary social studies: Juxtaposing historical master and counter narratives in picture books. *Social Studies, 109*(2), 64–73.

Derman-Sparks, L. (2016). *Guide for selecting anti-bias children's books.* Social Justice Books. https://socialjusticebooks.org/guide-for-selecting-anti-bias-childrens-books/

Derman-Sparks, L., & Olsen Edwards, J. (2020). *Anti-bias education for young children and ourselves* (2nd ed.). NAEYC.

Dunbar-Ortiz, R., Mendoza, J., & Reese, D. (2019). *An indigenous peoples' history of the United States for young people.* Beacon Press.

Duvernay, A. & Moran, A. (2016) *13th* [Film]. Netflix.

Edbuild. (2020). *Fault lines: America's most segregated school district borders.* https://edbuild.org/content/fault-lines/full-report.pdf

Egalite, A. J., & Kisida, B. (2017). The effects of teacher match on students' academic perceptions and attitudes. *Education Evaluation and Policy Analysis, 40*(1), 59–81.

Enriquez, G. (2021). Foggy mirrors, tiny windows, and heavy doors: Beyond diverse books towards meaningful literacy instruction. *The Reading Teacher, 75*(1), 103–106.

Erwin, P. G. (2006). Children's evaluative stereotypes of masculine, feminine, and androgynous first names. *The Psychological Record, 56,* 513–519.

Feltman, C. (2009). *The thin book of trust: An essential primer for building trust at work.* Thin Book Publishing Co.

Fernández, S. (2017, February 1). Schools in the city of Syracuse see no integration in sight. *The Daily Orange.* https://dailyorange.com/2017/02/schools-in-the-city-of-syracuse-see-no-integration-in-sight/

Figlio, D. N. (2005). *Names, expectations and the Black-white test score gap.* NBER Working Paper Series.

Freire, P. (2000). *Pedagogy of the oppressed* (30th anniv. ed.; M. B. Ramos, Trans.). Continuum.

Freire, P., & Macedo, D. (1987). *Literacy: Reading the word and the world.* Bergin & Garvey.

Glaze, L. E. & Maruschak, L. M. (2010). *Parents in prison and their minor children.* US Department of Justice Statistics.

Greenwald, A. G., & Banaji, M. R. (2017). The implicit revolution: Reconceiving the relation between conscious and unconscious. *American Psychologist, 72*(9), 861–871.

Guttman, A. (2020). *Spending on advertising to children worldwide from 2012 to 2021.* Statista. Retrieved July 17, 2022, from https://www.statista.com/statistics/750865/kids-advertising-spending-worldwide/

Hammond, Z. (2015). *Culturally responsive teaching and the brain: Promoting authentic engagement and rigor among culturally and linguistically diverse students.* Corwin.

Hannah-Jones, N. (2021). *The 1619 project: A new origin story.* Random House.

Hass, C. (2020). *Social justice talk: Strategies for teaching critical awareness.* Heinemann.

Humphries, T. (1977). *Communicating across cultures (deaf-hearing) and language learning* [Doctoral dissertation]. Union Institute and University, Cincinnati, OH.

Janks, H. (1993). *Language and position: Critical language awareness.* Hodder & Stoughton.

Janks, H. (2010). *Literacy and power.* Routledge.

Janks, H. (2012). The importance of critical literacy. *English Teaching: Practice and Critique, 11*(1), 150–163.

Janks, H. (2014). *Doing critical literacy: Texts and activities for students and teachers.* Routledge.

Jones, S. (2006). *Girls, social class and literacy: What teachers can do to make a difference.* Heinemann.

Keene, E., & Zimmerman, S. (2007). *Mosaic of thought.* Heinemann.

Kendi, I. X. (2019). *How to be an antiracist.* One World.

Kleinrock, L. (2021). *Start here, start now: A guide to antibias and antiracist work in your school community.* Heinemann.

Kucsera, J., & Orfield, G. (2014). *New York State's extreme segregation: Inequality, inaction and a damaged future.* The Civil Rights Project. https://civilrightsproject.ucla.edu/research/k-12-education/integration-and-diversity/ny-norflet-report-placeholder/Kucsera-New-York-Extreme-Segregation-2014.pdf

Ladson-Billings, G. (2014). Culturally relevant pedagogy 2.0: a.k.a. the remix. *Harvard Educational Review, 84*(1), 74–84.

Ladson-Billings, G. (2021). *Critical race theory in education: A scholar's journey.* Teachers College Press.

Laminack, L. (2019). *The ultimate read-aloud resource* (2nd ed.). Scholastic.

Laminack, L., & Kelly, K. (2019). *Reading to make a difference: Using literature to think deeply, speak freely, and take action.* Heinemann.

Lane, H. (1992). *The mask of benevolence: Disabling the deaf community.* Knopf.

Leitich Smith, C. (2021). *Video interview with Colorín Colorado.* https://www.colorincolorado.org/videos/meet-authors/cynthia-leitich-smith

Lipkin, G. (2018). Exploring equity issues: Teaching kids about identity and bias. *Anti-Defamation League,* 1–6.

Love, B. (2021). *Lessons in liberation: An abolitionist toolkit for educators.* AK Press.

Luke, A., & Freebody, P. (1997). Shaping the social practices of reading. In S. Muspratt, A. Luke, & P. Freebody (Eds.), *Constructing critical literacies: Teaching and learning textual practice* (pp. 185–225). Hampton Press.

Luke, A., & Freebody, P. (1999). Further notes on the four resources model. *Reading Online, 3,* 1–6.

Manvell, L. (2022). Part one: From bystander to ally—The roles we play in bullying. *School Climate.* Retrieved July 20, 2022, from https://schoolclimate.com/2013/04/17/part-one-from-bystander-to-ally-the-roles-we-play-in-bullying/

McDaniel, C. (2004). Critical literacy: A questioning stance and the possibility for change. *The Reading Teacher, 57,* 472–481.

McDavid, J. W., & Harari, H. (1966). Stereotyping of names and popularity in grade-school children. *Child Development, 37*(2), 453–459.

McLaughlin, M., & DeVoogd, G. L. (2004a). *Critical literacy: Enhancing students' comprehension of text.* Scholastic.

McLaughlin, M., & DeVoogd, G. L. (2004b). Critical literacy as comprehension: Expanding reader response. *Journal of Adult & Adolescent Literacy, 48*(1), 52–62.

McLemore, L. (2018). *Historical perspective or racism in* Little House on the Prairie? Little House on the Prairie. https://littlehouse-ontheprairie.com/historical-perspective-or-racism-in-little-house-on-the-prairie/

Mendoza, J., & Reese, D. (2001). Examining multicultural picture books for the early childhood classroom: Possibilities and pitfalls. *Early Childhood Research & Practice, 3*(2), 1–32.

Moll, L. C., Amanti, C., Neff, D., & Gonzalez, N. (1992). Funds of knowledge for teaching: Using a qualitative approach to connect homes and classrooms. *Theory into Practice, 31*(2), 132–141.

Muhammad, G. (2020). *Cultivating genius: An equity framework for culturally and historically responsive literacy.* Scholastic.

Mulcahy, M. (2021). *Unearthed map from 1919 became precursor to federal housing programs segregating Syracuse.* CNY Central. https://cnycentral.com/news/the-map-segregated-syracuse/unearthed-map-from-1919-became-precursor-to-federal-housing-programs-segregating-syracuse

Noe-Bustamante, L., Gonzalez-Barrera A., Edwards, K., Mora, L., & Hugo Lopez, M. (2021). *Majority of Latinos say skin color impacts opportunity in America and shapes daily life.* Pew Research Center. Retrieved July 12, 2022, from https://www.pewresearch.org/hispanic/2021/11/04/majority-of-latinos-say-skin-color-impacts-opportunity-in-america-and-shapes-daily-life/

Norris, K. E. L. (2020). Using the read-aloud and picture books for social justice. *Kappa Delta Pi Record, 56*(4), 183–187.

O'Brien, J. (2001). Children reading critically: A local history. In B. Comber & A. Simpson (Eds.), *Negotiating critical literacies in classrooms* (pp. 41–60). Lawrence Erlbaum.

Radesky, J., Reid Chassiakos, Y., Ameenuddin, N., & Navsaria, D. (2020). Digital advertising to children. *Pediatrics, 146*(1), e20201681.

Reading Rockets. (2015, January 30). *Mirrors, windows and sliding glass doors* [video]. YouTube. https://www.youtube.com/watch?v=_AAu58SNSyc

Reese, D. (2016). *Mirrors, windows, sliding glass doors, and curtains.* Writing Native American Characters Master Class. https://writingtheother.com

Reese, D. (2019a). An indigenous critique of whiteness in children's literature. Arbuthnot Honor Lecture. *Children & Libraries,* 3–11.

Reese, D. (2019b). Highly Recommended: FRY BREAD: A NATIVE AMERICAN FAMILY STORY. American Indians in Children's Literature blog. https://americanindiansinchildrensliterature.blogspot.com/search?q=Fry+Bread+update

Rhodes, M. (2017). Combatting stereotypes: How to talk to your children. *The Conversation.* https://theconversation.com/combatting-stereotypes-how-to-talk-to-your-children-71929

Roberts, L. M., Nelson, R., Purcell, C., & Harbin, B. (2020). Teaching beyond the gender binary in the university classroom. Vanderbilt Center for Teaching.

https://cft.vanderbilt.edu/guides-sub -pages/teaching-beyond-the-gender-bina ry-in-the-university-classroom/

Romano, T. (2004). *Crafting authentic voice.* Heinemann.

Rosenblatt, L. (1995). *Literature as exploration* (5th ed.). Modern Language Association.

Saad, L. F. (2020). *Me and white supremacy: Combat racism, change the world, and become a good ancestor.* Source Books.

Social Justice Books (n.d.), https://socialjus ticebooks.org

Tatum, A. W., & Muhammad, G. E. (2012). African American males and literacy development in contexts that are characteristically urban. *Urban Education, 47*(2), 434–463.

Tatum, B. D. (2017). *Why are all the Black kids sitting together in the cafeteria? And other conversations about race.* Hatchette Book Group.

Taylor Bullock, R. (n.d.). *We Are.* www .weare-nc.org

Teaching Tolerance. (2019). *Let's talk: A guide to facilitating critical conversations with students.* The Southern Poverty Law Center.

TED. (2018). *How my transgender son negotiates visible invisibility | Courtney Farrell* [Video]. YouTube. https://www .youtube.com/watch?v=NW7aodLnYWk

Vasquez, V. (1994). A step in the dance of critical literacy. *UKRA Reading, 28*(1), 39–43.

Vasquez, V. (2010). *Getting beyond "I like the book": Creating space for critical literacy in K–6 classrooms.* International Reading Association.

Vasquez, V. M. (2014). *Negotiating critical literacies with young children.* Routledge.

Vasquez, V. M. (2017). *Critical literacy across the K–6 curriculum.* Routledge.

Vasquez, V. M., Harste, J. C., Albers, P. (2021). *Using art critically: Volume 1.* CCC Press.

Vasquez, V. M., Janks, H., & Comber B. (2019). Critical literacy as a way of being and doing. *Language Arts, 96*(5), 300–311.

Vasquez, V. M., Tate, S., & Harste, J. C. (2013). *Negotiating critical literacies with teachers: Theoretical foundations and pedagogical resources for pre-service and in-service contexts.* Routledge.

Vasquez, V. M., Woods, B., & Felderman, C. (2022). *Technology and critical literacy in early childhood.* Routledge.

Wallace, S. (2018, September 12). *Autism and aggression—What can help?* Autism Speaks. https://www.autism-speaks.org/autism-and-aggression#:~:- text=Among%20those%20with%20autism %2C%20common,to%20identify%20the% 20underlying%20cause

Waech, G., & Hoog, C. (2014, April 1). *Violence in the lives of the deaf or hard of hearing.* VAWnet Special Collections. https://vawnet .org/sc/violence-lives-deaf-or-hard-hearing

Winkler, E. (2009). Children are not colorblind: How young children learn race. *PACE: Practical Approaches for Continuing Education, 3*(3), 1–8. https://nmaahc .si.edu/sites/default/files/downloads/ resources/children_are_not_colorblind.pdf

Wood, K., Taylor, B. & Stover, K. (2016). *Smuggling writing: Strategies that get students to write every day, in every content area.* Corwin Press.

Wright, J. P., & Laminack, L. (1982). First graders can be critical listeners and readers. *Language Arts, 59*(2), 133–136.

Yates, T. M., & Marcelo, A. K. (2014). Through race-colored glasses: Preschoolers' pretend play and teachers' ratings of preschooler adjustment. *Early Childhood Research Quarterly, 29*(1), 1–11.

Index

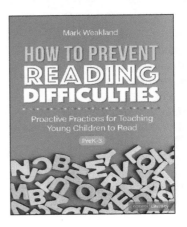

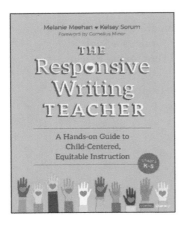

At Corwin Literacy we have put together a collection of just-in-time, classroom-tested, practical resources from trusted experts that allow you to quickly find the information you need when you need it.

DOUGLAS FISHER, NANCY FREY, NICOLE LAW

Using a structured, three-pronged approach—skill, will, and thrill—students experience reading as a purposeful act with this new comprehensive model of reading instruction.

PAM KOUTRAKOS

Packed with ready-to-go lessons and tools, this user-friendly resource provides ways to weave together different aspects of literacy using one mentor text.

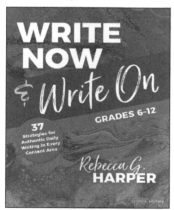

REBECCA G. HARPER

Customizable strategies turn students' informal writing into a springboard for daily writing practice in every content area—with a focus on academic vocabulary, summarizing, and using textual evidence.

MELANIE MEEHAN, CHRISTINA NOSEK, MATTHEW JOHNSON, DAVE STUART JR., MATTHEW R. KAY

This series offers actionable answers to your most pressing questions about teaching reading, writing, and ELA.

CORWIN

A SAGE Publishing Company

Helping educators make the greatest impact

CORWIN HAS ONE MISSION: to enhance education through intentional professional learning.

We build long-term relationships with our authors, educators, clients, and associations who partner with us to develop and continuously improve the best evidence-based practices that establish and support lifelong learning.